The Fastest Hike:

Quest for the Pacific Crest Trail Record

The Fastest Hike:

Quest for the Pacific Crest Trail Record

by
Raymond Greenlaw

Roxy Publishing, LLC
Savannah, Georgia

Copyeditor	Hugh Willoughby
Cover Design	Caroline Harrington
	Workhorse Creative
Additional Design	Ben Page, Ruslan Hristov
Photographers	Liz Chiz, Karen Gerbs
	Paul Goransson, Laurel Greenlaw
	Raymond Greenlaw, David Meehan
	Adrian Plante, Peter Solomon
Proofreader	Jenny Blackmore
Text Design	Raymond Greenlaw
Typesetting System	LaTeX
Assistants	Sandi Lott, Tunishe Timmons

Roxy Publishing, LLC
Apache Avenue, Box 411
Savannah, Georgia 31419
912 / 961-1767
USA

The publisher and the author do not advocate the backpacking practices described in this book. Extreme ultralight backpacking can be dangerous. Anyone utilizing the techniques described in this book does so voluntarily at his/her own risk.

The trade names and trademarks of several companies and products have been used in this book. No endorsement of them nor any association with this book should be inferred.

ISBN 1-59028-045-8 (paper)

To those who supported me, and
to those who hiked with me.

For You

You made it beautiful,
Worthwhile, fulfilling, and special.
You enhanced my dream.
You are one with me.

Manning Park

Rainy Pass

Stevens Pass

Snoqualmie Pass

Seattle

Goat Rocks Wilderness

Washington
508.4 miles

Cascade Locks

Portland

Mount Hood

Crater Lake

Oregon
457.4 miles

Sky Lakes Wilderness

Pacific
Crest
Trail

Seiad Valley

Burney Falls

Lake Tahoe

Belden

California
1,693.7 miles

San Francisco

Kennedy
Meadows

Agua Dulce

Mojave

Idyllwild

Los Angeles

Campo

Acknowledgments

I poured my heart into this hike and into this book. Without the support of Laurel, Celeste, my family, and those listed below, I would have accomplished little. I love you; I thank you. A deep thanks to my hiking partners, Peter "Fish-out-of-Water" Solomon and Paul "Superman" Goransson. A deep thanks to James "Jimbo" Wogulis for his support and for maintaining a "live updates" Web-site throughout the duration of my hike. A heartfelt thanks to Jenny Blackmore for her careful reading and thoughtful comments on an initial draft of the manuscript. Her suggestions have greatly improved the text.

My sincere thanks to Jim Leisy of Franklin, Beedle & Associates, Inc. for his friendship, and interest and support of this project. Thanks also to Tom Sumner. A sincere thanks to Hugh Willoughby for copyediting the manuscript two times. Thanks to Glen "Fiddlehead" Fleagle, Glenn van Peski, Henry Shires, and Garrett Graubins for their support, friendship, and advice. A warm thanks to Ben Page for his work on the front and back covers, and for scanning in images of the hike. Thanks to Mark Burge for help with LaTeX. Thanks to Caroline Harrington of Workhorse Creative for her work on this project. Thanks to Adrian Plante, who helped get the trip underway. Thanks to Greg Geller for his comments on the initial chapters of the manuscript. His ideas helped to shape the overall text. Thanks to Sandi Lott, who assisted me with entering edits to the manuscript. Thanks to Tunishe Timmons for her drawing of the Pacific Crest Trail map.

Thanks to all hikers who provided me with encouragement, support, and company. Thanks to all volunteers and trail angels who make the Pacific Crest Trail a great place to walk. Thanks to the Pacific Crest

Trail Association. Many others have contributed to this project, and a warm thanks goes to all of them.

 Contents

The Fastest Hike:

Quest for the Pacific Crest Trail Record

1 Quest Preliminaries

The *Pacific Crest Trail*[1] (*PCT*) is a 2,659-mile-long national scenic trail that winds over mountains from the Mexican border at Campo to the Canadian border near Manning Park. Campo is a tiny nondescript town located one hour's drive east of San Diego. Manning Park is a small tourist town located several hours' drive east of Vancouver, British Columbia. These towns would have remained anonymous to me, if not for their being the beginning and ending points of the PCT. This book was inspired by my attempt to hike between Campo and Manning Park via the circuitous mountainous PCT in record time.

Flyin' Brian Robinson, the only person to have hiked the *Appalachian Trail*, Pacific Crest Trail, and *Continental Divide Trail* in a single year, owned the PCT record. His incredible three-trail achievement had expanded the realm of human endurance; he'd walked 7,400 difficult trail miles in one year. Flyin' Brian had hiked the PCT in 86.5 days. I planned to hike the PCT in 85 days. A couple of months before departing, I'd announced my intentions (to ensure credibility in case I broke the record) by placing my demanding hiking schedule on the World Wide Web. The schedule called for super-human mileages in remote, rugged, mountain terrain.

This book was written entirely from memory; I didn't take *any* notes while on the trail. The book is not about the hike. Rather, the story describes my searching, coping, escaping, overcoming, and pushing myself to the absolute limit—mentally, physically, and spiritually. This narrative is a tale of discovery, endurance, and personal achievement. I sincerely hope that you can share in this journey and will laugh and cry and walk with me. I hope this quest inspires you.

---

[1] Appendix H contains a glossary of trail jargon. We place trail terms defined there in italics on their first usage in the text.

1

The epic adventure unfolded as I departed from Campo . . . .

On May 12, 2003, at 7:30 am, my Rhode Island high-school English teacher, Dr. Adrian Plante, who resides in San Diego now, drove me to the monument marking the PCT's southernmost point. I had prepared for and had researched my upcoming *thru-hike* of the PCT, but far less than one would expect—especially for a person as detailed as I usually am and for someone holding a PhD in computer science. I wanted a true adventure, and slightly less-than-rigorous planning had guaranteed one.

My mentor, also a highly-skilled photographer, carefully framed a few photos of me with the Southern California desert as the backdrop. I wouldn't carry a camera during any part of the trip in order to keep my *pack weight* down. Would these shots be the last pictures of me alive? I wondered. Adrian quipped, "Better you than I." I smiled, nervously. As far as I knew, close to the Mexican border was where people posed the biggest threat to my life this summer, so I anxiously anticipated leaving the trail's southern terminus far behind.

While firmly shaking hands and exchanging eye contact, Adrian wished me the best. I thanked him for his hospitality in San Diego and for the ride to the PCT's southern trailhead. My excitement peaked. "Here I go," I said, speaking my last words for a long time. "Good luck, Ray," rang Adrian's final words of encouragement. I walked 100 yards into the unforgiving desert and glanced back at a 25-year-long friend, a friend whose interest in me at a young age had shaped my future, and a friend who had helped me to understand the world better. My thoughts overloaded my mind; my legs trembled. I'd been anticipating this moment daily, and now my eight-year-long dream commenced. While choking back tears, I summoned my courage. I strode forth completely alone and into the unknown; I didn't glance back a second time.

I felt nervous and scared. Would I finish the PCT? Would I die of dehydration in the Mojave Desert's heat, fall off a mountain in the High Sierra, drown crossing a swollen creek in Northern California, be grabbed by a hungry Mountain Lion in the Sky Lakes Wilderness Area of Oregon, or be mauled by a Grizzly Bear in the rugged North

Cascades of Washington state? Perhaps a wacko would knife me, rob me, and leave my body to rot in a shallow grave never to be found. Other than Flyin' Brian, who really knew what extreme challenges I would face? I certainly didn't.

Could I survive my ambitious hiking schedule, or would that paper cloud my judgment and push me to the breaking-point? If I died, people would surely say that I was under-prepared. Thoughts spun in my head. At that moment I promised myself that I wouldn't quit this endeavor, unless I sustained a serious injury. My opportunity to hike the trail seemed like now or never. Restructuring my life a second time in order to make an all-out attempt at the PCT record didn't appear possible. My motivation shot off the charts, and I felt unsure if I would ever again reach this extraordinary level of desire, for anything. My age would become a factor in a few more years, too.

As I disappeared into the arid brush among unfamiliar desert plants, I reflected back briefly to my sign-in at the Campo Post Office earlier that morning. The entry read as follows:

5/12/2003

Wall here.

I am planning an 85-day thru-hike and expect to arrive in Manning Park, Canada, on August 5th. Feeling great, feeling excited. Just happy to stand here. My dream is beginning.

Best of luck to all hikers.

Happy trails.

Thirty or so locations along the PCT house *trail registers*. In these notebooks hikers write messages for friends, describe their plans, indicate what they've found on the trail, and explain how they feel. Trail registers serve as the only means for hikers farther along the trail to communicate with those behind them. This mechanism is a one-way communication. Trail registers become a major focus of any long-distance hike, providing an important avenue for expressing one's thoughts.

Thinking of hikers whom you met and passed along the trail occupies much time, and engages the imagination fully. Lack of information about new-found friends taunts the solo *thru-hiker*. As in daily life many unanswerable questions arise: Did they quit? Are they okay? Will they avoid this pitfall? Where are they? What are they thinking? Will I ever see them again? How are their feet? Not having any substantive information regarding people you care about licenses the mind to fill in the blanks either optimistically or pessimistically. I tried to think optimistically. The sweeping emotions that a hiker experiences, when wondering about fellow hikers, are similar to those experienced by friends back home who are thinking of you. Uncertainty bothers most people, and coping with the unknown successfully doesn't just happen. One must possess and maintain courage, strength, faith, and a positive outlook.

A person walking transforms into a thinker. Whom would I meet? When and where? Where would I camp? Would the water-sources be located where I expected? How many rattlesnakes would I encounter? What would the weather hold? My mind emptied of the usual day-to-day self-talk and filled with questions such as these. While many questions flew around in my head, few answers arrived. Somewhat surprisingly, this gap didn't trouble me.

I had laid out a close-to-impossible challenge for myself, had told people what I planned to do, and now attempted to achieve my goal. Not completing the hike in record time would mean not achieving my goal. That outcome would be hard for me to accept. However, I needed to see things realistically in order to survive. If I placed too much pressure on myself, I was doomed to failure. A mistake on the trail could have serious consequences. I tried not to think about all the things that could go wrong. That list was long.

Traditionally, a hiker assumes a *trail name*. This alias isn't to conceal one's true identity, but rather to indicate a noteworthy trait. Trail names consist of catchy or interesting phrases such as "Free to Go", "Lady in Red", or "Shade Boy". Eventually, if you answer to only your trail name, your real identity slowly fades. This transition provides anonymity and allows you to establish a new persona. Upon returning from the woods, the readjustment usually takes awhile before a hiker begins to answer to his/her given name. A hiker's identity is never the same afterward, though.

Where did my trail name "Wall" come from? Many readers of this book will recognize the familiar expression *hit the wall*, which signifies that a person lacks any energy and has encountered a barrier to physical performance. The expression occurs most commonly in the context of 26.2-mile marathon runners, who typically hit the wall around mile 20 and then trudge in the last 6 miles painfully slowly. Long before Clif Bars, Power Gel, and Quest, and for that matter prior to Sports Medicine evolving as a discipline, I'd attempted many crazy endurance feats—a one-day 200+-mile bike-ride as a teenager (on a heavy Schwinn Continental with a friction light, kick-stand, and a friction odometer), a 75-mile run on one candy-bar, a handful of Ironman triathlons, and many 100-mile runs, too. I'd suffered many *bonks* leading me to scrape dirt off and then eat banana crud from a discarded peel, obtain crusty salt off my own sweaty face, and view bugs for their caloric content. These experiences and some other failed athletic attempts had led a good friend to nickname me Wall. The name had stuck, and I had accepted it.

As far back as I could remember, a passion for fitness and adventure had burned inside me. I loved physical challenges and loved exercising. Knowing that I would never become tired gave me a welcomed self-assurance. I liked to travel into the mountains and had often strayed from the trail. Unlike other aspects of my life, I never worried much about what would happen to me in the woods. I always felt safe and comfortable in mountains, at peace and at home.

I'd been dreaming about hiking the PCT for many years. The seeds had been first planted when I'd spoken to a hiker named "Fiddlehead" during my 1995 97-day thru-hike of the Appalachian Trail (*AT*)—the shorter and more popular east-coast version of the PCT. Fiddlehead had invited me to join him and his friends for a PCT thru-hike during the summer of 1996, but unfortunately, life's circumstances didn't permit my venturing out on the PCT then. I knew that the PCT offered spectacular beauty, and my burning desire to hike the trail consumed me. It was always merely a question of when I would hike the PCT, not if.

At the outset of my trip, I felt ill-prepared regarding resupplies and trail details, both important, but to me not paramount. I'd channeled all of my energy into building up will-power, courage, and determination for my arduous journey. Extreme weather, loneliness, hunger, dehydration, discomfort, bad luck, and pain became my major nemeses. The hike would involve calculated risks, too. Still I felt optimistic about my prospects. Deep inside me I believed that good things happen to those who are happy, receptive, and paying attention. I walked "smilin' and stylin' ", as another of my Southern California register entries would note. Leaving the border at Campo, I possessed a lot of spring in my step. I pondered and looked forward to many discoveries. In making my way north, I never really knew what type of challenge or adventure I would face next. I knew only that they would be grand and welcome.

In my life I have covered over 65,000 miles on foot and have surpassed the marathon distance (26.2 miles) in a single day more than 500 times. I've participated in many strenuous endurance events, where I've pushed myself to the edge. During my more than 30 years of running, hiking, and training, I've developed two strategies for maximizing life's opportunities and for coping with difficult times. I call these two processes my *library* and my *switching network*. The discussions in this book are an introduction to a complex psychological framework; a continuum of strategies blends together and interacts in symbiotic ways.

My "library" occupies a region of my mind where I stash important life experiences and then "check them out" in times of need. Sections of my library house sayings, audio clips, hero profiles, images, songs, and personal encounters as well as other items. The material is comprehensive and vivid. The categories are recursively subdivided, forming a "directory structure". My library holds all of my good memories and experiences, and I have complete access to its shelves. In times of intense struggle I withdraw appropriate items from my library to alter my consciousness. The ability to retrieve the materials that I require and at exactly the right times took decades to perfect—meditating, experimenting using trial and error, performing careful monitoring, and making sensitive adjustments. The *matching algorithm* that "knows" what material needs to be checked out and when is the key component of the system. I constructed my life's card catalog, and know it intimately. Throughout my journey, I will describe various checkouts and acquisitions to my collection.

My "switching network" consists of a grid that I've set up throughout my being. Hundreds of pain switches, which I can flip "off" and then toggle back "on", line key junctions all over my body. Another group of switches controls my senses. Many additional switches pertain to feelings. It has taken a lifetime to develop my switching network and to employ the system effectively. Of utmost importance is the thought process required to know when to toggle a switch from off to on and then back. Without periodic monitoring of, for example, pain switches, it is easy to injure one's self and to cause permanent physical damage.

Setting the thousands of switches in combination creates "interference". However, when the switch-setting technique is properly mastered, interference can be eliminated, and one can program one's self and control pain, emotions, and thought-processes. When the switching network has "leaky circuits" or signals become distorted, desired manipulations may not happen, and the resulting situation can become dangerous. The outcome could be a complete mental breakdown or even worse. Throughout this journey, I will share with you when I throw certain switches and their positions.

I'd left my world behind in Savannah, Georgia, by adjusting my switching network. Thoughts of family and friends danced in my mind, but my concerns, out of necessity, turned to walking, staying on the trail, obtaining food and water, avoiding creatures like snakes, and locating places to sleep. Those familiar with Savannah know that that historical city sits in a plain at sea-level. To prepare properly physically for my summer-long mountain trek from Savannah had seemed like an impossible challenge. However, I'd tried my best by repeatedly running Savannah's *only* hill, the Talmadge Bridge to South Carolina, which rises a mere 180 feet.

The Savannah Striders run the bridge on Sunday mornings to avoid traffic, and I'd become a group regular. With great interest my training partners had questioned me about the hike and eventually kept track of me via a weekly updated Web-site. (The site is still accessible via my personal-page which can be found through Google.) My friends felt concerned for me because of the awesome task that I faced and, well, because I resided in Savannah—a moss-covered city almost as laid back as Key West, Florida.

My family, my job as Dean of a College of Computing, my work as an author, and my hobbies don't leave much time to reflect on my life. I'm living and doing, but not planning to the degree that I would like nor discovering as much about myself as I would like. What's the old saying? "Know thyself". I wanted to know more about who I really was and find the answers to the following questions: What are my greatest fears and how can I overcome them? Am I kind, caring, considerate, happy? What are my weaknesses and my strengths? How can I contribute more to loved ones, society, and the world? Is my life valuable and moving forward along a good path? Am I using my abilities? How can I improve myself? What are my mental and my physical limits? The high-altitude PCT and my demanding mileages would help reveal the answers to these and other questions that I viewed as fundamental. I also realized, though, that I am just a small piece of a complex puzzle, so naturally similar lists of questions existed regarding the context of my life—family, friends, and environment. I felt nervous about the answers that I would find, but my apprehension didn't deter me from searching.

One valuable lesson which I'd learned while hiking the AT told me to ignore conventional wisdom, or at least to make sure that it didn't prejudice me in decision-making. This rule worked particularly well, for example, in the domain of gear selection. Most backpackers wear hiking-boots, shoulder a bulky pack having a padded waist belt, and carry the so-called "ten essentials". I'd decided to walk in running-shoes, to cut the waist belt off my backpack (Would you cut up your 200-dollar pack, voiding the warranty, just to save weight?), and to leave the "ten essentials" at home.[2]

I'd focused on keeping my pack weight minimal since my feet are my physical weakness, and I did everything possible to reduce the stress on them, even to the detriment of the rest of my being. One of the reasons that I'd decided to walk with trekking-poles was to decrease, by a couple of pounds per step, the weight supported by my feet. My Leki Super Makalu poles also helped me with balance and would allow me to incorporate the upper body, required for a Savannahan, while climbing steep mountains.

I've never been afraid to go against the grain. My parents instilled in me a sense of right and wrong. When I know that something is right, I believe in it. I trust my intuition, but not blindly. Throughout the years, I've listened to advice from others, read, and acquired knowledge

---

[2] I don't advocate this strategy.

through life experiences. For these reasons I felt comfortable standing up to criticism of gear selection and negative comments concerning my ambitious schedule. I believed in myself; those who knew me believed in me, too. Long ago, I had learned to listen more to those who really care about me and to listen less to those who don't.

My stomach housed a funny feeling as I stepped forward into the desert near Campo. An overwhelming sense of freedom swept over me, and I felt a great joy but also a great sadness. I was headed smack dab into the unknown without carrying a single map. On one inquiry to Fiddlehead, he'd indicated that I would be okay taking just the *Pacific Crest Trail Databook* (or *Databook*, for short). This convenient light-weight book summarizes important locations along the trail.

Figure 1 shows a few typical entries from the book. These items are not successive *Databook* entries but merely representative ones. The first entry pertains to Arrastre Trail Camp, one of my favorite campsites. The detailed information following the location name for the Arrastre Trail Camp is interpreted as follows: 'w' means that water is available there, 0.9 indicates the distance from the previous point of interest, 257.9 is the mileage from Campo on the trail, 7605 is the elevation in feet, and C5 refers to the corresponding map in the *Pacific Crest Trail, Volume 1, California* (or *Volume I*, for short) where Arrastre Trail Camp is located. New items in the Silverwood Lake entry are interpreted as follows: 'G' indicates that groceries are available there, 'M' stands for meals, 'sh' represents shower, 'R' signifies road, and 1.70mE means that the items preceding this notation are found 1.7 miles east of the trail. The other entries are interpreted similarly. The map entries for Oregon and Washington refer to the *Pacific Crest Trail, Volume 2, Oregon & Washington* (or *Volume II*, for short). The *Databook* doesn't provide a route description, nor does this little guide contain any maps.

In my never-ending quest for lightweight gear, I'd searched the Internet thoroughly. Savannah offers absolutely no market for specialized hiking-products and obviously none for cold-weather equipment, either. The temperatures in this charming southern city rarely dip below 40°F in winter. The Internet served as my store. I already owned a $350 feather-weight Clip Flashlight tent; however, I wanted a product even lighter than that. After a couple of hours of Internet surfing in mid-

. . . .

Arrastre Trail Camp	w		0.9	257.9	7605	C5
Silverwood Lake State	w,G,M,sh,	0.1	331.1	3390	C15
Recreation Area's	R: 1.70mE				
entrance road					
Angeles Crest Highway 2	R		1.3	391.0	6670	D6
Junction to South	w: 0.10mW	1.5	1765.5	5360	B8
Branch Mountain Shelter					

. . . .

Figure 1.1: Representative entries in the *Databook*.

March, Google had found a product called the *tarptent*. The two-person version of this shelter, named the *Squall*, weighed in at only 31 ounces. This total improved upon my Clip Flashlight tent by over a pound, so after having viewed an impressive set of jpegs of the Squall pitched all over the globe, I'd decided to order it. This carefully-engineered shelter appeared to be reliable and durable.

Pack weight concerned and consumed me. About two months prior to my departure for California, I'd purchased a highly accurate postal scale for weighing mail or, I guess, backpacking gear. Initially, I'd kept a handwritten record of the item weights. After five minutes, I'd realized that maintaining records electronically worked better. Firstly, my handwriting qualifies as hieroglyphics and becomes hard for me to read even a day later; and secondly, I had continually modified individual pieces of gear, a process which had resulted in saving tenths of ounces and which had generated many list cross-outs. This editing had produced an ugly record-keeping system, so I'd created an HTML[3] file and viewed my gear list on the Web. Having 24-7 access to the developing list from everywhere had allowed me to record any new creative ideas before they'd slipped my mind.

In my home office I had carefully weighed all of my gear, repeatedly. Equipment had sprawled all over a large and infrequently used second-story room. It had soon become clear that the way to reduce pack weight involved leaving items behind. After all, even small pieces of the lightest materials such as ripstop nylon, Kevlar, graphite, and titanium still weigh something. I'd eliminated many "essential items",

---

[3]The language that Web pages are coded in—HyperText Markup Language.

going against conventional wisdom. For example, when I departed from Savannah, I'd already decided not to take a compass, any maps, a camera, a journal, or a pen. I'd chopped the tops off plastic bags, shortened shoelaces, trimmed excess material off the straps on my *GVP* custom backpack (which itself with sleeping-pad weighed only 25 ounces), eliminated the dental-floss container, broke the tooth-brush in half, hacked 10 inches off my hydration-system drinking-tube, scraped the labels from all containers, ripped the sizing labels off my shirts and shorts, unwrapped my Band-Aids, squirted out extra tooth-paste, left the stove behind, and so on. (The final gear list at the time when I'd started the trip appears in Appendix F.)

Luxury goods stayed home. Each item that I shelved had resulted in a strategic compromise—either in comfort, safety, or function. An example of the latter situation meant not taking pictures. Although embarking on the most incredible journey of my life, to save weight I'd sacrificed sharing images of the trip. I would deposit many scenes in my library, so that I could describe the trail to friends, but I wouldn't have any photographs that had been snapped by me. I felt meticulous and obsessive about weight minimization. Would I jettison other items along the way?

Originally, I'd planned to hike the trail in 90 days. Each year I work on a nine-month job contract and had decided to use the full summer to enjoy the trail. Fiddlehead once more had intervened. I should point out that we'd met only once (on the AT eight years prior to the commencement of my PCT hike) but have kept in touch during the past decade via email. My respect for Fiddlehead had grown immensely. He is an extraordinary hiker, having completed the *triple crown* and then almost having completed it a second time in a single year. Fiddlehead is knowledgeable about the PCT and other long-distance trails, so I always listened carefully to him and sought his advice. When he'd heard that I'd planned to hike the trail in 90 days, he suggested that I chase the existing record of 86.5 days. "You can break the record if you want," he'd written in an email. On his recommendation I'd decided to prepare a revised 85-day schedule.

To develop my schedule, I'd relied entirely on the *Databook*. As noted earlier, this hiker's companion describes locations near the trail where a hiker can obtain groceries. Food and water topped my list of priorities and had governed the schedule-building process. I'd bucked the trend by deciding to send only three *mail-drops* rather than the thirty which most hikers use and that several experts recommend. My plan included drastically fewer packages, and this fact should have alerted me to future problems.

The reasoning that I'd employed which convinced me to utilize so few mail-drops proceeded as follows: post offices are typically open only from 9-to-5 M–F, and in small "towns" maybe open only from 12-to-4. Saturday hours might be from 9-to-12, if at all. If I had sent dozens of mail-drops, I knew that over the duration of the summer several situations would arise when I would have to push hard to arrive at a post office by 5 pm on Friday or perhaps even have to layover until Monday morning to pick up a package. I didn't want to find myself in either of these undesirable circumstances. In my mind, I simply couldn't afford to lose any hiking time due to waiting for a post office to open. Additionally, I didn't want to package my food for May, June, and July before the trip even started. Nor did I want to devote the time and the energy required to prepare 30 boxes for mailing.

I've witnessed thru-hikers retrieving packages a few weeks in to their hikes, and uniformly they seemed disgusted with the types of food that they'd packaged pre-hike. Sending out mail-drops can also mean sacrificing variety. Besides, accurately gauging the number of calories to include in each package challenges the best planners since this amount can vary widely as a hiker loses weight, as temperatures change, and as daily mileages and terrain fluctuate. Mailing out dozens of packages also requires a reliable support person who will hang around for most of the summer. If a box arrives general delivery, a post office will usually hold the item only for two weeks. Packages can vanish without a trace or be ripped open by security, and small critters can sneak into the tasty-smelling mail-drops at their destinations. For these reasons I'd decided to rely primarily on stores.

My schedule had zero rest-days. That is, I planned to hike *every* single day of the summer. I wanted to average 31 trail miles per day, or 50 kilometers, and figured that I would average another two miles per day heading into towns, finding water, locating bathroom sites, and in getting lost. No rest-days meant that I could never recover properly, nor could I afford any delays. Building no down time into the schedule also meant that I had no cushion, no margin for error. To illustrate how critical having no rest-days was, with my relatively short trip-duration and the length of the PCT, if I took a *single* day off, my *average daily mileage* for the summer would need to increase by almost a half mile to make up for the off day. I worried more than usual about a friend dying or a family member getting ill. If I needed to leave the trail for even a couple of days, my dream would be over. I hoped and prayed that everyone, including me, would stay healthy.

My schedule called for me to hike 180.5 miles during the first week for an average daily mileage of 25.8. The first seven days of the schedule balanced nicely, with days ranging from 23.8-to-26.9 miles. Pre-hike training had involved running 80-to-90 miles per week in Savannah's heat and humidity. Taking my German Shepards out twice a day at home and going between buildings on Armstrong Atlantic State University's campus had accounted for another 30 miles per week. In total I'd traveled roughly 120 miles per week on foot. My (faulty) logic had led me to believe that my full-time job accounted for the equivalent of another 60 miles per week, and this thinking had led me to settle on 180 miles for the first week of the PCT hike. Fortunately, the initial part of the trail is well-graded and possesses a good walking-surface.

A few months prior to departing for the hike I'd decided to have lasik corrective eye-surgery. For my entire adult life I'd been wearing glasses, and my eye-sight had measured only 20/1,000 without glasses— what I saw from 20 feet a person with normal vision saw at a distance of 1,000 feet. This meant that if I lost or broke my glasses, I would be essentially blind. While hiking, keeping glasses clean and from getting badly scratched involves a monumental effort. For these and other reasons, I'd opted for the painless eye-surgery. I worried about the surgery contributing to dry eyes in the desert. My vision had stabilized near 20/20, granting me a new-found freedom in not having to be continually occupied with glasses. I approached the hike with fresh eyes.

Part I

SOUTHERN CALIFORNIA

The arduous Southern California segment of the trail stretches from the barren Mexico/United States border at Campo to the far-greener Kennedy Meadows. Much of the 697 miles that this section covers has burned in the last 10 years. The lowest elevation sits at only 1,000 feet above sea-level, while the highest stands at a lung-bursting 9,000 feet. The majority of the terrain consists of mountainous desert. Many beautiful flowering cacti, including the Beaver-tail and Banning Prickly-pear, grow trailside. Fires raise a constant alarm; burned-out trees called "widow-makers" can fall on an unsuspecting hiker at any time. Hikers walk among millions and millions of wild flowers and bees through blackened trees. Lizards, snakes, ants, and beetles thrive. A limited water-supply along the trail tests all hikers, and the heat beats down intensely. I'd planned to resupply about nine times during this stretch. The longest haul that I'd planned to go without resupply extended 150 miles. The biggest day that I'd scheduled measured 32.9 miles. My first mail-drop waited for me at Kennedy Meadows. I'd started May 12th and hoped to reach Kennedy Meadows on June 8th, day 28 of my journey.

15

2 The Adventure Begins

My hike began on May 12th, which overshoots by three weeks when the bulk of thru-hikers leave Campo. This year 160 hikers dreamed of walking the entire width of the United States along the demanding PCT. As best I knew, only one person set out to break the speed record: me. Fiddlehead had reasoned that with my late start I could literally follow in the footsteps of the others. His suggestion did work in many areas; however, obviously this strategy didn't work well on grassy parts of the trail or on segments of the trail north of me where rain had washed away all footprints. The tracks of those ahead of me could disappear in a flash. Why hadn't I realized this fact pre-trip? I'd expected the trail to be far better marked than I found it, so I had mistakenly never addressed this important issue.

Within a mile after departing from the southern terminus, I lost the unmarked trail. This confusion disturbed me and worried me. I became frustrated. My God, can I make it to Canada? This is totally ridiculous. Adrian had been driving away for a mere 15 minutes, and here I was lost. I mumbled choice words for those "marking" the trail, and added a couple of expletives directed at Fiddlehead. One thing I realized early on was that I always needed to hike somewhere. While the bright sun scorched me, I couldn't stand around feeling sorry for myself, and wait to be rescued. So, even when I didn't know where the trail went, I walked "forward".

Since I was hiking the trail *pure*, meaning that I planned to walk northward continuously (without "leap frogging" and then returning to any sections) and to cover every step[1] of the PCT all the way to

---

[1]Where there is deep snow, the PCT itself and its trail-markings are buried, so

17

Canada, mistakes meant that I needed to backtrack, even if a mistake had fortuitously led me to rejoin the trail. If I intended to set a record, the hike needed to be as pure as possible. Otherwise, the effort would have no integrity and would be meaningless.

During the initial five miles of walking, I made countless wrong turns, retreated, and re-found the trail. I encountered only Border Patrol personnel throughout the early part of the first day. They stared me down, but I was never directly questioned. Surprisingly, I saw no other hikers. I did see footprints and occasionally an arrow drawn in the sand, indicating which way the trail went. I came to depend on and to trust completely such impromptu markings. The arrows were drawn in sand using boot-heels, formed with sticks, constructed from rocks, and sometimes scribbled on paper and placed inside a plastic bag beneath a single small stone trailside.

I was thankful for the resourcefulness and kindness demonstrated by those hikers ahead of me. Each time I spotted such a trail indicator, it brought enormous joy to me; I was heading the right way. I can't overemphasize how much this reassurance meant. Such affirmations gave me hope and strength. People were helping me, and my loneliness dissipated. I became part of a community of like-minded folks. I also left markers in ambiguous areas, often backtracking to do so. While walking past the temporary markers, I filed many images in my library.

The weather on day one cooked me. Although I carried little food because my schedule called for me to reach a grocery store early the next day, my light food load was more than compensated for by my heavy water load. The eight liters of water that I carried seemed more than necessary, but I feared running out of fluids and dehydrating in the desert. A pinched nerve in my neck, which I'd been seeing a chiropractor for in Savannah, tormented me under the strain of my pack. Unaccustomed to wearing a pack all day, my back hurt, too. I became concerned about my forearms and hands, which were now busy 12 hours a day holding trekking-poles.

While worrying about meeting desperate folks who were trying to sneak into the United States, I plodded along the dusty trail. Many

---

this process means following the trail to the best of one's ability. Walking the trail in deep snow is far more dangerous, difficult, and time-consuming than walking a snow-free trail.

times I noticed torn clothing and *cache* remnants where people had deposited supplies for someone trying to come into the country. I also saw many empty water-bottles. Thoughts of Mexicans who had died in this inhospitable area while following their dream of finding a better life and a better home troubled me. I held a moment of silence for them.

The knowledge that perhaps as many as 1,500 other people had successfully hiked the PCT from Mexico to Canada over the years comforted me, and I thought that surely I hiked as well as the weakest of them. If they had done it, I could do it. At the time I didn't mention to myself that only a handful of people had ever hiked the entire trail in fewer than 100 days.

A computer geek from Savannah, untrained for mountains, with a pinched nerve in his neck, no maps, hiking solo, relying on footprints as trail-markers, not carrying the "ten essentials", and trying to set a speed record for one of the longest hiking-trails in the world—what's wrong with this picture? Of course, I realized that the odds were stacked against me; however, I knew deep-down that I possessed great mental strength. My switching network and my library, developed over the course of a lifetime, assisted me. I possessed will-power; I felt indefatigable; I believed in myself. I marched north.

Late during day one as the temperatures finally dipped under 100°F, I encountered my first thru-hiker. I caught up to him on a flat brushy section where he struggled a bit. Having company gave me a good feeling. I quickly learned that this thru-hiker's name was Joe, that he'd graduated from Cornell, that he'd been employed at an outfit to help rich kids improve their SAT scores, that he'd wrestled in high school, that he'd run out of water the day before, that he'd already ditched his hiking-poles, and that he was hurting from a few blisters. He learned that my trail name was Wall. Joe said that he'd been hiking faster than I was, but was taking longer breaks. I wondered about this statement since I'd just hiked in one day the same distance that he'd walked in two. We continued north together.

I guessed that Joe was 22 years old. His dark hair already appeared oily, and fell just short of his strong wrestler's neck. Since his hiking experience seemed limited, not yet having completed one of the mega trails, I wasn't sure if he would finish the PCT. He may have doubted my abilities, too. If people compared us, a majority might have put their money on Joe's finishing. I rooted for him. I told Joe that I'd previously hiked the AT. He was glad that the first thru-hiker whom he'd met was experienced. My new friend asked for hiking tips, and I gave him some, primarily on pack weight-reduction and maintaining a flexible state-of-mind.

I know a few professors in Cornell's well-respected Department of Computer Science, so we talked for awhile about Joe's alma mater.

"Do you know Hartmanis?" I inquired about Cornell's Turing Award winning professor and co-founder of the field of complexity theory—my primary research area.

"I may have heard of him."

Joe wouldn't know anyone else in the department by name if he didn't know the superstar Juris Hartmanis. I didn't bother to ask about anyone else.

"My roommate studied computer science for awhile."

"Really? What happened to him?"

"They make that program so damned hard that no one can get through it. Not sure why they do that," Joe noted with disgust, indicating that his roommate was an excellent student, despite his lack of success in the Department of Computer Science at Cornell.

"At the undergraduate level in a tough program like Cornell's, they really stress foundations."

"He programmed constantly."

"I made the mistake of taking an undergraduate CS course at the University of Washington once. We wrote 3,000 lines of code per week," I sympathized.

"My roommate changed majors. When do you plan to finish?"

"August 5th."

"Wow, that's quick! I hope to finish in September. I heard the record for the trail is 83 days. You must be coming close?"

"I thought the record was 86.5 days by Brian Robinson. Where did you see 83? I'm trying to break Flyin' Brian's record and walk the trail in 85 days."

"You are! Don't remember where I saw 83—maybe on the Internet."

The number 83 worried me. I'd heard that someone had claimed completing the trail in 83 days, but had taken 9 rest-days that he'd not counted. His hike took 92 days as far as most hikers were concerned. For the moment, I didn't give Joe's comment further consideration. We continued talking while plodding north.

Joe thought it interesting that my schedule called for breaking the PCT record by only a day-and-a-half. I explained to him that this amount seemed huge to me and would be difficult to achieve, if not impossible. No one ever breaks a world record by more than the smallest of margins. My schedule already called for a 260-plus mile week, and the biggest week that I'd ever hiked previously measured 215 miles on the AT. Knowledgeable hikers considered a 215-mile week on the AT insane. I'd be delving into uncharted territory just to come close to the record. If I landed in the ballpark, I thought that I could always push one *huge* day to better the record.

My itinerary called for me to camp at Boulder Oaks Campground. (See Appendix E for my complete initial schedule plus planned camping areas.) I knew nothing about this campground other than the fact that it lay 26.1 miles north of Campo, as mentioned in the *Databook*. Upon approaching the campground, I felt more than ready to put my pack down and set up my tarptent for the first time on this trip and for only the second time ever. To our dismay, the campground was closed and wouldn't open for another month. We needed to push ahead.

The impetus to continue north once one has been preparing to stop isn't easy to muster. The body has already begun to shut down, so the mind must take over and restart the body. I adjusted my switching network to facilitate such restarts. While a large black watchdog barked violently at us, I found a water spigot, refilled my water-containers, and walked on with a tired Joe. We dragged our weary bodies another three miles north and arrived at a ravine that overflowed with Creosote Bushes, Peppergrass, Burroweed, and Brittlebushes. Although the spot barely qualified as reasonable, we camped there since we didn't want to walk any farther and since we didn't want to spend the night much closer to the upcoming road.

Joe needed to go to the "bathroom" and dropped his heavy pack in some tall dry grass. I'd reconnoitered for a flat spot, and busily erected the tarptent on the one I'd found. While I climbed into my spacious silver-colored shelter for the first time all summer, Joe's worried voice called out asking if I'd seen his pack. I hadn't. He frantically searched around for awhile, and, fortunately, found the gear that he'd based his life on for the next four months. I could only imagine what thoughts had bounced around inside his head during those disheartening moments. If his pack hadn't been recovered as darkness settled, Joe could have crashed without a sleeping-bag in my two-person shelter. In daylight we surely could have located his summer's supply line, but undoubtedly this nervous young man wouldn't have slept a wink.

Joe's pack incident reinforced the idea of never letting my backpack out of my sight. I planned to adhere to this axiom for the remainder of the summer, as the pack contained the success to my trip. In particular, my little yellow stuff-sack contained all my cash ($1,500), credit cards, and identification. I would never let this precious bag be separated from me. As long as I possessed the stuff-sack's contents, I could purchase whatever I needed, although the highly specialized and customized gear that I carried probably couldn't be replaced in less than a month. If I lost everything, I would have continued with off-the-shelf equipment. Acquiring such replacement gear would have taken a couple of days and required hitch-hiking to a store and back. That detour would have been a great disruption to my trip and to my state-of-mind. I feared losing time. A delay of *any* sort would make breaking the record impossible. I didn't want to fall too far behind my schedule at any point.

The first day of hiking, despite my wrong turns, yielded almost 30 miles, so I found myself several miles ahead of schedule. My feet felt good with no hint of blisters. This fact temporarily reinforced the notion that my decision to wear trail-running shoes rather than hiking-boots had indeed been a wise one. I had successfully set up the tarptent and had enjoyed a good night's sleep. The hot sunny weather suited me. In addition, I was with a new friend and so felt safe. Everything progressed well and according to plan.

Late on the morning of May 13th, Joe and I reached the Mount Laguna grocery store, at mile 42.9. While Joe found a seat outside, I entered the small store and inquired about a trail register. They maintained one, and I scanned the book with great interest to see whom I would be meeting in the upcoming weeks. Several entries piqued my curiosity. My sign-in read something like the following:

5/13/2003

Wall here.

Left Campo yesterday morning. Hiked in today with Joe. Everything is going great. No blisters.

I love this trail.

I purchased food for three days, making several rounds of the store, and sat down on the front wooden porch to refuel, repack, and rehydrate. I'd already started improvising my schedule due to water weight and planned to buy food in Warner Springs, at mile 110.6, rather than carrying supplies all the way to Idyllwild, at mile 180.2. The Mount Laguna Post Office didn't open until noon, so Joe sat and waited for his mail-drop. Several other thru-hikers had arrived at the store, too, and we'd introduced ourselves. We chatted mainly about gear, footwear, and future plans. While the others waited impatiently for the post office to open, I hiked the road back to the trail and headed north alone. Would I ever see any of these hikers again?

Many people are unaware of how beautiful a desert can be. The word "desert" conjures up an image of a desolate, dry, and undesirable place. In the Anza-Borrego Desert plentiful wild flowers, including Desert Primrose, Spotted Langloisia, Desert Aster, and Desert Mariposa captured my attention. While moving brush aside with my trekking-poles, I walked through vast seas of purple that covered several square miles in area. When a light breeze blew, the purple mountainsides appeared to shift downhill. As the wind direction changed, the synchronized purple fields shifted uphill. I added many of these spectacular images to my library; I also added the sounds of the breeze and the croaks of the black ravens.

As the PCT meandered endlessly north, I could often see the trail unfolding for several miles. I loved seeing the narrow winding path ahead of me, as it disappeared toward the horizon. My favorite pastime became speculating on when I would reach the next point of interest. I'd say, "I'll be at that patch of yellow flowers in 10 minutes," or "I'll reach that valley floor in 25." The privilege of walking in the bright sunlight with a pleasant warm breeze on my face, coupled with a divine color-scheme, created precious moments. Other than my footsteps, breathing, poling, and singing, the only sounds that I heard came from ravens, insects, wind effects, and occasional rattlesnakes.

The desert bustled, remarkably full of life. Dozens of types of lizards criss-crossed, and ran up and down the trail, including Iguanas, Collared Lizards, Long-tailed Bush Lizards, Zebra-tailed Lizards, and Horned Toads. The Long-tail Bush Lizard raised up like a hydrofoil and would take off running in its elevated stance at speeds in excess of 30 miles per hour. Once a comfortable distance ahead of me, the foot-long lizards would stop again on the sandy trail. When I approached, they *motored* off rapidly, leaving tiny footprints and sinuous tail markings. Many of the lizards seemed to stray a half-mile or more from where I'd originally spotted them. I wondered if they lived in an adobe home and would return there, or if they simply raced around truly nomadic. I didn't pursue the answers to such questions. They merely entertained me.

After a few days on the trail, the desert sun turned my brown Savannah skin even darker. I wore a sombrero and a pair of Julbo Sherpa glacial glasses to protect my face and my eyes. The sun felt intense, but I enjoyed the heat and the sweating. Savannah's high heat-indexes had prepared me for the blazing conditions. Already, after just 72 hours on the trail, I could tell that my mental-stress level had dropped precipitously. Despite minor aches and pains, I felt good physically and at this time nearly always remained on a high. Being in nature, having a path to follow, enjoying freedom, and feeling in tune with my surroundings gave me a complete sense of happiness and satisfaction. I belonged in this setting, and lived blissfully.

On my sixth day of hiking on the trail my stomach craved real food, and I looked forward to eating a hot restaurant meal. This plan didn't come to fruition, though, as the place where I'd intended to dine served only lunch. Since I didn't arrive at the establishment until 3 pm, I missed out. This poor luck meant eating and drinking only cold items because I wasn't carrying a stove. I hoped my timing with restaurants improved over the course of the summer; otherwise, I would "skip" numerous planned meals.

At the end of the first week on May 18th, I hiked toward Idyllwild—a great name for a mountain village. I carried only pages torn from the *Databook* and not the more detailed *Volume I*, which elaborates on how to reach towns, contains maps, and includes verbose trail descriptions. As far as I knew, visiting Idyllwild required a 4.5-mile road-walk from the trail. For someone attempting to set a speed record, this distance seemed like a long way off trail, but I wanted to resupply frequently. Luckily, just at the right moment on the PCT, I encountered a weekend-hiker, who told me that I needed to take the Devil's Slide Trail spur for a little over two miles, and then do a similar-distance road-walk to reach Idyllwild.

Without the *spur trail* information, I would have completely missed Idyllwild. This mistake would have been costly, perhaps even hike-ending and certainly record-ending, since at this juncture I badly needed food. I started to accept that the trail was impossible to hike using just the *Databook*. Even though I'd reached this realization, that knowledge didn't strike me as hard as it should have, so I didn't acquire *Volume I*, yet. I felt fortunate in seeing the weekend-hiker, and felt as if a presence watched over me due to the uncanny nature of the timing.

A couple of miles later I hiked into the trailhead parking lot for the Devil's Slide Trail. This expansive lot sits near a popular rock-climbing area, and I observed many lean climbers walking around with ropes, carabiners, slings, and assorted protection. The weather enhanced the scene magnificently. That day being a Sunday, cars and SUVs occupied all available parking spaces. Overflow vehicles lined both sides of the road that led to the designated parking area. In fact, on the trail that day I'd encountered far more hikers than I'd come across in the previous six days combined.

I enjoyed an affable talk with three rangers, and they asked to see my PCT thru-hiking permit. All of them served as volunteers, but they looked official to me in their matching uniforms. An attractive blond-haired woman who split her time between the California coast and Idyllwild, a pudgy young man who immensely enjoyed the woods and hiking, and an older white-haired man who exuded a great affinity for the outdoors formed this ranger team. These three volunteers seemed full of life and energy, and just glad to be enjoying the woods. The large number of families and individual day-hikers kept them busy checking permits.

After I'd finished picking the trio's brains about nearby trail conditions, and they'd finished grilling me about my thru-hike, I continued my headlong descent. A warm feeling of optimism swept over me regarding my hitching into town. I'd walked only 200 yards on the pavement when another ranger offered me a ride to town in his green pickup truck. By my estimation this man was 40 years old, but his severely pock-marked face may have fooled me. I imagined that he'd suffered bad acne as a child and had been insulted by other children; perhaps those scars had driven him into the woods.

This talkative ranger told me that he had worked in Idyllwild for a long time and had witnessed many changes. He mentioned that a lot of Mexicans had moved into town, causing me to speculate how many of them had crossed into the United States on the PCT. He said this population change had meant that the police and rangers needed to enforce the laws more strictly. "We used to turn the other cheek, but now one thing leads to another. Drugs are a problem." He told me that rangers weren't allowed to give hitch-hikers rides but kindly dropped me on the outskirts of town, anyway. He knew how the system worked because of his longevity. We shook hands and, smiling, I said, "Thanks. Appreciate the lift." I grabbed my trekking-poles and pack from the truck, and walked downhill, looking forward to exploring the small village.

Idyllwild is a quaint mountain town which is becoming more and more tourist-friendly—that is, commercial and over-developed. The hamlet itself seems compact, being nestled in the mountains. I found a store and acquired drinks, and while quenching my thirst, walked to a phone to make a number of calls. Hearing familiar voices and receiving encouragement felt great.

I walked to a Laundromat, where I spoke to a woman and her teenage daughter. Based on the contents of their laundry basket, I deduced that they lived alone. The mother kindly changed money for me, providing lots of quarters. Feeling glad that I didn't have to walk back to the store to obtain change, I thanked her. I made a mental note to plan ahead next time. This cramped building, filled with sloshing washers and spinning dryers, seemed to be part of their weekly routine, but obviously it wasn't part of mine.

Not having washed laundry at a Laundromat for quite some time, the prices struck me as outrageous—two dollars per washing cycle and one dollar per drying cycle. I attributed the inflated prices to California's electric rates, a paucity of water, and greed. Since I carried minimal clothing and everything needed washing, I sat in the Laundromat barely covered up and at one point stripped completely. The women stole glances at me, but I pretended not to notice.

While waiting for my dryer to stop spinning, I befriended "Wild Bill". This lanky man, who was in his mid-forties, told me that he'd thru-hiked the PCT three times. This feat meant that he ranked as one of the most-experienced hikers in the United States. As we bantered back and forth, I learned that Wild Bill is an interesting character. I could see instantly that Wild Bill never would settle. He worked a temporary job in the nearby woods, cutting down diseased trees for fire prevention. Forest fires worried the locals. I prodded Wild Bill for information about the trail, and he obliged with many helpful responses, happily sharing his extensive knowledge.

With apprehension and great curiosity, I asked Wild Bill about rattlesnakes, one of my major concerns. He told me that in one section of trail I would encounter so many rattlers that the noise would "Sound like the Fourth oh July." I just laughed, and so did he, hard. Wild Bill lived out of a beaten pickup truck. He'd evolved a meticulous laundry protocol and rolled seven identical sets of clothing to perfection while chatting with me. They got housed in the cab.

Many of Wild Bill's stories involved near-lethal quantities of alcohol. My new mountain-man friend described the time when some hunters had given him a lift, had put their recently-purchased beer on dry ice to cool it extra quickly, and had proceeded to down a full case each. Subsequently, they had returned Wild Bill to the woods; he, not surprisingly, had seen double. "Instead of one bear, I saw two. Instead of one forest, I saw two," he said, again laughing wildly without restraint. I joined in the uproarious laughter of the fun carefree moment. Wild Bill was a neat character, and I felt good about having bumped into him. By the way, I never asked Bill how he'd acquired his trail name, nor did he ask how I'd acquired mine.

Once I'd finished my laundry, which had consumed an hour, I dressed my filthy body in the momentarily clean clothes and headed to a nearby campground. I paid two dollars for the privilege of taking a shower. Unfortunately, the campground clerk didn't sell soap or shampoo. Again, Lady Luck watched over me, and in the spacious handicap shower-stall, I found unopened soap and shampoo with the Sheraton Hotel label. I cleaned up in 20 minutes, thoroughly enjoying my first rinsing since hitting the trail, and stepped into the intense sun, drying off fast. Feeling and appearing like a new man and no longer stinking, I walked effortlessly back to the store, carrying an empty pack.

The Idyllwild market warehoused a good selection. At this stage of the trip everything whet my appetite. I circled the aisles of the store and nearly overflowed a family-sized shopping-cart with four days worth of food. My next intended resupply was at Big Bear, 96 miles farther north. I felt sure that I'd bought enough.

A thru-hiker must always spend time repackaging items post-resupply in order to save weight and to dispose of trash properly. Finding a "seat" on the hot asphalt outside the store, I began the repackaging chore. As I started ripping open packages, a middle-aged, blond-haired German woman approached me and began talking in a heavy accent. I tried out my rusty German; 20 years earlier I'd spoken fluently. She appreciated my broken sentences. The former opera singer now provided homeless people with food and shelter, and I gave her a small portion of my unopened food. I didn't replace the quantity that I shared. This lady seemed genuinely curious to learn more details about my hike, and I answered all the routine questions for her, in English. She told me about her former husbands, careers, and places of residence. I fixated on my groceries, so many issues that she talked about didn't fully register. Periodically, I would nod and smile; these gestures satisfied her.

The phone calls, laundry, shower, and shopping had all gone efficiently. Although my original schedule called for an overnight stay in Idyllwild, my Casio read only 4 pm, so I decided to return to the trail. Before proceeding north, though, I wanted to devour a real meal at a Mexican restaurant. I wandered into an establishment close to the Idyllwild market and ordered my food, and then continued with calls from the restaurant's pay phone, while the cooks prepared my meal. Friends whom I reached spoke excitedly to me and vice versa. A young boy tapped me on the arm to indicate that my food had arrived, so I cut my last call short.

I consumed an enormous plate of steak fajitas, executing the usual load-and-roll tortilla routine repeatedly, and drank several large beverages, while ordering an avocado burger and French fries for the "road". These American staples would serve as my dinner. I called the fajitas a (very) late lunch. As I exited the restaurant, I spotted a number of thru-hikers sipping lime margaritas on the deck. I felt tempted to relax with this young group for awhile, and a frosty margarita would have gone down smoothly, but I pushed on—much to their disbelief. Idyllwild is a town where many thru-hikers overnight, and a nontrivial percentage of these hikers never return to the PCT. I wanted to keep my dream alive.

After my Gargantuan meal of fajitas, I began the road-walk back to the trailhead. This time I went steeply uphill and carried a titanic-sized pack. The burger and the French fries together weighed close to four pounds. Even though I'd intentionally paid close attention to the winding route to town, I was mystified on how to return to the trailhead. Several unfamiliar intersections confused me. I asked a couple of folks for directions, which resulted in the proverbial "Do blah blah blah, and you can't possibly get lost." The clear implication being that if you did get lost, you possessed the intelligence of a cow.

Having walked a mile without recognizing any landmarks, I stopped a woman in a car who was pulling out of her driveway. The lady opened the driver's window a coat-hanger's width, and I asked her for directions. She told me where to go. I'd made a wrong turn leading up an incredibly steep hill; now I free-falled for a half-mile and walked toward the trailhead along another parallel road. My feeble attempt at hitching a ride came up short, since no one, except me, was heading back out onto the trail at 5 pm on Sunday evening. I eventually retraced my steps up the highly inclined Devil's Slide Trail and rejoined the PCT, where I'd seen the rangers hours earlier. I felt good about regaining the trail, and marched happily northward.

Nearly every resupply point along the PCT is reached via a long downhill, and sometimes via a *very* long downhill ... 8 to 10 miles with 3,000–4,000 feet of descent. This drop occurs because most of the towns sit in valleys. While in town, I always made a conscientious effort to super-hydrate on energy-replacements drinks and to eat a large quantity of (relatively) healthy food. Every return to the trail necessarily entails a big climb to obtain the crest. Needless to say, with a full stomach and a heavy pack, the returns to the trail involve stretches of the most difficult hiking that one must do. The pull that one feels to stay in town to remain comfortable only exacerbates the situation.

Being the "last straw", the unbearable weight of the avocado burger needed to go. So, at the first semblance of flat ground, I began munching my mega-calorie dinner. The cold burger would have filled a child's lunchbox, and its bun sprouted condiments, including lettuce, tomato, onion, pickles, and, of course, avocado. I forced the massive burger and as many French fries as possible down on top of the unsettled fajitas. The bag of fries must have been super-sized twice over. Cold fries don't turn me on, but I decided to take the uneaten portion with me, not wanting to discard anything containing calories. With a substantially-lighter pack and noticeably-larger stomach, I pushed on until darkness encroached. That night I found a spectacular place to camp.

I perambulated the area and set up my tarptent on a cliff's edge in a small sandy spot. My campsite was not an established one. This virgin *stealth camp*—a campsite off the trail that is completely hidden from view—suited me perfectly. Having consumed a few more fries, I walked barefoot over to a rocky outcropping and climbed up, gazing down on the valley and across at the shadowy mountains. I lay there for awhile on the rocks, letting my mind wander. The evening felt peaceful and beautiful, as the orange light slowly faded.

While little animals and unfamiliar-looking birds kept me company, I meditated. This gorgeous evening reinforced one of the main reasons why I wanted to hike the trail—to commune with nature. I turned in at around 9:30 pm, put in earplugs, and slept in what would likely be one of my most comfortable campsites for the remainder of my summer. In the morning, as I would always do throughout the trip, I made sure that my campsite was returned to its pristine state. This simple task took little time since the light-weight tarptent's footprint could barely even be detected. I never planned to start a fire. Mine was low-impact camping.

————————————————————

The first week on the trail flew past. Although I'd made some wrong turns, I found myself ahead of schedule, and my plan seemed effective. My equipment hadn't let me down, and my extensive mental preparation had helped me to remain focused and positive. Physically, I'd conquered the soreness of mountain-climbing, and my feet looked and felt, amazingly, like new. The speed-record dream lived! I fully expected the remainder of the summer to unfold as smoothly, to find beautiful camping areas, to stick to my schedule, and to develop few foot problems.

3 Unforgiving Desert

Following my wondrous night of camping north of Idyllwild, I ate a breakfast of cold French fries and crushed PopTarts, broke camp, and hightailed it north. Although I was hiking at an elevation between 8,000 and 9,000 feet, the altitude didn't bother me because of my previous mountaineering experience. Another splendid sunny morning had greeted me, and the initial part of the day had unfolded excellently. This calm start made me feel carefree.

Having walked a few hilly miles through evergreen forest, I emerged into an open sandy section where I couldn't tell which way the trail led. The PCT had vanished. This disappearance created anxiety and took me out of my comfort zone. I discovered a large semicircle and an arrow drawn in the dirt with the label "PCT". Nevertheless, I couldn't determine which way to proceed, as the direction in which the arrow pointed didn't seem to lead to a trail.

I began hiking down a declivity, and my track angled more steeply than any previous part of the PCT. Still I kept hiking. I soon found myself in no man's land and decided to continue downhill until I reached a trail-marker. On my precipitous descent, prior to my believing that I was lost, I'd found a pleasant place to kick back, relax, and enjoy songbirds. Lost, I felt far from relaxed and was thinking about the time that had been spent sitting.

As my knee-damaging descent continued, I began to get even more suspicious that I'd walked off trail. I encountered a man named Larry, who'd just hiked up the trail that I was sailing down. Larry appeared to be in his early fifties and in great shape, but he seemed totally worn out from his ascent. His breathing was labored, and his chest heaved. The

33

high altitude as well as the steepness of the climb had affected him. He told me that his son had wandered off to climb boulders nearby. Glancing around, I noticed some interesting rock formations that I'd missed earlier. I asked Larry if the trail we stood on was the PCT. He didn't think so and said that his son would be back shortly, and perhaps he knew.

Larry asked if I was doing a thru-hike of the PCT, and when he learned that I was, he immediately became interested and posed lots of questions. One query was, "What are you carrying to protect yourself?" When I told him "Nothing", he lurched sideways with surprise. Larry whipped out a large buck knife and said that if a Black Bear or a Mountain Lion attacked him, he would defend himself. I thought how unlikely that would be—both the attack and the successful defense—but said nothing.

Larry seemed surprised to hear that I was drinking the water from streams. In *Outdoor Magazine* he'd read about certain types of bacteria that can completely immobilize you. Chris McCandless (the protagonist of *Into the Wild*) came to mind. McCandless had become sick from eating the wrong types of seeds, and later had tragically died from starvation. I told Larry that I wasn't concerned, and that I sure hoped that nothing like that would happen to me. Larry was also shocked that I hiked alone. I answered that I didn't know anyone who wanted to hike the PCT on a similar schedule. All-in-all, Larry seemed to be in a state of disbelief concerning my hike. Naturally, his questions helped little in putting my own mind at ease and erasing my personal doubts.

When our conversation ended, Larry's son appeared out of the blue. He was also named Larry. He sported many tattoos and piercings, looked to be in his mid-twenties, and was totally ripped. Larry Jr. wore no shirt and soaked up the intense rays. Neither of the Larrys carried a map, as they had planned just an out-and-back day-hike. Although the two tried to assist me as best they could, they didn't possess any truly reliable trail information. Both father and son thought that I'd veered off the PCT, but they seemed only 50% convinced of this possibility. The Larrys told me that they'd remembered seeing a trail-marker another mile or so downhill from our current position.

I decided to find out what the mysterious trail-marker read. Of course, I felt worried that I wouldn't find the trail-marker at all, and also that the estimated one mile might actually be more. "Thanks, guys. Good meeting you. Take care," I said, while wondering if I'd ever see these fellows again. With great trepidation, I proceeded downhill until finally reaching a trail-sign. I'd come down the Marion Mountain Trail. "S—!" In an instant it became clear that I'd detoured off trail— way off. My instincts had already been telling me this news for a long time. Grave disappointment and intense frustration swept over me, as I attempted to come to grips with the situation. I tried my best to let my blunder go, but for the moment I experienced difficulty in coping with my mistake. Losing my way ticked me off.

I felt demoralized. Uncertainty wreaked havoc in my mind and on my emotions. Without having enough information to decide which way to go, I'd simply guessed. Naturally, under such circumstances, I would chose correctly only half the time. I now relied on my fitness and my mental toughness to get me back on schedule. I became a tracker, always looking for clues and trying to discern where the trail hid. At crossroads such as these, I tapped into my library and sang James Taylor's line "Keep your head together, and call my name out loud ..." While doing 25-mile days, a wrong turn would hurt less than it would while doing 45-mile days.

Coming to grips with my Marion Mountain Trail mistake and having settled my emotions, I needed to hike up the spur trail to regain the PCT. I pushed hard in going uphill, trying to minimize the amount of lost time, and also attempting to relieve the stress caused by the knowledge of being lost. In ascending I breathed hard, and more clearly understood why the elder Larry had been gasping for air. I thought that I would catch the two Larrys during this Lance-Armstrong-like effort, but surprisingly didn't see them on this vertical stretch. Eventually, I arrived back at the semicircle and arrow in the sand. This time the trail jumped out at me, and it was easy to see which way I needed to go. Nothing had changed, but my perception. Why had the obscure morphed into the obvious? "F—!" This five-mile detour pissed me off. It had drained valuable energy, particularly on the uphill, since I'd gone anaerobic.

I finally knew for certain that I'd reintegrated the PCT, and this knowledge made me happy. While starting across Fuller Ridge, at mile 188.3, I encountered melting snow. Clothed only in running shoes, shorts, and a T-shirt and obviously not accustomed to walking through snow in Savannah, I paid close attention to my footing. I saw a partially buried trail-sign that indicated the PCT headed downhill. On discovering the trail-marker I declared, "This can't be the PCT. The PCT is a crest trail, so it must go uphill here." I figured that someone had sabotaged the sign, so I proceeded sharply uphill, heading straight for the summit of Mount San Jacinto—one of the highest peaks in Southern California. (Although I should have known it, at that time I didn't realize the four-digit numbers in the *Databook* specified altitude.)

While I was pushing farther and farther uphill, as expected, the snow became deeper and deeper. Following two sets of footprints, I imagined that I might still be on the PCT. Must be thru-hikers' prints. The steep snow conditions became difficult and dangerous, and merited an ice axe, but I didn't carry one in Southern California. These guys are nuts I thought, but blindly plowed ahead. To my great chagrin, I eventually caught the two Larrys; I'd been following *their* footprints, not the tracks of thru-hikers! Holy s—!

The Larrys and I had said our goodbyes much earlier, and had never expected to see each other again. While shaking their heads, they told me that I'd detoured off trail, again. I'd been in denial about this fact but then admitted that I'd made another mistake. After a brief pause, we exchanged what I hoped were final goodbyes, and I descended back to the Fuller Ridge sign. If they'd been betting men, I don't think they would have wagered that I'd make it to Canada or for that matter even Oregon. Doubt didn't creep into my mind, though. I felt embarrassed, totally humiliated, but nevertheless was still on a mission.

One's thought-process works in strange ways. My earlier wrong turn down the Marion Mountain Trail somehow blocked me from heading downhill to Fuller Ridge, where I'd first laid eyes on the perfectly good PCT sign. I couldn't fathom the paranoid logic which I'd employed that made me ignore this trail-sign. For almost 200 miles I'd followed arrows drawn in the sand, but in this case I had disregarded a well-placed official trail-sign.

Another couple hours had vanished on my second detour. More costly, I'd burned a great deal of energy and done a prodigious amount of extra climbing. I'd practically returned to Idyllwild and almost summited Mount San Jacinto! These mistakes qualified as insane and never should have happened. Remarkably, I didn't let them get me too down. I used adversity to build my strength. I pretended that a grotesque adversary was trying to prevent me from completing the trail and that I would slay the monster. The mental games which I played along the way kept me going.

I'd lost so much time on my unintentional side trips that I'd fallen behind schedule. By hiking too fast to correct these screw-ups, I'd way overextended myself. To make up for the lost hours, I hiked until darkness that evening. At that point in the hike, I didn't carry a light. I descended steeply into a canyon. For 15 minutes I'd been speed hiking while simultaneously trying to look for a flat camping spot on the sides of the canyon walls. I learned that the big canyons in Southern California contain no flat ground, though.

Several times while glancing up at hillsides, I'd twisted my ankle and nearly lost my balance. A broken ankle here would mean a painful hobble out and the end to my dream. Because darkness loomed on the rocky trail and I wasn't yet accustomed to setting up the tarptent by feel, I resigned myself to accepting a less-than-suitable camping spot. The night after my perfect campsite, I "slept" on a 15° slope on a brushy and rocky canyon wall. I lay awake most of the night, and when, to my nickle-sized pupils, the trail looked illuminated enough to continue, I rambled.

I'd camped without any water. A dry camp is a situation which hikers fear and which I found myself in because of another miscalculation. I'd expected to get water from the *next* creeklet coming from a snowfield, but eventually, the snowfields ran out. Thirsty, I descended another 4,000 feet to a water fountain at Snow Canyon Road, at mile 208.4. A room-sized boulder sat 10 feet from the fountain and provided me comfortable shade. I rinsed my coolmax T-shirt off, rung it out, and tossed it on the boulder to dry. When the clean T-shirt landed in the sand, I repeated the process, being more careful. I forced myself to drink as much as possible, and then drank more. "One more liter," I directed. "Yes, sir." My exposed stomach grew round before my eyes, bulging like that of a hungry African child.

While sitting next to the gray boulder, as probably all previous PCT thru-hikers had done, I watched a multi-colored lizard, and it watched me. I drank even more, as the sun felt hot by 9 am. The next water-source, according to the *Databook*, was only 12.7 miles away. Since I'd just super-hydrated, I figured that five liters (just over ten pounds of water) would suffice for the four hours of walking. I even thought that this amount seemed excessive and considered taking less. At around 9:30, with a sloshing stomach providing music and a damp T-shirt cooling me, I marched on.

As I descended farther toward the superhighway I-10, I noticed that the temperature had increased dramatically. A strong wind usually blows through this pass, but on that day the windmills covering the mountainsides barely turned. The heat wasn't yet a significant factor, though, and I still felt good. In fact, so good that when I encountered a golf ball that lay one-quarter of a mile from the freeway, I wrote a heel-dragged note in the sand that read, "Wall hit this ball from the freeway." Joe would get a kick out of that, if he made it this far. My spirits soared. I remembered my late father and our CalTech field-trip years earlier to this region to study earthquake faults. My thoughts oscillated between happy and sad.

Leery of rattlesnakes, I worried that I might be entering the "fireworks" section that Wild Bill had mentioned. I didn't hear any rattlers, but this fact didn't free me from my hyper-alert state. The temperature increased further, and I drank water whenever I felt thirsty. I sipped fluid easily from my Platypus tube, which at all times hung only a foot from my mouth. The first three gulps contained liquid that the direct sunlight had almost boiled. Additional mouthfuls tasted cooler, since the Platypus itself was buried in a pack sleeve. I passed under the freeway, but the multi-lane road provided only moments of shade. It never occurred to me to hang out under the road until temperatures cooled, which would have been many hours henceforth. The smell, pollution, and vehicular noise bothered me, and subconsciously I probably worried about vagrants.

I climbed gradually uphill. A couple of hikers had earlier asked me if I'd planned to stop at the Pink Motel. Never having heard of the place, I naturally said "No". I passed a dingy-looking building that had a "Welcome Hikers" sign up on corrugated metal. The landscape imitated an abandoned-auto dump. Little did I know that this dwelling was the famous Pink Motel, where I could have filled my emptying water containers. At this point I felt more concerned about getting mugged, so I didn't slow down. My suspicions about people gradually faded as the summer progressed, and my faith in humanity was gradually restored. It took a long time to overcome societal training and stereotypes. For the moment, though, I lost out, more than I realized.

I hadn't really noticed that I was getting precariously low on water. While climbing uphill in the loose sand, the temperatures blistered me. The humidity read 10% compared to Savannah's 85%, and I told myself, "It's a dry heat." I laughed. "It's a dry heat," I said again, shaking my head from side-to-side and smirking. I passed a beat-up old car that was parked near the trail. It looked like the poor wreck had fried there overcooking in the brutal conditions. I wondered who'd abandoned the car, and if the vehicle's owner had made it out of the desert alive. The beater had probably sat there for dozens of years, and this inhospitable place was its unsavory burial-site; its license plates were tombstone inscriptions. While pushing on through the desert, I continued to overheat and rather seriously so. Suddenly, I laughed no more.

In my quest to find shade, I crawled under a spindly tree and rested there for awhile on, of all things, a torn black-plastic bag that I lay down on whenever my back hurt. (I'd been given the trash bag by two *section-hikers* a few days earlier at a water-cache where we'd become friends.) After five minutes of lying down, I began sweating even more profusely. My black-plastic sheet functioned as a ground-level oven. I took an inventory of my water and to my great dismay discovered that the precious-fluid supply had practically evaporated. At the rate I was dehydrating, I couldn't lie here too long. I soon rose and began hiking. "Come on, Wall!" I said forcefully, giving myself both encouragement and an order to push on strongly.

Time seemed to freeze somewhere between 12 noon and 1 pm, and with the sun directly overhead, no shade existed anywhere in this scrub desert. I hiked on a 12.7-mile waterless stretch and believed that my next water would be obtained at a creek. I told myself that I would arrive there soon, hoped that I could find the creek, and prayed that the small water-source hadn't already dried up for the summer. The trail rose continuously uphill and remained sandy, and I made poor time, much worse than I'd hoped. What if the water-source were dry?

After taking a few minuscule sips of boiling water, my supply seemed completely gone. I sucked desperately on the Platypus tube but ingested only air, as the Platypus folded and crumpled in a vacuum-induced state. This emptiness voided my hopes, and created a bad feeling. Not really sure how far I still had to hike to reach water, I speculated maybe an hour. In the extreme heat and with goose-bumps already forming, this stretch would be hard, dangerous, and life-threatening. Naturally, I thought that I should have left Snow Canyon Road with more water. I felt frustrated, stupid, and angry over my poor judgment, but my mistake had happened and couldn't be undone. "F—!" All of my mental energy now focused on events that I could still influence.

My tired legs became anchors in the desert sand; my swelling feet became slow-emptying hourglasses. The previous day's hard effort, when I'd red-lined my pace to make up for wrong turns, had totally zapped me. I hadn't recovered fully and felt baked. Splotches of salt outlined my clothing and my face. I went horizontal again on my black plastic in another spot having almost zero shade. This sunny place was, however, the best resting point that I could find. Feeling cooked and getting worse, I wasn't comfortable. Even the plastic melted in the extreme temperatures. I told myself to stand up and hike. I commanded myself a second and a third time, "Do it, Ray! Do it!" My will-power and experience with dehydration were all that I had to go on. I was in serious trouble and knew that no one would be coming by to assist me. I fiddled with my switching network, but my poor timing had reduced its effectiveness.

I dragged myself north. Hallucinations entered my mind with regularity—rocks became pools of blue water; cacti became water fountains; lizards became St. Bernards carrying water. I needed to concentrate intently on hiking. Another steep section faced me. I ordered myself to walk as efficiently as possible and began poling more rhythmically. This stretch felt like the terribly vertical Caneleta on Aconcagua, the tallest mountain in the world outside of Asia, that I'd climbed in oxygen-starved air at 22,000 feet. "Keep moving, slowly, slowly," I encouraged myself. Then the fact dawned on me that I could still make sounds. Hermann Buhl, the great Austrian climber, during his solo alpine ascent of Nanga Parbat in the 1950's had been so horribly dehydrated that he couldn't utter a single sound. As long as I could still speak, I believed that I could endure. I pulled the Buhl volume from my library and kept moving forward, periodically making an inane comment to assure myself that I wasn't dead.

My pace degenerated to that of a disinterested toddler. The clock continued to tick: 1 pm, 2 pm, 3 pm, ... The temperatures continued to escalate. On the cold side there is a coldest temperature known as absolute zero, but on the hot side, there is no such corresponding upper limit. I wished that there were. Tremendous cotton mouth plagued me, and my lips cracked deeply. Thoughts of water flooded my mind. Unable to salivate, I could only think how good even a tiny sip would taste. I was beyond desperate and close to falling down.

I must be getting close to the creek—at least I believed and hoped that this thought held true. Constant reassurance kept me hiking, just another 15 minutes, just another 10 minutes, just traverse this wasteland, ... Then I struggled over a big rise and in disbelief gazed on a long set of *switchbacks* wrapping hundreds of feet downhill into a bone-dry canyon. The limited vegetation was shriveled and brown, and there was *no water* in sight, anywhere. This desolate place depressed me. My spirits sank as reality whispered that this grueling descent would take another hour of hiking at my snail's pace. I doubted that I would last for that duration. I felt sad. This lonely ending, shared only with ravens and lizards, wasn't the final scene I'd envisioned.

Then the thought to dump my pack occurred and to head directly for the creek. Encouraged by rational thinking, I felt hope. If I did rid myself of the pack, I would have to return for it. I really had no sense of the gap size between me and the creek. My highly-erratic pace and warped sense of time confused me. For all I really knew, the water was still another hour after the massive descent. I decided not to jettison the pack, yet.

I was miserable and a beaten man. My fear of death turned more to a feeling of acceptance. If I was to die that day, I was to die. To save myself, though, I needed to reach water. I decided to carry my pack Tanzanian-style to create shade for my head. After an hour or so of this technique, with aching back, I staggered to a creek. My eyes felt weepy, but no tears fell. The creek appeared suddenly—perhaps too suddenly? The urge to cry dissipated, though, even as I thought that I was seeing a mirage. It was a mirage. "No! Oh, no!" I shouted without making a sound. It wasn't. Thank God, I saw a real creek!

I stripped naked and lay horizontal in the cool narrow creek. With water streaming over my goose-bump-covered body, there I lay submerged for an hour-and-a-half, drinking animal-style. During many of these moments, I cramped up and writhed in agony—like a poor squirrel emerging from underneath the wheel of a speeding auto—had I already left my body? I yelped and whined. Various body parts became badly sunburned, and my feet softened up. However, these discomforts held absolutely no concern. I drank, drank, drank, and then chugged more. Ants scurried all around me on the nearby shore.

While filling all of my water-containers to the brim, I tried to eat salty foods. After this life-threatening bonk, a long time elapsed before I could upright myself and walk. Despite my misery, I felt happy to be alive. In fact, I experienced a great joy at being alive. Tears of joy fell, and my emotions flowed unchecked, as all my senses returned. My dream breathed, too. This time I'd returned from the edge.

The thought to camp near the friendly creek never even occurred to me. Once recovered enough to rise to my feet, I pushed north. I didn't hike too much farther that day, but a moral victory had been won in just hiking again, at all. The day ended with a mileage total of only 25. Thanks to Larry Sr. I worried about dying from the life-saving water because I hadn't taken the time to treat it. However, the creek's water never did bother me, and I felt a presence watching over me. I continued to guzzle vast quantities from my vessels. While forcing myself to swallow more, I thought of chocolate milk, root-beer soda, pina coladas, Chimay ale, and icy Del's lemonade. Despite the huge volumes of fluid, I never urinated that day or that night. As the sun illuminated a morning scene that I felt happy to play a role in, I drank more water and ate my sunflower seeds to acquire salt. When I did pee, the liquid flowed an ugly, grainy, brown color. I looked away, feeling sick.

The day subsequent to my cruel dehydration, after I'd been hiking for a couple of hours, I encountered a fellow going south. The white-haired outdoorsman appeared to be around 70 and looked hardy. Eventually I learned that the old car which I'd been mystified by was his; he took great pride in his relic. "Has 400,000 miles and runs great." I asked him where we were on the PCT, and he pulled out his *Databook*. His copy wasn't cut up, like mine. He taught me about the altitude column in the *Databook*, and from then on I paid close attention to elevation as a means of knowing where I was. Why hadn't I noticed the elevation column up until now? I couldn't even speculate. The hiking veteran wore a wrist altimeter, too.

My latest instructor said that he'd passed a petite Asian woman earlier that day. "She was going gangbusters up the trail. Saw her come out of a dry wash this morning where she'd camped. I asked her why she didn't come up to the campsite only one-hundred yards farther up the trail. She just said that she didn't know about it." I wondered if I would meet her later that day. My new friend, the mechanic, pressed on south with a grave warning from me regarding the water situation that he'd be facing. Obviously, he'd already been over this terrain and was doing an out-and-back trip, but I was too far gone to realize his itinerary at the time. This experienced back-woodsman surely didn't need my warning. He probably thought I was nuts.

Amazingly, I hiked 32 miles the day following my epic dehydration. As the sun disappeared from the sky, I dragged my battered body into a pine-needled campsite. The "Asian woman" rested there at a picnic table, and sat all bundled up to protect herself from the freezing temperatures. Her dark balaclava disguised her as Ninja-warrior. I startled her by my late arrival, as darkness fell, and perhaps because she was alone and hadn't anticipated any other hikers arriving at camp this late at night. My war-worn appearance probably didn't comfort her, either. I sighed deeply; I felt wasted. We exchanged pleasantries, and pointing, I asked, "Do you mind if I pitch my tent over there?" She was fine with that. I told her that I needed to establish camp right away since I didn't have a light.

As I was setting up the Squall, the woman finished eating a cooked dinner. I learned that she planned a thru-hike and that her name was Jenny. Like Joe, not everyone uses a trail name, especially at the beginning of a hike. I needed to lie down before I fell down, and, as an afterthought, I asked her if she would like to start off hiking together the next day. Jenny remarked that she liked to get going early. We agreed to start hiking by 6 am, and said goodnight.

I slept well that night, and when Jenny called to me at 5:40 am, I was dreaming of water. Fortunately, my internal clock still ran on eastern standard time. The camp where we'd stayed sat at 7,600 feet, and the crisp morning air chilled us. I filled my Platypus with clear water from a faucet, and Jenny needed to close the container for me. My numb fingers wouldn't cooperate enough to press the zippered seal tight. Jenny told me that she'd been rock-climbing for seven years, and this fact showed in her hand strength. For my part I wouldn't make the same mistake of getting icy water on my hands when refilling water-bags.

Jenny and I hiked together and shared friendly conversation. She'd started her solo journey on the evening of May 9th, ignoring grave warnings from Border Patrol personnel, and planned to finish the PCT in mid-September. I informed her of my goal to complete the thru-hike in early August. We shared similar interests in music, and we sang our way north together. Jenny possessed a melodious voice that was well-suited to songs by Janis Joplin, Joni Mitchell, Paul Simon, and others. She demonstrated a gift for lyrics and knew the full words to many songs. I could usually recall only the chorus and one or two verses, so chimed in sporadically. Miles passed quickly and happily for both of us.

Although Jenny hadn't completed a mega trail, she was a strong and experienced hiker. She'd done two multi-week trips in preparation for her PCT hike. This diminutive powerhouse had soloed the 235-mile Superior Hiking Trail in Minnesota traversing along the northern shore of Lake Superior to the Canadian border and the 223-mile Ouachita Trail in the Ouachita Mountains spanning Oklahoma and Arkansas. Since Jenny had worked at REI, she knew the "in's and out's" of gear, too. Her meticulous planning and skillful preparation showed, and her hiking résumé impressed me.

No doubt ever crept into my mind as to whether Jenny would finish the PCT or not. Obviously, she possessed great courage to hike alone in the wilderness. People had questioned her sanity for going solo, just as they'd questioned mine. The only thing that concerned me about Jenny's journey was that she lugged close to 50 pounds. For any hiker this amount is a back-breaking load, but for a 5-foot 1-inch, 105-pound person the weight seemed enormous, and I worried about her sustaining a foot or a leg injury. I learned that Jenny intended a true wilderness experience and planned to resupply only every 12 days. This plan I found truly remarkable since I intended to obtain new supplies essentially whenever feasible, thus at all times carrying the least amount of food possible.

We arrived at a ranger station and were refilling bottles when another thru-hiker asked us our names.

"I'm Jenny."

"I'm Ray."

"You're not Ray and Jenny Jardine, are you?"

We both smiled and said "no" simultaneously. The Jardines are the most famous hiking couple in the world, and Ray Jardine is considered by many to be the father of ultralight-backpacking techniques.

Jenny confided later, "I never thought of that before."

When Jenny and I parted company, I felt sad and lonely. I think she did, too. Jenny had taught me a great number of things. I wished that our schedules had meshed better. Destiny pulled me inexorably north, though, and Jenny followed her own carefully thought-out itinerary. Throughout the trip I would often think of Jenny and wonder how she was faring. I hoped that she found her way and was successful. Jenny inspired me.

From Idyllwild I'd planned to hike 100 miles before resupplying in the town of Big Bear, at mile 276.3. When nearing the approach for Big Bear, my food stores ran low. Nevertheless, I decided to skip this resupply point and push two more days without food to Silverwood Lake, at mile 331.1. I turned off the hunger switch. During those two days, I burned almost all my remaining body fat while consuming only 2,000 calories. This episode hurt, but had definitely toughened me up for any future lack-of-food dramas. Despite the struggle, I was happy that I'd skipped Big Bear.

I'd actually traveled to Big Bear before, and even under similar circumstances. When I'd first moved to California from Rhode Island to attend Pomona College in 1979, I'd often explored Southern California alone by bicycle. One day while sitting in my dorm room, I'd looked at a California map. At the time I'd assumed that the scale matched the one for Rhode Island (as most Rhode Island teenagers probably would have done), and had found Big Bear Lake nestled in the mountains. The alpine lake had fascinated me since I'd never seen one. I'd decided to ride my bike to the lake from Claremont.

The mammoth ride had tapped all my reserves, and I hadn't brought enough fluid or food with me. The last 17 miles had involved tortuous climbs, and I'd completely bonked. My plan had been to ride from Claremont to Big Bear and back to Claremont on the same day. The route I'd cycled went on forever, and it hadn't been physically possible for me to turn around and immediately pedal back to my dorm. Fortunately, I'd carried a credit card with me. I had checked into a motel, had devoured a huge meal, and with extremely sore knees had pedaled back safely to Claremont the next day. This trip, better than any geography class, had helped me to understand the relative sizes and the relative elevations of Rhode Island and California.

In Southern California the PCT is arid, so locating water is a formidable task. The *Databook* describes where the next available places are to pick up water, and most hikers rely heavily on this light guide. I realized that losing a single desert page of the *Databook* would put me in a potentially life-threatening situation. With gaps in water's availability as wide as 30 miles and temperatures over 120°F, dangerous predicaments can arise. In the desert I often carried my maximum possible water-load of 11 liters (approximately 22 pounds).

Hiking a waterless stretch of 30 miles, while walking three miles per hour, consumed 10 hours. In the soaring desert heat I needed at least one liter per hour. Thus I would typically find myself out of water by the time I reached the next water-source. If I missed that creeklet or spring, it could have meant another 30 miles without any water. This distance wasn't doable except at night, and I carried no light, so I simply couldn't miss *any* refill opportunities. Finding some water-sources challenged me, and without the *Databook*, I wouldn't have known where to search. I kept a watchful eye on the pages of the precious *Databook* to avoid a disaster.

4 Trail Angels

Trail angels are people who enjoy assisting hikers out of the kindness of their hearts. Along the PCT in Southern California, a number of trail angels regularly put out water-caches for thirsty hikers. These caches, although they can't and shouldn't be relied on, make crossing the parched desert soil much safer. Unexpectedly discovering a cache, when one needs water, is a great blessing. The people who take the time to restock these caches served to remind me that most people mean well. Many caches that I saw seemed positioned in the middle of nowhere. How people hauled 50 to 100 gallons of water into inaccessible harsh terrain puzzled me. These amazing folks deserve much credit and thanks.

I felt lucky to meet trail angel John at one point as he replenished water and candy at a cache. He epitomizes generosity and regularly restocks water-caches for hikers in Southern California. John has thru-hiked the PCT himself and possesses an excellent appreciation for what hikers experience. His concern for hikers went a long way toward improving my faith in people. Simply stated, John is a good-deed doer. This next story recounts another meeting with a trail angel.

On my way to Silverwood Lake, I'd pushed hours beyond the bonk point, having bypassed an intended resupply at Big Bear. I concentrated hard to keep my overworked and underfed body moving forward. I muttered some nasty phrases concerning the food that I'd given to the German woman at Idyllwild. I desperately hoped to resupply at Silverwood Lake. Unfortunately, I arrived in the vicinity of the lake shortly after its snack-bar had closed for the day. I mumbled. Prior to this discovery a couple whom I'd made friends with on the trail had offered me a sandwich, but obtaining it entailed a 15-minute detour to their car. Maybe I should have gone with them, but that opportunity to refuel had been missed. More mutterings passed through my quivering lips. I walked on hungry, searching for a place to camp. Suddenly, Lady Luck changed my situation for the better.

Upon entering a small picnic area after Silverwood Lake, I ran into "Fire-Walking Bill" and his gang. They invited me over for the feast of the summer and one of my greatest feasts of all-time. The all-you-can-eat fruit, potato chips, dill pickles, barbecued chicken, smoked salmon, juicy steak, corn-on-the-cob, baked potatoes, and pudding tasted great. I'd been so ravenous that I ate for hours down-shifting my chewing rhythm as my stomach began to fill. I consumed a vast amount of food, and felt energy surging back into my bloodstream. The ice-cold bottled water, sodas, wine coolers, and Southern Comfort hit the spot, too. Evidently, I wasn't going to push on that night, and ended up camping near Fire-Walking Bill and his wife, and two other couples who were their friends. Without this *trail magic*, I would have spent an unpleasant evening.

How did the trail angel Fire-Walking Bill acquire his nickname? He wasn't a hiker. At the picnic area where I'd encountered Bill, a concrete fire-ring four feet in diameter sat in the middle of the group's campsite. As the alcohol in the Southern Comfort bottle vanished, Bill's surfing instincts emerged. With Madonna providing background music, Bill danced, surfed, and walked in the fire—his shoes and his pants occasionally igniting. Based on his blazing performance, I dubbed my partying friend Fire-Walking Bill.

After the Sumoesque feed with Fire-Walking Bill, my hunger pangs left, and I reached my resupply point the following day at Interstate 15 in Cajon Canyon, at mile 344.7. My overnight stay in town there revitalized me. From Cajon Canyon I continued north through the desert, experiencing happiness and joy while hiking. My next stop occurred at Agua Dulce (Sweet Water) on Darling Road, at mile 454.9. I knew absolutely nothing about this town, except that the Saufley family there assisted hikers. Before trying to find their place, though, I visited the well-stocked market in Agua Dulce and completed another extensive shopping spree.

At the pricey Agua Dulce market I encountered a hiker who informed me where the Saufleys lived. In the cozy hiker-friendly town, I succeeded immediately in hitching a ride to their house. Trail angels Jeff and Donna Saufley open their home to hikers, and in the comfort of their residence, I read email for the first time since I'd departed from Savannah. This communication allowed me to catch up on news, and let my friends know that the PCT had already exceeded all expectations. Shortly following my marathon email session, I headed back to Agua Dulce proper. Donna couldn't believe that I was pushing on so soon and not taking more advantage of their hospitality. "This is the best stop on the trail," she said repeatedly with conviction.

I thanked Donna profusely for her kindness. While I proceeded north, 20 hikers remained at the Saufleys' scattered everywhere: eating, playing cards, watching TV, or catching up on correspondence. I hitched a ride back to Agua Dulce for a humongous pizza lunch, and, after a long brutally-hot road-walk (which many hikers skip), resumed my journey on the hot dusty trail.

My spirits flew incredibly high during this time, and little discouraged me. I brushed off wrong turns, rattlesnakes, out-of-food episodes, and blisters. My switching network aligned perfectly. I completed the hike into Lake Hughes, at mile 485.2, on Saturday afternoon, May 31st. At the Harley Bar, I consumed another memorable meal: a jumbo shrimp cocktail, garden salad with blue-cheese dressing, beer-battered fish-and-chips, and frosty draft beer. The trail dramatically improved the taste of all food. From Lake Hughes via phone, I finalized arrangements with "Fish-out-of-Water" (or "Fish", for short) for our rendezvous in the town of Mojave, California. Fish is my lifetime friend, Peter Solomon, who planned to join me for two weeks of adventure starting on June 2nd.

I'd fallen slightly behind schedule on my way to Lake Hughes, so to meet Fish on time I needed to hike 72 miles in a 34-hour period. During this span, I would cover over 50 miles in a 24-hour period. On the afternoon stretch out of Lake Hughes, I hiked with a woman named Sharon. She told me about "Jack's Place", where we could acquire much-needed water. Sharon carried *Volume I* with her and thus could determine where the trail meandered. All of the day's relevant pages she'd torn from the heavy book and stashed in her pocket. Without the assistance of her book, I couldn't have negotiated that section of trail. The PCT simply followed too many unmarked turns.

Sharon worked as a nurse. She could find employment anywhere, and enjoyed a flexible job situation. If Sharon wanted to take extended time off, she simply requested leave and was guaranteed a position, whenever she returned. I learned that Sharon loved adventure and had traveled the world. Sharon hiked strongly. Like Jenny, this woman amazed me with her courage and determination in hiking the trail alone. I found hiking solo very challenging and very demanding.

Sharon and I eventually found what was formerly Jack's Place, and, when we walked up, the greeter's first words sounded friendly, "Would you like a burrito?" I hadn't turned down any food offer yet, and certainly wasn't turning this one down, either. Quickly I replied, "Sure", and the man handed me a paint brush, and said, "I'll go fix the burritos while you're painting." What the hell just happened? I wondered.

Sharon followed the man into the house. Since I'd already hiked 35 miles that day and planned to hike another 9 miles with Sharon, I wasn't really in the mood for painting. We stood, at mile 516.0, near Highway 138 in the desert, and the 100°F temperature did little to stimulate my interest in work, either. I brushed 10 pickets, splashing white-paint droplets on my green shorts, and then entered the house to collect my burrito.

The fellow living at this dwelling wasn't Jack, but Jack's successor. He opened his front yard to hikers and asked that hikers construct a "hiker-town" for themselves. I wolfed down three burritos, red licorice vines, tortilla chips, and a bowl of mango ice cream. Sharon consumed the same items, matching me bite for bite. The three of us chit-chatted for awhile, but I felt eager to return to the trail. I signed the register in hiker-town, wishing my hiking friends good luck, and while exiting the premises, we filled our water-bottles, which an hour earlier had been the main reason for our stopping.

A mile later we caught up to two hikers who'd intended to visit Jack's Place but had missed the water stop. We told them how to find Jack's, and they reluctantly backtracked with the intention of spending the night there. I'd filled them in on the work detail and its rewards. So far, once I'd passed a hiker, I never saw him/her again. I doubted that I'd encounter these two fellows farther up the trail.

At one point, for conversation, I asked Sharon if she'd hiked any other trails. Her 10-minute answer mentioned practically every long-distance trail in the United States, including the AT, *CDT*, Superior Hiking Trail, Ice Age Trail, and many others. With this hike she would complete the triple-crown. Sharon's goals involved enjoying the trips rather than building an impressive hiking résumé, although she'd accomplished the latter feat as well. She hiked powerfully.

Fortunately, Sharon possessed a headlamp, which we used to consult her map when the sun disappeared. One civilian we'd passed on a dirt road told us that this area wasn't a safe place for hiking and that a lot of "crack houses" operated in the area. I felt glad that we hiked together; I think she felt safer, too. We didn't hike with Sharon's light on, as this beacon would have made us conspicuous. The moonlight shone sufficiently to guide our walk on the roads in the cooling Mojave Desert. We camped together, setting up at around 9:45 pm. I slept in my tarptent, while Sharon crashed on the ground without a shelter. She spent quite awhile ensuring that no rattlesnakes lurked in the area before bedding down. Sharon slept under the stars, whenever possible. I admired her strength and courage.

In the morning Sharon departed early, saying that I would catch up to her soon, since I was hiking faster. My day began 45 minutes after the departure of one of the country's most-accomplished hikers. This stretch through the anhydrous Mojave Desert consisted mainly of flat dirt roads. Occasionally, I caught a glimpse of Sharon up ahead. She motored and walked perhaps a mile-and-a-half ahead of me. Once the road started undulating, I could no longer see her. About two miles later I made a wrong turn. Speeding cars flew by on the dirt roads, and they completely wiped out all footprints as they drove past, throwing thick clouds of dust into the air and into my lungs.

Getting lost in the parched Mojave cost me an hour. Three or so hours later, I caught and passed Sharon. She'd wandered a quarter mile off the PCT into an arroyo, presumably looking for water, when I went ahead. I shouted and waved, but I don't think that she saw me. I knew for sure that Sharon would finish the trail. She would hear from me via future register entries, but would I ever again hear from her? We never said goodbye.

I continued on, hiking quickly in the ridiculous heat, and finished almost 30 miles by 4 pm. This distance brought me to the Tehachapi-Willow Springs Road, at mile 555.1. Arriving there on Monday June 2nd, day 22 of my hike, I had kept on schedule. From this desolate piece of boiling blacktop, I needed to hitch-hike 12 miles to the town of Mojave, where I'd meet Fish. A paucity of cars on the hilly road, coupled with my haggard condition, reduced my chances of being offered a lift.

To walk into the town of Mojave in the stifling heat would have taken me another three hours, and since I'd run out of water, this strategy didn't seem like a good option. Just prior to reaching the road, I'd passed up a water-source because of the number of cattle that appeared to have used the small pond for a toilet. If I was offered a ride within two-and-a-half hours, the choice to hitch would have been justified. I stuck out my thumb, and glancing down at the grizzly digit made me realize how sunburned I was. My charred thumb resembled a young boy-scout's first campfire hot-dog.

Cars sped passed at the rate of one every two minutes. While standing on the scorching-hot, heat-radiating asphalt, I uttered various impolite phrases as people accelerated by me without stopping. I continuously mulled over whether or not to begin walking toward the distant town. The locals were probably used to PCT hikers hitching from this location, I reasoned, so I remained at the point where the trail crossed the road.

A couple from Mojave rescued me from the heat after only half-an-hour. I tossed my smelly salty backpack and fast-wearing trekking-poles into their compact trunk, and sat in the back seat with their panting dog. I missed my two dogs back home, Dottie and Julie, who always showed me unconditional love. They continually filled my thoughts, and I hoped that their summer was fun. While the back-seat dog slobbered all over me, the three of us humans chatted during the winding drive into town.

My chauffeurs described a PCT-thru-hiking couple from Edmonton, Alberta, whom they'd driven many days earlier, and how they'd invited the Canadians over to their home for dinner. Clearly, they hoped to stay in touch with their new friends. Their talk of food had made me hungry. The Californians kindly dropped me off right in front of my destination, White's Motel. I felt grateful for the ride, for the conversation, and for the chance to pet a dog. My new friends were two more down-to-earth Americans for whom I possessed good vibes.

I looked around, eagerly anticipating my reunion with Fish—a true friend. We'd hiked together for six weeks on the AT in 1995, but due to family and job commitments hadn't seen much of each other over the past few years. We've always kept in close touch, though, via email. Fish and I had grown up close, and our friendship, as of this writing, already spanned more than 35 years. Fish was taking two weeks out of his busy schedule to join me. During the summers, he leads bicycle tours in Vermont, and spends time with his family. During the academic year, he serves as the swim coach at Middlebury College in northern Vermont.

Fish was an exceptionally talented swimmer, explaining how he'd received the trail name "Fish-out-of-Water". He has held numerous swimming records for over 30 years. In most Olympic Games world records are set in virtually every swimming event; rarely do records last more than a year or two in this dynamic sport. Since training methods and the strokes themselves have completely changed, the longevity of Fish's results is astounding. Fish had also completed a double-Ironman triathlon. Most athletes feel that the Ironman, consisting of 2.4 miles of swimming, 112 miles of biking, and 26.2 miles of running, is the ultimate endurance event. Imagine doing a double! The longer event ranks probably 20 times as hard, not merely twice. Fish knew mental and physical conditioning intimately; he was a world-class athlete.

Fish had cashed in frequent-flyer miles to reach Bakersfield, and from there would catch a bus to Mojave. He had to change aircraft three times to utilize his miles. Fish would arrive tired and jet-lagged. When I reached White's, I inquired if Peter Solomon had checked in yet. Sadly, the woman "helping" me couldn't. She wasn't able to determine who occupied a room at the motel or who had reservations. My feet ached, since I'd just hiked 72 miles in less than a day-and-a-half, and they told me in one-syllable words to sit down. I'd flipped the pain switches back on for monitoring and found out quickly that damage existed. I decided to book a room.

I asked if the motel accepted credit cards, as I wanted to conserve my cash. Thus far, I hadn't seen an ATM near the trail. Although

I'd formulated several contingency plans to acquire more cash, none seemed particularly satisfactory. First, I inquired with the clerk about American Express, and her response took three minutes. Then I asked about Mastercard—another two minutes, this time a "yes". I handed the clerk my Mastercard card. After 10 minutes of her fumbling around, I said as politely as possible that I'd pay cash. I handed the poor woman two 50's for a charge of $53.99. Five minutes later, I requested my money back. While handing her three 20's, I said, "Please, keep the change." Thank God I hadn't tried to use traveler's checks! Believe it or not, I left a message for Fish with her.

I bolted to my second-story room (on the way meeting "Yogi", a thru-hiker and a close friend of one of my former University of New Hampshire students, AT and PCT thru-hiker "D-Low") and performed the usual preparations for returning to the trail—washing hiking-pole handles, airing out the sleeping-bag, rinsing my water-containers, dumping trash, cleaning sun-glasses, and so on. I jumped into a hot shower, getting only partially clean, while totally dirtying the stall. Next I dialed the usual phone numbers.

My hunger surpassed the acceptable threshold, and I decided to eat dinner straight away. I hoped that the woman at the front desk remembered to send Fish to my room once he'd arrived. I possessed nothing to write with, and this stripped motel room didn't, either, so I scratched a note on a piece of old newspaper using my toenail clippers. Going to find a pen was out of the question since that actively entailed additional walking. I deposited the barely legible broken sentences on the pillow of the twin bed closest to the door. Would Fish find it and join me for dinner?

While all my preparations were taking place, unbeknownst to me, Fish had actually arrived. On his inquiry, the woman at the front desk had told him that I hadn't arrived yet. He'd checked into a room three doors down from me, unnoticed. Fish had left a note with the desk clerk to direct me to his room when I showed up. I checked back, but she indicated that he hadn't arrived. I walked to dinner on my own and enjoyed a colossal feed at a country-style restaurant. The mid-America salad with ranch dressing, buttery vegetables, butter-soaked corn bread, and steak cooked in butter were all welcomed with open arms at my booth. During the meal, I also polished off two thick milkshakes that were topped with several inches of whipped cream. Glimpsing at the customers, I noticed that everyone outweighed me by at least 50 pounds. In the establishment's background music I heard a few favorites that I'd been singing on the PCT. The Left Banke's "Just Walk Away, Renee" aired: "... you won't see me follow you back home ..." The one-hit wonder brought a smile to my face.

On the way back from the restaurant, with aching and bulging stomach, I popped into a convenience-store to purchase ChapStick and Gatorade. A short while after returning to my dismal room, a grinning Fish appeared at my door. We exchanged handshakes, pulling each other close for a hug and a pat on the back. Our much anticipated reunion happened at last, and we both felt very happy to see each other. Fish's arrival had cured my loneliness. The cure would last for two weeks. I'd enjoy his excellent companionship hiking through an arduous section of the PCT. Fish loved the woods and seemed excited about the return of the "Fish and Wall" team to the trail. When best friends reunite after years of separation, happiness and excitement abound. Our time together would undoubtedly be an extremely special two weeks in our lives.

As we exchanged horror stories regarding the motel check-in, we learned that Fish had arrived shortly after I did. We sighed because we could have easily shared dinner together. Nevertheless, we laughed ourselves silly over this travesty. Our script could have been the basis for a gut-busting short. Energy filled the air, as we became each other's realities. Since gear lay strewn all over the floors of both our rooms, we kept them rather than consolidating—not to mention the difficulties which we would have suffered with the clerk, if we'd attempted to put a room back into her inventory.

Fish had brought a box of trail supplies for me that I'd mailed to Vermont prior to departing from Savannah. As I repackaged those goods, Fish asked me about what other items he might need. I detected a cautious anticipation about the arduous high-altitude terrain and challenges that we would face. We'd be hiking 8 times the length of our home state, climbing 16 times as high, traversing snowfields the size of its counties, and encountering wildlife seen there only on TV. Based on my advice, Fish performed a few last-minute pack adjustments.

In catching up with other hikers at White's Motel upon his arrival, Fish had learned that a thru-hiker had committed suicide in an adjacent room just the previous day. The trail could be cruel. We both felt terribly saddened by this distressing news, and spent a joint moment of silence remembering someone whom we'd not met, but who'd shared our love for the outdoors. We turned in early. The desert and the mountains awaited us the next day.

Awakening to a tequila sunrise the next morning, Fish and I grabbed a ride back to the PCT, to the exact point that I'd hitched from 16 hours earlier. Two other hikers accompanied us in the full SUV. The talkative hiker-friendly driver dazzled us with his knowledge of windmills in the area. Fish and I chatted about our resupply point to occur in 150 miles at Kennedy Meadows. My first mail-drop, which contained my ice-axe, waited there. We envisioned a lovely place straight out of the "Sound of Music". The schedule called for hiking this distance in six days, walking approximately 25 miles per day.

I felt pretty comfortable in intolerable desert heat by now, but Fish had arrived fresh "off the couch" from northern Vermont. Questions that we both thought about, but didn't discuss, loomed: how would Fish handle the distance, altitude, heat, cold, fords, and snowfields? The real answers would come soon. We tipped the driver and continued on our way. We carried heavy food bags, and, since the sun beat down super hot, we also hauled a great volume of water. At that moment I enjoyed total happiness; Fish did, too, I think. I made many additions to all types of media in my library, for these days were the best of times.

During this unforgiving desert stretch, Fish hiked amazingly and provided great companionship. His sense of humor, athletic prowess, positive attitude, and adaptability made for a wonderful time. We caught up on recent details of each other's lives, and that knowledge was special. Fish picked my brain about my experiences over the first few weeks on the trail, and I shared many laughs and trail stories. The hiking felt difficult to us, but we wouldn't have traded it for anything.

On one of our first days, Fish overheated on a huge climb—an "hors category" in Tour de France language. The climb featured no shade, and, conservatively speaking, temperatures in the sun broke 125°F. I listened to Fish's irregular breathing, which became heavy and labored. Sweat poured off his forehead, streaming over his eyebrows and into his eyes. The salt burned beneath his sunglasses. I knew that Fish's experience, determination, and mental toughness kept him going. Physically, he should have stopped much earlier.

Upon reaching the top of that nasty drag, Fish stated pellucidly that he needed to lie down. The Casio read 5 pm, and even the ants still struggled to locate adequate shade, hopping from twig to twig with great agility to avoid foot burns, and then ducking under tiny tinder before scurrying off again. The sun seemed positioned directly overhead, and, although this fact defied the laws of nature, we suffered from intense sunlight. We crawled ranger-style under a spiked and dangerous Joshua tree, the kind Fish and I knew only from Dr. Seuss books, and garnered an iota of much-needed shade.

After rolling onto his back, Fish stared at me intently and said, "Ray, all I can do is give you 100% each day, and today, I've done more than that." His words touched me deeply. Feeling as though I'd pushed my lifelong friend too hard, my insides ached. Speaking from my heart, I told Fish not to worry about my schedule and that we'd just hike as much as he could. Under no circumstances would I separate from my trusted friend. We rested awhile longer, almost in a stupor, and ate dinner cautiously beneath the Joshua tree. After a short spell, we resumed hiking. The slight temperature drop assisted us greatly.

Fish and I would usually break for half-an-hour for dinner at around 6 pm. Then we'd hike another two-and-a-half hours. This schedule allowed us to rest, re-energize, and walk six more miles for the day. In addition, since we didn't eat in camp, no loose bear-attracting tidbits littered our campsites. I liked this practical approach and planned to adopt it for the remainder of the summer. The method worked well, and I never went to bed on a full stomach. In fact, several nights I needed to put my earplugs in because my stomach's growling kept me awake.

Fish quickly adapted to the heat. His sense of humor never wavered regardless of bodily trauma. One day, as we sat taking a breather, he remarked, "Wall, there's an alien trying to get out of my calf." His overworked muscle twitched uncontrollably. We laughed at the unnatural vibrations, thinking something would pop out. Another time, after a bowel-movement, he nonchalantly said, "Seeing that completely changes my opinion of humanity." I suggested that he box up the discovery for the Smithsonian. When I went to the bathroom, he would inquire with great sincerity while suppressing laughter, "Wall, what's your midwife's name?" I occasionally caused Fish to roll as well. "What are the triplets' names?" I inquired after one of his noisy stops. Another time I asked, "Remember in 11th grade when the mustached girl from Barrington . . .?"

Fish and I laughed ourselves silly and enjoyed great fun—our senses of humor had been warped by too much trail time. Our natural endorphin highs contributed to our giddiness. Lady Luck watched over us, and several times we found caches of water at just the right moments. Most evenings we spooned down seafood dinners that consisted of seven-ounce packets of tuna or salmon, the new type that leaves no mess. Since these meals contained only 400 calories in them, Fish dropped weight quickly—losing a pound per day. With Fish's permission, I have included an excerpt from his journal detailing this first week—June 3rd to June 8th.

Begin Fish's diary excerpt, week one:

Daily temperatures above 100°F, lack of shade, and limited water provided the biggest challenges of the week. The landscape was dotted with chaparrals, yucca plants, Joshua trees, and enormous windmills that help meet the electrical needs of the greater LA population. Daily encounters with snakes kept Wall and me on our toes. With one encounter, Wall noticed a rattlesnake under his feet and stopped short using his hiking-poles. The snake mistook the pole for his leg, launched, and bit the pole. Another hiker we encountered this week wasn't as lucky and was actually bitten in the hand by a rattlesnake. His hand and arm were swollen considerably, but he would make it.

The climbs this week were long but gradual. The numerous switchbacks were made that much more arduous by a heavy carry of a week's worth of food and enough water to get to the next filling-point. There are approximately 40 thru-hikers ahead of Wall at this point. After 162 miles over our first six days, we realized a 27-mile per day average, and Wall a 25.5-mile per day average for his first 28 days on the trail. Amazingly, there hasn't been a trace of rain thus far on the trip for Wall.

Our conversations ranged from past childhood adventures, which we now laugh about, to the recent loss of a parent, who we mourned together. With all the food for the week consumed, we enjoyed the relative weightlessness of our packs on the last morning and made our way to Kennedy Meadows General Store.

Kennedy Meadows is the last stop on the trail prior to the High Sierras, so many hikers spend a few days there to rest up, recharge their batteries, and socialize with fellow thru-hikers. We spent four hours there to make calls back home, hydrate, eat, and pick up food and equipment for the upcoming week. Wall picked up new sneakers as well as his ice-axe and fleece jacket for the higher elevations.

The dinner location after Kennedy Meadows gave us a taste of things to come as we sat on a foot bridge overlooking Monarch Meadows (elevation 7,500 feet), which is the largest mountain meadow in the Sierras and also the headwaters of the mighty Kern River. Nesting Cliff Swallows buzzed overhead, while the trout scurried about the tranquil icy waters below. We were hoping that the hikers ahead of us would lay down some good tracks through the snow-covered passes to come.

End Fish's diary, week one.

Our first week played out according to script. Fish's companionship kept me strong, focused, and loving life. I felt secure hiking with him, and he with me. Fish was certainly experiencing all that he'd signed on for and more. We moved out of Southern California's searingly-hot desert and headed into Central California's frigidly-cold snowy mountains. How would we fare in one of the country's most demanding mountain ranges?

During the first phase of the hike, I'd resupplied far fewer times than I'd expected. Although my biggest planned day had been only 32.9 miles, I'd already put in a 50-plus-mile day. Rattlesnakes and poison oak had tried hard, but had missed me. I felt healthy and happy, and still believed that I could break the thru-hike record for the PCT. My thinking said: another relatively easy week, and then a sustained all-out effort. Having already spent five weeks on the trail conditioning, I believed that I could handle the upcoming weeks both mentally and physically. This time *was* one of the most upbeat periods of my life. I felt privileged and humbled to be hiking the PCT.

Part II

CENTRAL CALIFORNIA

The rugged Central California section of the PCT extends from Kennedy Meadows to the deep-valley town of Belden. This stretch covers a grueling yet marvelously beautiful 586.1 miles. The lowest elevation sits at just over 2,000 feet, and the highest elevation reaches over 13,000 feet. Much of the terrain involves treacherous snow-covered mountains. Forester Pass at 13,180 feet measures the highest point on the PCT, and in heavy snow much time was spent finding Forester. Great snow-depths and few hikers passing through spell difficulty in spades for this section of the trail. Late snow blanketed the PCT in the High Sierras in 2003, and I was one of the first 15 hikers heading north. Here frequent big passes rise over 10,000 feet in altitude. The trail traverses many famous parks and wilderness areas, including Sequoia National Park, Ansel Adams Wilderness, John Muir Wilderness, Kings Canyon National Park, and Yosemite National Park. Many raging rivers block the trail, and their fording difficulty hinges deeply on the time of day when they are encountered. Later in the day the rivers catch snow-melt and become more dangerous. My plans called for five resupplies during this stretch. The longest segment that I'd scheduled without resupply measured a double century. The *biggest day consisted of 35.6 miles. My second mail-drop waited at Belden. I started this section on the afternoon of June 8th and hoped to reach Belden, at mile 1,283.1, on day 47, June 27th. At the completion of this section, 56% of the trail would remain, but 60% of my time would have passed.*

5 Wild and Snowy High Sierras

Fish and I were actually over half-a-day ahead of schedule when we arrived at Kennedy Meadows, at mile 697.0, on Sunday, June 8th, at 8:30 am. The store opened at 9 am. While waiting to purchase breakfast, we each caught up with a few calls from the General Store's pay phone. Everything hike-related proceeded excellently, and we enjoyed a good time. Reaching Kennedy Meadows provided a psychological boost. I'd already completed over one-fourth of the trail, and the desert lay behind us. My feet had held up well, as did my equipment. Fish thrived in the wild. The vast open spaces of the west coast as compared to the over-developed east coast showed us how America once was. The remote and undeveloped PCT impressed us. I'd met many wonderful people and loved the trail. My dream flourished.

Fish and I'd engaged in eight years worth of catching up that first week. Now we waited to pick up our new supplies, gorge ourselves, and return to the trail. We anticipated beautiful scenery in the High Sierras, but we also knew that snow factored into the equation. We didn't, however, know the actual snow depths, since we couldn't obtain reliable information. We'd heard that the snow level stood at 7,000 feet from one person, and at 10,000 feet from another. We expected to find snow at 7,000 feet on north-facing slopes, where it melts slowly.

I'd prepared myself mentally in case my mail-drop had disappeared between Savannah and Kennedy Meadows General Store. Fish anticipated a resupply package, too. Luckily, our boxes had arrived intact, and we successfully collected them, for a small fee. Hikers began to trickle into the store, as we repackaged our supplies on the adjoining deck. The majority of these hikers had milled around the area for a few

63

days and hadn't come off the trail with us. Several more folks that we'd seen on the trail drifted in, too—Nikki, Dave, Triathlete Dave, Split Pea, Tin Cup, and Jeff. Many hikers who we encountered at Kennedy Meadows had departed the Mexican border three weeks prior to me. They sat tight waiting for the snow levels to drop in the High Sierras before pushing ahead. Everyone appeared sunburned and fit, and full of anticipation and apprehension regarding the upcoming mountain passes.

When Nikki, Dave, and Triathlete Dave noticed how little weight Fish and I carried, a gear-related discussion ensued.

"Yeah, we trimmed our shoe-laces, cut the tops from plastic bags, and burned loose threads from stuff-sacks," I said.

"Are you carrying dental floss?" Dave asked.

Fish chimed in, "Just a single piece. I wash it."

Our three new friends smiled. I applied ChapStick to my sunburned lips, slightly easing their pain.

Triathlete Dave said in a shocked but joking voice, "You didn't remove the label from the ChapStick?"

"Not yet," I responded while peeling.

"You could get rid of the cap on that, too. Just wind it down lower."

"Since I've already removed all the lint from my pockets, that'd work," I said, as I faked a toss of the cap.

While laughing and thinking of other extreme measures for saving grams, we talked about life experiences and personal philosophies. Fish, Triathlete Dave, and I also talked about the Ironman, and about the possibility of competing together in the fall at the Greater Floridian Race. Our group got along well. I think Nikki, Dave, and Triathlete Dave eventually ended up leaving Kennedy Meadows with far less weight than they'd originally planned.

For breakfast Fish and I feasted on baloney-and-cheese sandwiches, consuming an entire loaf of bread in the process. We hydrated well and luxuriated in hot open-air showers. I loaded my pack with as much food as I could carry, causing me concerns that the straps might rip or that I might injure a shoulder. Fish copied me. Buckling under heavy loads, we struggled off with great expectations. I never expected to see any of those hikers who rested at Kennedy Meadows farther north on the PCT.

My schedule called for us to hike 175 miles in six days. This distance averaged out to 29 miles per day over rugged terrain. Many consider this stretch the most demanding and the most beautiful section of the PCT. When I developed my hiking schedule, I thought that Fish could hike 25 miles per day for week one, and then 29 a day for the following week. I knew that his second week would be tough, but also knew that he was a great athlete and competitor. We'd actually averaged 27 miles per day during week one; if we could do that again, we'd meet my plan.

The schedule that I'd prepared in Savannah in March obviously didn't account for the arrival of huge late-April snows in the High Sierras. I'd predicated my schedule on a low-snow year, which based on the winter weather up through March, had seemed reasonable. The terrain never factored into my schedule; I figured that we could hike uphill as fast as we could hike downhill. This fact wasn't quite true. I didn't take into account altitude in my schedule, either, nor Fish's attrition. Good thing that Fish hadn't carefully researched my plan prior to joining me, for he might have entertained second thoughts.

The 175-mile segment which we embarked on included Mulkey Pass at 10,380 feet, Cottonwood Pass at 11,160, Forester Pass at 13,180, Glen Pass at 11,978, Pinchot Pass at 12,130, Mather Pass at 12,100, Muir Pass at 11,955, and Selden Pass at 10,900. Nearly all of the trail between the passes reached over 10,000 feet, too, and Fish had never spent time over 5,000 feet. Every pass also meant many river *fords*, since the snowfields melted fast in June. In exposed places the snow disappeared at the rapid rate of five inches per day. The thru-hikers following a week behind us would encounter an entirely different setting. With three feet less snow on the ground, the trail would be significantly easier to find and to hike. Our footprints would be long gone. We climbed over Mulkey Pass at 10,380 feet and Cottonwood Pass at 11,160 feet without much difficulty.

Fish and I forded many churning rivers in the High Sierras. Creek-lets became raging torrents because of the vast amounts of late snowfall and the massive run-off. New rivers simply emerged wherever Mother Nature had earlier dumped snow, so we never knew when to expect fords. At each dangerous river we would scout around, discuss our crossing-strategy, come to an agreement, and proceed with extreme caution. If Deet coated our legs to ward off hungry mosquitoes, we suffered the added whammy of the poisonous chemical running into dozens of open wounds. This burning inflicted searing pain.

One river we encountered appeared particularly nasty. I dropped my pack and bushwhacked downstream to search for a crossing. Returning, I told Fish that it didn't seem too promising. He set his pack down and checked upstream. His description sounded even worse. Fish then hiked downstream and took a gander. I followed silently. Where he'd stopped, a tiny island divided the river into two. The raging whitewater measured around 35°F, and ran waist-deep. We agreed to attempt to cross on the island spot. Fish and I couldn't do anything for each other in the event of a slip, but mutual emotional support had always helped us through such times.

On this wavy crossing I felt that one of us would fall in, so I suggested that we strip down and stuff our clothes in plastic bags. Since we didn't have *any* backup garments, if we did "lose it", this strategy meant that we could dress in dry clothes. Hypothermia appeared certain without any dry clothing articles. Fish bought my logic, but in reality, if someone fell, he wouldn't be getting dressed again. Fish unstrapped his pack for quick release in the event of a topple. No thought was wasted on how to retrieve the packs, if we jettisoned them. All energy focused on the crossing. I felt a great clarity at such demanding moments.

Fish may well have been the strongest swimmer ever to attempt to ford this creek. I swim well, too. If we lost our balance in this crossing, swimming to safety in the raging river seemed doubtful. The two of us were, however, unlikely to drown panicking if the situation deteriorated. Successfully wading through the waist-deep whitewater on the algae-glossed rocks would require total concentration. Fish and I executed the dicey crossing safely in two stages, having paused only briefly on the island to regroup. I wouldn't have wanted to ford here alone. We'd submerged to waist-level—what Fish coined a "scrotum washer"—during a few touch-and-go moments. The ice-cold water numbed everything, so I formed the habit of peeing before attempting such crossings.

On the north shore, we dried off in the sun for a spell and redressed. We always forded wearing our running-shoes, and they dried far faster than boots would have. Since slime grew on many of the rocks, even small creeks couldn't be crossed barefoot. Our feet felt like boards we resumed walking after fording a big river. The lower-leg muscles froze and didn't fire properly, if at all. This meant adjusting our gait to a post-Ironman-like shuffle. Our feet screamed at us, as they thawed.

Fish and I agreed that ice water felt therapeutic. The chill reduced the swelling in the feet and in the lower legs. Perhaps iced-over nerves conducted less electricity, too. We stopped postulating theories after awhile. Whatever felt good, was good. Amazingly, I sustained no foot injuries in the High Sierras. I never even developed a blister from the dozens of river crossings. When one steps onto the bottom in a fast-moving river, the foot acts as a small dam, so shoes always fill with sand. I rarely stopped to dump out my shoes, nor did Fish, since the crossings happened so frequently. Blisters should have covered my feet. Fish suffered gobs of blisters, and his feet became a mass of silver duct-tape.

One night Fish helped me hang our food for bear-protection. With two heavy food-bags to counterbalance each other, this task wasn't a one-person job. Fish and I wore just socks on our feet at the time, having stripped off our wet sneakers. I accidentally stepped on his foot, and he let out a hideous scream. Glimpsing down, I saw that the front half of his white sock appeared red—completely soaked in blood. I apologized and felt terrible. Fish asked for more Advil, and we continued to hang the food. He never mentioned the incident.

On one particularly gorgeous evening, Fish and I passed the spur trail to Mount Whitney, at 14,492 feet the highest point in the continental United States. We encountered three thru-hikers there, a woman and two men, who planned to climb Mount Whitney the next day. I'd never entertained thoughts of climbing Whitney on this trip and certainly not now with our food-supply dwindling rapidly. With my tight schedule, *no* detours were possible. The nighttime sky influenced our decision to sleep out that night and gaze at the universe. We felt as though a far-away voice called to us, and that we were not alone. Since the weather seemed perfect, I didn't even bother to set up the Squall.

The stars reached for infinity. Mount Whitney and other peaks rose fabulously from the earth's surface. When the moon appeared, a crisp lighting-effect created impressive shadows that altered our consciousness. We felt that the moon, the stars, and the planets floated within our reach. I actually lifted my hand forward once or twice to touch them. Frigid temperatures raided our high-altitude camp during the night, and when we woke up (if we ever fell asleep), Mother Nature's frost fingerprints covered us. Recalling a late-night ford from the previous evening, I worried about our shoes.

I habitually cinched my shoelaces up tightly during the day. That morning, realizing my worst fear, I discovered steel beams where I'd left my New Balance 806s. In the icy morning's thin air, I forced my crying feet into the frozen beams. My internal switching network didn't function properly, and the pain that I experienced during the first hour of hiking devastated me—frozen feet, icy shrunken shoes, and rocky terrain. Fish pitied me, but his feet fared only a little better. From that night onward, I slept with my shoes inside my sleeping-bag whenever the remotest possibility of freezing occurred.

As we approached 13,180-foot Forester Pass the next day, we confronted massive amounts of snow. We abruptly realized why hikers sat back at Kennedy Meadows. Snow consumed the trail, and we relied primarily on the footprints of a few other hikers to guide us. Naturally, this reliance worried us terribly. The tracks always seemed to keep us directly on trail, though. This fact eased our minds slightly. Only occasionally did we actually see a small patch of the PCT. "Got trail" became a joyous phrase.

When we landed in the proximity of Forester Pass, I thought that I noticed *switchbacks* weaving steeply up a skyward-reaching mountainside, but what I saw looked too ominous to be the PCT. We didn't believe that the trail could possibly ascend that forbidden slope. At that time we lost track of all footprints. Fish and I wandered around in deep snow for three hours searching for the pass. "Where do you think it goes?" "Where do you think it goes?" We repeatedly asked each other without resolution. *Postholing* to the point of extreme fatigue, and getting cold from wearing just running-shoes, shorts, and T-shirts, we eventually concluded that we needed to explore the area which had earlier looked like switchbacks. This entailed crossing over another big snowfield.

An Herculean effort put us close to the angled lines on the expansive mountainside. The peaks soared thousands of feet above us in all directions, and with their white snowfields contrasted starkly with the deep-blue sky. From our new vantage-point we immediately saw that the angled demarcations were indeed the PCT's switchbacks. We felt frustrated at the lost time and energy, but that feeling didn't dim our spirits. Fish and I encouraged one another. Neither one of us would ever let the other one down. The security that we provided each other was immeasurable. I felt deeply responsible for Fish's well-being.

Fish had carried his ice-axe since Mojave, and I'd picked mine up at Kennedy Meadows. I'd taught Fish how to use his ice-axe. The situation that we faced on Forester developed into a dangerous one, and his new skills would be required. In several places we needed to traverse switchbacks that lay buried underneath snow angled at 60°, where a slip guaranteed a long accelerating slide ending on rocks. I coached Fish on what to expect and how to cross safely. In the process I tried to calm his racing mind. A hiker mustn't panic or freeze during such high-wire acts because accidents tend to happen under those circumstances. While we moved through tough sections, talking relaxed us. I dreaded calling family and friends in the event of an accident. A world without Fish seemed unimaginable. I led the way across, inquiring how Fish felt, and we passed our first challenging snow test.

The key to the difficult traverses involved making sure that we obtained a good purchase with our ice-axes in advance, so that we could immediately stop ourselves if we slipped. If one of us lost his footing, a self-arrest would have been impossible on these slopes, due to their steepness and the poor snow conditions. Where advance security appeared infeasible, I kicked plentiful steps. Crampons would have comforted us tremendously, but the running-shoes worked surprisingly well. Boots, of course, would have facilitated kicking steps; still, we didn't feel too handicapped, except when walking on ice.

Fish and I continued upward through falling-rock areas, crossing several stone-filled snow patches. With the loose-rock projectiles aiming down, we didn't want to hang around, so we hiked fast. I borrowed a line from a former Swiss mountain-guide, "Why should it fall now?" This mantra could work only so many times, but we employed it anyway and carried on. Fish felt the altitude with our quick pace, and he also burned nervous energy. At the top of Forester Pass, towering 13,180 feet, we firmly embraced each other, feeling dramatically relieved. Fish snapped an arms-length joint picture, his highest ever.

We abruptly learned that descending the passes involved even more danger than ascending them. The descents occurred on the north faces, which typically held more snow. During this time, we followed The NorthFace's motto, "Never stop exploring", like a religion. Mid-day descents tested Fish. His combined pack and body weights surpassed mine by a good 50 pounds. The postholing break-point seemed somewhere near my total of 170 pounds. At Fish's total weight, postholing became inevitable. Repeatedly falling through the crusty snow horribly beat up his legs and his ankles. Both the fronts and the backs of my ankles dripped blood as well. Fish left red splotches on the snow, and I felt his pain. We pushed north steadily, the next day making it over two huge climbs—Glenn Pass at 11,978 feet and Pinchot Pass at 12,130 feet.

Rivers as wide as 20 feet often formed beneath the snowfields. Occasionally, the snow would collapse, thereby exposing the frigid fast-moving water. We frequently had to cross snow-bridges over such rivers. Fish and I never really knew how secure the melting bridges were. We probed with our trekking-poles to gauge their stability—many times being forced to shift our route. One of our greatest fears was falling through such a snow-bridge and never popping back up. Our minds tortured us by following through on such thoughts. A single leg would punch through several times a day and find a river. We felt extremely lucky to have avoided a serious incident on the delicate snow-bridges.

Fish and I tackled Mather Pass next, or should I say that Mather Pass tackled us? On the approach to the 12,100-foot Mather Pass, for already the second time in the High Sierras, we found ourselves in denial about where the trail wandered. "No way!" We both exclaimed. The two of us believed that we saw footprints heading straight up the mountainside in a rock-fall area. Upon closer inspection, regrettably, our eyes hadn't lied. Fish and I climbed straight up the soaring face, and again the ice-axe plantings alone kept us secure. I made an extemporaneous comment by Jerry Mather from the show "Leave It to Beaver", "That's a lovely dress you have on, Mrs. Cleaver," and even in our dire situation, while imitating June's voice, Fish chimed in "Why, thank you, Eddy." We laughed about our favorite childhood TV characters.

I asked Fish for his disposable camera, motored ahead, turned around after firmly planting my ice-axe, and snapped a memorable picture of him. The slope seemed vertical. I filed this picture and other images of the High Sierras in my library. We'd become more comfortable on snow and ice, but we felt relieved to summit Mather Pass. The airy mountain-range views in the bright-blue skies rewarded us. We admired dozens of snow-covered peaks in every direction. A long grueling descent awaited us.

During Fish's second week, we often camped high, especially if we'd taken more time than expected to summit one of the gigantic passes. One night I looked far down the mountain from our camp at a completely iced-over lake. On freezing mornings clothed only in shorts, T-shirts, and windbreakers; we struggled at daybreak. Once we could con ourselves into moving and the sun came out, we warmed up surprisingly fast and sometimes even overheated in the high-altitude sun. My scabby ears, nose, and hands all lost multiple layers of skin due to sunburn.

The snow felt crusty in the mornings and in the evenings, so postholing affected us little except at midday. Danger increased on steep slopes in firm-snow conditions. We just proceeded since trying to time when we reached somewhere seemed impossible. Our declining food-stores didn't permit sitting around, nor did my ambitious schedule. Fish and I fell behind my schedule, but we didn't talk about it. Staying safe in these dangerous conditions remained foremost in our minds. The blue skies, white mountains, and green trees soothed our spirits. We were two men extending and strengthening an eternal bond.

Fish and I performed an epic climb of 11,955-foot Muir Pass, crossing massive snowfields. On the way up our favorite saying became "What the hell was John [Muir] thinking?" At the top of the pass we met Freefall, Mr. Tea, and the Japanese couple Tomo and Masa. Freefall hiked for a charity and jumped out of airplanes for fun. A reverend by vocation, he sometimes gave sermons in trail towns. Mr. Tea wanted to become the first Japanese person to thru-hike the PCT. Tomo and Masa had met their countryman Mr. Tea on the trail. They hoped to fulfill a long-term dream by finishing the PCT.

When we first met Tomo and Masa, I'd remarked how well they'd taken care of their equipment and that their gear looked unused. In fact, only three days earlier, they'd replaced all of their original gear with new lighter-weight equipment. We played photographer for one another in front of the Muir Hut, posing in every conceivable hiker subset. Mr. Tea possessed a timer on his camera and affixed the digital device to a snowbank tripod. He dove into the scene just seconds before the click resulted in a successful group shot.

At the summit of Muir Pass, I'd been food-less for awhile. I felt hungry, but knew that I wouldn't be eating for a long time. My sign-in at the Muir Pass register read as follows:

6/14/2003

Wall here with Fish.

Enjoyed an epic climb up Muir Pass with huge amounts of snow. What the hell was John thinking?

Been out of food for awhile. Heading to Vermillion Valley Resort to resupply tomorrow. Looking forward to getting out of the snow.

Good luck to all thru-hikers I've met.

Hunger-switch off.

Several reasons pointed to my premature food-shortage. The short answer read "bad planning", but let me elaborate. We'd left Kennedy Meadows the day before I'd originally planned, but I'd neglected to add another lunch and another dinner to my pack. Realistically, I couldn't have carried more food, anyway, as I'd completely maxed out on weight leaving Kennedy. I'd also expected to reach Vermillion Valley Resort at least a full day earlier. With Fish and me becoming lost several times, we'd used incredible amounts of energy plowing through deep snow and had fallen over a day behind schedule. We'd burned far more calories than anticipated, due to the cold weather, too. Fish and I had simply consumed our food faster than we'd thought possible. Finally, the mail-drop that I'd prepared pre-trip for Kennedy Meadows contained only 5,000 calories per day, but I'd required closer to 7,000 during this arduous stretch.

Many backpacking "experts" recommend that a hiker always carry at least one extra day of food. This suggestion never seemed feasible.

I usually left a resupply point with all the weight that I could lift. My record-breaking strategy involved trade-offs among comfort, acceptable risks, and safety. More weight meant hiking slower, which meant more food, which meant more weight .... Resupplying more often in remote stretches would have cost me too much time. Before the trip, I'd prepared myself mentally for some serious bonks. I also thought of the characters in *The Longest Walk*, who walked many days without food or water—several of them dying during their impossible journey. I tried to focus only on the survivors.

Having turned off the hunger-switch at Muir Pass, I successfully stopped food from consuming my thoughts. My energy level plummeted, of course, but I totally blocked eating from my mind. I regulated the pain switches all over my body, turning them off to shut out pain, and back on when I needed to monitor how bad something really hurt. The switch to my feet usually remained in the off position. As long as my switching network contained no "leaky current", the system worked.

Fish and I had lagged behind when the others had left the old stone hut at Muir Pass. The Japanese couple had preprogrammed their *GPS* unit with the coordinates of the passes and so knew exactly where they needed to descend. We intended to follow their tracks down the mountainside. All of the Japanese weighed so little that they almost never postholed. They skimmed along the snow's surface, leaving barely enough footprints for us to follow. I postholed occasionally on the descent, and Fish plunged through with great regularity. Fish demonstrated unbelievable guts on this descent and others. We fell far behind our new friends, as Fish painted the snow red.

During the descent of Muir Pass and other big passes, we often found ourselves side-stepping on 40° snow slopes. These slopes sometimes ran out to frozen lakes that had just begun to thaw. A slip could have easily resulted in a situation where one slid into a turquoise-colored coffin, breaking through the brittle ice. Although exhaustion dominated our thoughts, we watched out for each other on these dangerous run-outs. Once off the snowfields, we breathed a sigh of relief. We soon caught up to our Japanese friends. They'd just forded Evolution Creek, at mile 844.1 and at an elevation of 9,210 feet.

The water-level of a snow-melt creek depends significantly on the time of day and the cloud cover. We reached Evolution Creek on a sunny day at around 5 pm, and the high water flooded its banks. The "creek" classified as a wide and fast-moving river. We dwarfed the Japanese hikers, and thought that if they'd forded the river here, we could cross successfully as well. The 30-yard gap and deep water prompted Fish to say, "Another scrotum washer."

Fish led the way, and as he exited the water just 10 feet in front of me, he turned back to see me almost lose my balance. Apparently, my legs had been far more fatigued than I'd thought. I recovered and barely dragged my weary body out of the fast-moving, waist-deep, ice water. Fish's glance had saved me. He willed me out of the water. Trembling, I thanked him. My gaze into his eyes revealed the entire story. A presence once again seemed to watch over me.

While still soaked and numb, Fish and I rested briefly. In an effort to restore our core body temperatures, we stood up to resume hiking. Due to a lack of blood in the head, I almost fell down. The sooner we reached Vermillion Valley, the sooner I could eat again. During this stretch, Fish did a good job conserving his food, and he generously gave me whatever calories he could spare, which unfortunately wasn't much since he found himself a day short on food, too. Fish possessed a few more bodily reserves than I, but those disappeared quickly.

A couple hundred feet farther along the trail we paralleled Evolution Creek. To our horror, just several hundred yards below where we'd crossed, bubbling rapids and a cascading waterfall churned and fell dramatically. In all likelihood, if I'd slipped, Fish wouldn't have seen me again. Later we talked to Freefall and learned that the appropriate place to cross lay much farther upstream, which is where he'd wisely crossed. We all agreed that the creek had been aptly named, for survival of the fittest.

Hikers can follow a spur trail a mile off the PCT to a ferry pickup, and obtain a boat-ride across Lake Edison to Vermillion Valley Resort. The ferry left daily at 4:30 pm and saved five miles of additional walking on the spur trail. On the day when we headed to Vermillion Valley, we needed to bear down hard to arrive at the pickup point by ferry-departure time. We'd already summited the 10,900-foot Selden Pass that day, and as far as we knew, no major obstacles lay ahead. As our energy levels dipped to record lows, Freefall, whom we'd repassed the night before while he cooked dinner, powered by us, hiking strongly. We latched onto him, imaging that a chain linked our waists, and he brought us home down a gravity-fed, 47-switchback descent.

The three of us reached the ferry docking-point at around 4 pm. We sat down on some big lakeside boulders, and watched the wind effects on the largest body of water we'd remembered seeing in quite awhile. Our frazzled minds could do nothing other than register the waves. Freefall gave me a Clif bar and cooked us his last packet of noodles, which Fish and I split. Another hiker waiting for the ferry gave us a little cereal, and we ate the crushed flakes dry from a plastic bag. Both Fish and I felt grateful for the calories and the friendly gestures. We could make it to the resort now. Brain and body functionality would be restored soon.

Seven other hikers waited with us for the ferry. They consisted of most of the first hikers through the High Sierras that year, and traveled as a group. The leader explained how they would fan out and walk seven separate lines in the snow while searching for the trail, essentially using a crime-scene technique. When one of them located the trail again, shouting "Over here!", the others would rejoin and rejoice. We thanked them profusely for leaving footprints, which served as our *only* guide. Without having any prior knowledge of the trail, leading the way through the snowbound High Sierras alone would have been impossible.

The refreshing 20-minute boat-ride to Vermillion Valley Resort provided an alternative perspective from hiking high up in the mountains. A bushy-bearded hiker named "Floater" had earlier arranged for a bottle of wine, cheese, and crackers to be on board our ferry. We toasted to friendship, and I welcomed the calories. Everyone felt relaxed, having hiked through the spectacular High Sierras without a serious incident. My right ankle hurt and swelled badly from sideways walking on steep snow slopes, but I felt lucky.

Fish and I booked a room at the run-down resort. Along the PCT the term "resort" applies to any structure possessing a roof. Most of the resorts are little more than hiker hostels. We still felt glad to have showers, laundry facilities, and beds, and the friendly staff made us feel welcome. Although Fish had been planning to hike another 64 miles with me, he thought it best to stop at Vermillion Valley. He'd covered 326.2 trail miles in 13 days for a 25-mile per day average. This great accomplishment satisfied him. I'd dropped behind schedule and needed to push on hard to keep my dream of a new record alive. Fish's mushy feet and swollen ankles hurt. He'd toughed the last days out, but hiking had passed the stage of being much fun. His muscles ached, too. Fish had shed 15 pounds and joked that his wife intended to send him with me every summer.

We ordered mountain-man dinners at the rustic restaurant at Vermillion Valley Resort, and as we progressed through our meal, the three Japanese unexpectedly arrived. We'd passed them the night before, where they'd camped south of Freefall. They'd missed the ferry and had hiked in along another spur trail. They seemed excited to reunite with us, and joined us for the last part of our feast. The Japanese astonished us by eating as much as we ate. None of them weighed over 120 pounds. Since we carried no stove, hot food seemed like a real treat, and we thoroughly enjoyed our dinner. The frosty beer helped, too, and Mr. Tea held his own in that department. From my trips to Japan, I'd already realized that Japanese businessmen often consume voluminous amounts of beer. However, I still felt amazed to see someone so small quaffing so many beers.

After showers and a good night's sleep, we devoured an over-sized breakfast with Reverend Freefall as our guest. When I thanked him with a couple of Clif bars, he seemed pleased. I had resupplied, had made phone calls, and had taken care of gear-preparations for my morning departure. During that time, Fish had been successful in arranging transportation out of the nearly inaccessible Vermillion Valley. He accompanied me on the return ferry ride, while most hikers at the resort slept and planned a rest day.

Fish told me that I was the only person with whom he would have completed this section of the trail. His kind words moved me. I felt sad to be parting from his company and knew that I would hike solo for most of the remainder of the trip. I'd also found out that only a handful of thru-hikers remained ahead of me on the PCT. One group—Pacific Beast, Rye Dog, and Tutu—had left Vermillion Valley about five days earlier. I felt scared about facing the upcoming heavy snow and river fords alone. The knowledge that I'd gained about the trail conditions troubled me.

The following excerpt of Fish's diary from week two, June 8th to June 15th, describes his perspective on our High Sierra experience.

Begin Fish's excerpt diary, week two:

The week started off in an exciting manner as we hiked past Mt. Whitney (elevation 14,492 feet), the highest mountain in the contiguous 48 states. Despite choosing not to take the extra day required to summit it, we did sleep under the stars at Sandy Meadow, which provided us with an 11,000-foot-high front-porch view of Mt. Whitney as the sun descended. With the magnificent sights, brilliant stars, freezing temperatures, and the initial threat of bears stealing our food that evening, we stayed awake most of the night.

With Forester Pass (elevation 13,180 feet), the highest point on the PCT, looming in that morning's hike, we shook off the ice from our sleeping-bags and got an early start on the challenging day. Initially, the deep snow prevented us from finding the trail that would lead us over the highest pass in the Sierras. After much denial and three hours of exploring other options, we started up the steepest wall toward what we thought was a switchback over 1,000 feet above us. Because of the lack of oxygen at that height, the steepness of the slope, and the depth of the snow, it took quite a while to get up the courage to make an ascent up and over Forester Pass. Once on top, a few victory photographs were taken to prove that we'd made it.

The next day held two 12,000-foot mountain passes (Glen Pass and Pinchot Pass). Ideally, hikers plan only one pass per day so that they can go over early in the morning. That way snow conditions are still firm enough to support their weight. Later in the morning, once the sun starts melting the snow, the consistency of the snow becomes loose and mushy. Consequently, a lot of postholing occurs. We often found ourselves waist deep in snow when trying to get from point A to point B.

Glen Pass wasn't too steep, so our climb of it was relatively uneventful. The Rae Lakes (a popular camping area with over 60 lakes) on the other side rewarded us with much beauty. As we left this area, it was hard not to wonder if our life paths would enable us to ever get back to these tranquil locations. Yet, with Pinchot Pass still to do that day, we had little time to ponder such questions. In fact, it wasn't until 7 pm that evening when we eventually did reach the top of Pinchot. Exhausted, with temperatures plummeting, and only an hour left before the sun went down, we were able to work our way down about 1,000 feet to a camping-spot. It felt good to be safe and relatively warm again in our sleeping-bags that evening, despite being camped above the completely frozen Lake Marjorie, which was at 11,160 feet.

The next day featured Mather Pass (elevation 12,100 feet). For the second time in the same week, we were in denial about where the actual trail crossed over the mountain. Once again, after much speculation and debate, footsteps of previous hikers were spotted, and they confirmed that our route went vertically straight up a wall of snow and ice that was 1,000 feet directly above where we stood. Because of the steepness, hard snow, and icy conditions over this part of the trail, previous hikers had graciously taken the time to cut steps. The only problem was that any mistake by a hiker climbing these steps would result in a fall of at least 1,000 feet. Needless to say, it was a relief to make it over the pass and down the other side safely to camp. In fact, we slept at a mere 8,750 feet that night; this was the first time during the week that we were able to sleep at under 10,000 feet. The warmer temperatures and additional oxygen made for some of our best sleeping conditions.

After a good night's rest, we embarked on a climb of another huge pass, Muir Pass (elevation 11,955 feet). The ascent was a long one, but snow conditions remained firm as we made our way up the bowl to Muir Hut. With rising temperatures and softening snow conditions, much of the afternoon was spent trying to get off the mountain. I had an exceptionally difficult time with postholing on the north side of the pass. I found myself belly-deep in snow with almost every other step. With much persistence, and a quickly fading sense of humor, we were soon back on the trail and moving north. The end of the day held a final challenge as we forded our widest and fastest river of the trip.

After six long, arduous, adventurous, exciting, and harrowing days with (literally) breath-taking scenery, we found ourselves still one day away from our next resupply and one day short on food. We retired that evening shy of where we'd hoped to be when we'd left Kennedy Meadows six days earlier. Between our next resupply, Vermillion Valley Resort, and us remained 22 more miles, including one more mountain pass, Seldon Pass (elevation 10,900 feet), and a few more challenging river fords. Despite the lack of food and energy, we pushed a quick pace all day and arrived at the shores of Lake Edison, where a ferry took us to the resort.

We arrived to our first hot meal in two weeks, cold beers, and an expensive night's stay in a motel room. In fact, the room looked more like it should have been charging by the hour rather than by the night. Mainly because of a few physical injuries and difficulties with my asthma during the week, I decided not to try to lick the remaining 64 miles to Tuolumne Meadows that I'd initially planned. It turned out to be the best decision for both of us. A day behind his schedule, Wall was determined to get through the final few High Sierra passes and get back on pace. Additionally, I discovered that my sore ankle, which I'd twisted back on Muir Pass while postholing a few days earlier, was now the diameter of a softball.

The following morning, after a great feast, Wall pushed north by himself, leaving me and a group of thru-hikers at Vermillion Valley Resort. With only a half-dozen hikers still ahead, a few especially dangerous river fords, and the last two remaining Sierra passes, it was with much apprehension that Wall took the ferry back to the trailhead to continue his dream of completing the PCT in record time. I took the boat-ride with him that morning to help send him off.

For us it was a great 13 days on the trail together. We got to visit and re-live many great moments in our lives (including our '95 AT thru-hike together). In the course of two weeks we'd laughed, cried, and sung ourselves up the trail. Before the boat pulled away, we shared a final embrace and reminded each other of how proud we were of the other's accomplishments. I was uncertain if I would ever see my childhood friend again.

End Fish's diary, week two.

I reminisced about Fish's first week on the PCT and compared it to his second week. During the first week, we'd caught up on each other's lives and what had happened to me thus far on the trail. The hiking had been far easier during week one, and we'd almost sung our way northward. We'd played name that tune, posing and answering many rock-trivia questions. Hundreds of songs had passed over our lips. Such games had kept us occupied. Fish had suggested that if I ever wanted to change my trail name, "Jukebox" would be an appropriate one.

The second week of our trip had brought us sky high, with so many dramatic climbs that we didn't have enough oxygen left for singing. The scenery had been spectacular, but we'd faced many extraordinary challenges. We'd talked philosophy during the hard times. Fish and I had grown up in the blue-collar, sea-level town of Riverside, Rhode Island. Whenever we'd accomplished a collaborative feat that we'd felt proud of, we'd would say in unison, "Not bad for a couple of kids from

Riverside". In fact, those words rang in harmony when we'd parted company for the final time on the breezy shores of Lake Edison.

6. Alone Again

On June 16th, at mile 871.3, I shook hands with Fish and stepped off the ferry, leaving him and the boat's operator on board. Fish seemed concerned about me, and he could tell that I felt worried, too; we both knew that what I faced ahead would be difficult, and to face it alone would test my limits. My minimal gear troubled us both. As I climbed back over the rocks where the group of us had sat the previous day, I turned and saw Fish's pensive expression one final time. I waved good-bye and turned my attention to the trail.

I powered back to the PCT off the spur trail, leaving the only other thru-hiker from the morning's boat ride, "Just Mike", behind. The wooded path to return to the PCT over the rolling terrain measured a mile, and took 15 minutes to master. The Casio read 10 am, and my schedule required me to hike a 29.4-mile day. Achieving this mileage would merely keep me from falling further behind. In reality, I knew that with the late start and the tough terrain, I couldn't possibly meet the schedule. My dream seemed to slip away. I became predominately concerned with survival.

Several people who worked at Vermillion Valley Ranch had warned me about two dangerous fords that I would encounter in the next stretch of the PCT. The North Fork of Mono Creek, called a Class Five rapids by Vermillion's employees, worried me. Walking northward to the creek, I speculated on what I would find and if I could handle the crossing by myself. I hoped for a low water-level and thought about selecting a place to cross which would minimize danger. The idea of falling in and losing all gear preoccupied my mind. The uncertainty and anticipation mounted, while all my neck and back muscle fibers tightened up to piano-wire tension. I missed Fish, and I faced my substantial fears alone.

The North Fork of Mono Creek raged wildly, and I heard the creek long before I reached it. The PCT stretched straight across the creek, and I could see the path emerging on the opposite side. The water appeared far too deep and far too swift to ford where the trail crossed. Downstream didn't look promising, so I began to explore upstream. This tactic involved bushwhacking along the inside of a 200- to 300-foot vertical rock wall. While making my way upstream, many times I hung from a brittle tree limb or a questionable rock handhold. A slip caused by a small tree uprooting or a piece of rock crumbling would have sent me spiraling into a boiling rapid. In all likelihood I'd have drowned, if I didn't die from the fall's impact. The ensuing newspaper headlines upset me: "Missing Savannahan's Body Located in High Sierras" or "Savannah PCT Hiker Found". I couldn't imagine what date would accompany these "news" items.

As I moved up the right-hand-side of the creek, the elevation changed drastically, oscillating hundreds of feet. Even from my eagle perches, I couldn't see any feasible place to cross. I discovered another trail that led away from the creek. In following the trail steeply uphill, I hoped to find a return path to the creek at a reasonable point to ford. Well, unfortunately, that prayer wasn't answered. I decided to retrace my steps, which I always disliked doing, and to cross at a place that I'd previously deemed too dangerous to ford.

As I worked my way back to an aerie near the creek's edge, I spotted a point where the creek momentarily split into two channels. The location wasn't so much an island as a debris pile of big rocks and giant broken logs. I concluded that this monkey-barrel heap was the best place to attempt to ford. Usually when I strayed off trail, I hiked steep terrain. This time satisfied the norm, and I felt exhausted from my search for a satisfactory crossing.

My heart thumped and my chest bellowed, as I descended a rock face to creek level. I down-climbed a 5.3 pitch with my pack and, of course, no protection. This incident took me far from my comfort zone. When I reached the planned crossing-point, the creek appeared much more dangerous than it had seemed from afar. The waves rolled larger than anticipated, and the water rushed faster than I'd guessed. I should have known that from a distance the true circumstances would have appeared gentler. Had fear sabotaged my reasoning abilities? The creek shore sounded noisy, as the crashing turbulent water pounded in my echo chamber. This churning chaos added to my distress and to my confusion. Should I risk this ford?

Retreating wasn't an option I'd permitted myself, and I'd seen no more-promising place to ford, so I reaffirmed my decision to cross here. I looked at the unappealing spot closely, planning my move sequence. A large half-submerged boulder that I needed to reach split the first gap in two, and from this giant wet rock I could make an all-or-nothing lunge to the "island". I didn't look ahead to the second smaller portion of whitewater. Entering the foaming water caused immediate numbing of my feet, ankles, and calves. I continued across, hammered by a walloping river surge. Glimpsing down and registering the astounding water velocity produced intense vertigo. I quickly looked up and recovered. The crux of the crossing hinged on my next move.

While stepping forward, I planted my foot securely on a rock, or so I thought. I slipped and almost went down. My flailing hiking-poles found no purchase. The water's force violently vibrated the poles, resulting in an eerie disturbing noise. I slipped further, torquing all my muscles to remain upright. Boom! My pack, which still rested on my shoulders, suddenly disappeared half underwater. The water exerted a tremendous amount more force on me now. "S—! S—!"

With my strength ebbing, only one last glimmer of hope remained. If I didn't risk everything and move immediately, Mother Nature would make my decision for me. I lunged hard toward the island and pulled myself from the creek's grip, with my hands spinning circles to balance forward. A syringe of adrenalin shot into my bloodstream. Powered by that incredible rush, I moved ahead directly. I normally would have carefully scouted this next crossing, too, but with my super-human, chemical-induced strength, I simply walked straight across without incident. Glancing over my shoulder, I felt shocked. No logical explanation existed for my actions. I could find no reasons.

Shaking, I emerged from the creek. As icy water poured off me and my pack, I glimpsed up to see what lay ahead. A 30-foot, 5.4 rock-climb guarded my creek escape. Only now, for the first time, did I look beyond the creek itself. That was a foolish mistake, I thought. I scoped my predicament thoroughly, but all other potential exits seemed even more treacherous. While looking around, I instinctively stuffed my hiking-poles into my pack. Once I began climbing, I would be committing myself since no strength existed to climb down. If I fell from above 20 feet, I'd be in serious trouble. I stood a good half-mile off the PCT at this point, and with decreasing water-levels imminent, perhaps no one would venture to this location until next season.

I selected a line and began climbing a promising crack. About two-thirds of the way up, a burning sensation permeated my fatigued arms and back. In a lapse of judgment, I reached too quickly for a handhold, and tore a gash in my arm on a sharp rock edge. When I witnessed the blood squirting out, I felt another massive adrenalin rush, and flew the last 10 feet over the top. The 30-foot ascent had wasted me— a Savannahan rock-climbing at 10,000 feet. The stress and effort had sucked away my already waning energy. After some direct pressure, the blood stopped flowing from my arm. I spent only 60 seconds catching my breath, and bushwhacked back to the PCT near the creek. This hard hiking restored my core body temperature. From the opposite side of the creek, where I'd stood hours earlier, I resumed my northward journey.

The PCT wasn't a trail that allowed me time to pat myself on the back. There was no time to reflect. I began to contemplate what the next crossing would be like. My imagination utilized my new perspective fully, thereby producing deep worries. This second ford had been described to me as a precarious step across a 90-foot waterfall, where you stood only a foot-and-a-half from the 90-foot drop. I'd heard that at the crossing-point the water reached mid-thigh. The short ford involved only one or two important steps, but the consequences of a mis-step loomed large. During the subsequent few miles of hiking, I visualized the scene. My thoughts troubled me. I never tried to distract myself from unnerving thoughts, though, but simply let them run their course. This way I found that they didn't return as quickly.

When I approached the day's second dangerous ford, the spot appeared exactly as anticipated. I fearfully watched the water gush over the trail and drop (a vertical) 90 feet. I studied the situation, but only one avenue presented itself. It was impossible to go above the falls, as another dangerous waterfall and rock wall blocked that direction.

Attacking from below was impossible, too, for that choice entailed a dangerous down-climb, ford, and ascent. No other options existed to continue northward at this moment. Having decided my fate, I summoned my courage, taking cliff-diver breaths, and went for it.

Once I stepped into the deep water, the current pushed me aggressively toward the drop-off's edge. Standing mid-thigh in the ice-cold water, I kept moving forward, paying close attention to the situation at hand. Step one. A long dicey step two, the crux of the matter. "S—! Whoa!" Step three. I'd crossed safely. Thank God. I stared back in disbelief at the crossing, and exclaimed "I hope no one dies on that this summer!" I worried about those behind me, especially my shorter friends. If they found this crossing at this height, ... I couldn't force myself to complete that thought. Through rocky forests and with frayed nerves, I continued northward, wondering what challenges I would face on my approach to the road near Tuolumne Meadows, at mile 935.7.

My New Balance running-shoes had fallen apart from kicking steps in the snow and ice, and from fording too many rivers. I'd tried to repair them earlier at Vermillion Valley, but the rubber-cement had held for only a few hours. I planned to pick up new shoes at Yosemite's Tuolumne Meadows, which Road Runner Sports had "overnighted" to me. The promise of new footwear meant a lot to me. The sole on my right shoe had been flopping all the way to the center of my foot for quite awhile. On dangerous terrain, this situation only exacerbated my problems. Fortunately, I'd tackled the 10,900-foot Silver Pass and the 11,056-foot Donohue Pass already. At the road to Tuolumne Meadows I stuck out my thumb, and a young guy in a pickup truck offered me a ride.

When I arrived at the tiny Tuolumne Meadows Post Office, I anxiously inquired to see if my package had been delivered. The clerk at the post office said "No". Simultaneously, a young man in a station wagon pulled up with the daily deliveries. I smiled and marveled at my good timing. My shoes would surely be in this new load. As the final thru-hiker mail-drop hit the curb, my heart sank. In disbelief I even searched the "mail truck" myself, poking my head around in the back of the empty station wagon. My anticipation and desire for the new shoes had been so piqued, that I felt sick to my stomach, when I realized that they'd arrive the next day. If I hadn't been pursuing the record, I could have sat around and enjoyed Yosemite for a day, while I waited for the shoes. But what would I do now? Where and when could I get new shoes? I felt sharply disappointed.

I'd hitched in a mile to reach the Tuolumne Meadows' store, but from the *Databook's* entry I thought that the ride should have been only a third of a mile. In fact, I'd missed three-quarters of a mile of trail. Dammit! Now, with my pack fully loaded from my Tuolumne shopping-spree, I did a one-mile road-walk "south", rejoined the PCT where I'd exited prematurely, and walked back along the section that I'd missed. This mishap put me further behind schedule, but I'd caught the mistake. With my feet and my body falling to pieces, my integrity remained whole. I felt good about that fact.

Another hot sunny day presented perfectly-clear skies. I passed a number of day-hikers and climbers in the Tuolumne Meadows area, as I reintegrated the PCT. I'd missed the shoes this day; they'd miss me the next. Who knew where that pair of shoes would end up? I'd never see them—what a shame! Overnighting packages to remote PCT locations meant three-to-four days for delivery. I had made good time for the remainder of this day, and had already eaten my heaviest food items. Although the shoe dilemma upset me, I hiked well and enjoyed Yosemite.

At around 8:30 pm as the sun was disappearing, I encountered a large Black Bear whose thick brown fur stood on end; the brown-colored bear looked like a medium-sized Grizzly. I'd startled him, and he began running north on the PCT. His acceleration and top speed awed me, as he ran faster than a track dog. I marveled at his limitless display of force. In spite of my extreme fatigue, the sheer power of that animal willed me to push on farther than I'd planned. The bear made me nervous, and I didn't have the security of being with another hiker.

I didn't cease hiking that night until I'd reached what appeared to be a wide-open field. While constantly scanning the perimeter of my camping area, I hung up my food and set up my tarptent. I worried about "Brownie", and assembled a small stack of rocks to scare him off, if he did enter my camp. I didn't put my faith in the rock pile, since stopping this bear with a bazooka seemed doubtful. Nevertheless, the rocks comforted me.

Many deer decided to visit me that evening and even peer into the Squall. Each time I tossed and turned, I spooked the deer, which in turn spooked me. I slept little that night and felt relieved to find my food intact when I arose. With cold fingers, it took a sustained effort to untie all the previous evening's knots. Losing my food to a bear at any time during the hike would have curtailed my record bid. I felt lucky, but I also felt that a greater presence had intervened again. At daybreak I realized that I'd camped in a glorious meadow.

Early one morning a day or so later I noticed two hikers camped 50 yards to the side of the PCT. They appeared to be thru-hikers. Who else would be out here pre-season? Since it seemed that they'd resume hiking shortly, I stopped. I shouted "Hello", and minutes later they rejoined the trail. Their names were Graham and Falcor, and they thru-hiked. We agreed to walk together. This decision was one of the best that I'd made all summer.

Graham possessed superb navigational skills, and Falcor possessed an uncanny knack for spotting the trail. Both of them seemed fit, having already hiked on the PCT for almost two months. As of late, they covered about 25 miles per day. I'd been lost several times in deep snow since leaving Fish, and I thought that these guys could help me to stay on trail.

Throughout the summer, I would be lost on many occasions. These times became a true test of courage. Keeping my head and retracing my steps to the last point where I knew for sure that I stood on trail became my sole purpose. Each mistake meant hiking additional hours, lost energy, and a greater risk of injury. My most difficult times involved junctures where I couldn't decide which way to go, proceeded forward, went backward, and still seemed stuck. I never felt in a position to wait for another hiker to come by to offer guidance. If trail-markings even existed, they sat invisible beneath the white surface. I would literally walk around at random until I located a speck of trail. Eventually I began to fear snow and always hoped to escape my white nemesis as soon as possible. Having hiking partners alleviated my fears.

In his early twenties and a landscape architect from Maine, Graham had attended Utah State University in Logan. I guessed that his passion for rock-climbing had brought him west for college. Graham appeared wiry and strong. He said that after the hike he and his girlfriend, who was finishing a PhD at Princeton, would head off on a four-month climbing-tour through Mexico. Graham had completed a multi-week glacial NOLS (National Outdoor Leadership School) course in Alaska. I admired his snow, ice, and survival skills. Graham had fashioned a tiny alcohol stove from two food cans. A friend of his from Utah had sewn his light-weight custom pack. He traveled light and seemed knowledgeable about gear.

Falcor looked to be about my age. His family owned and operated a rice plantation in California. He applied his encyclopedic knowledge of rice to answer my questions about this swamp grass. I learned about various types of rice—how to plant and to harvest the Far East's staple food, and that California produces more rice than most countries in the world. Falcor told me that five years earlier he'd quit his job as an engineer and had been living out of an RV. Since his till ran dry, he'd be returning to the workforce after the hike.

Falcor owned several pure-bred Irish Wolfhounds that he showed. His engineering background, combined with his failing RV, had led him to develop mechanic's skills, and while on the road, he would often earn extra cash repairing other campers' RVs. Falcor hiked with two flexible bows which he'd fashioned from young trees, but said that he would purchase trekking-poles at his next opportunity. His gaiters consisted of a pair of black dress socks with the fronts cut out. Falcor carried a lightweight stove, and sometimes cooked both lunch and dinner. He enjoyed heated food.

The three of us traversed many areas where snow obscured the trail. We usually relied on Graham's maps to keep us on track. He had painstakingly marked his maps in *Volume I* with highlighters, depicting the PCT in yellow and spur trails in pink. Taking an intersecting trail by accident always seemed possible. In numerous places the PCT abruptly turned off the "main trail", so a mistake could easily happen. Graham's maps alerted us to potential problems.

Graham had also written mileages on his *Volume I* maps. When Graham pulled out a *Volume I* page, Falcor and I huddled around and stared over his shoulder, curious to see any significant landmarks that Graham had noted. If the publisher's versions of *Volume I* had contained the map features which Graham had introduced, thru-hikers would have benefited significantly. Having three pairs of eyes helped dramatically with navigation, and I was thankful to have paired up with Graham and Falcor.

The first day that Graham, Falcor, and I hiked together, I'd walked 31 miles, while they'd pulled their customary 25. My earlier start and timing had worked out well. The next day Falcor and Graham agreed to do 32 miles. This mileage fit in better with my schedule, and I thanked them for extending their normal day. We enjoyed each other's company and got along well. Over the course of our 32 miles, one gurgling river ford stood out.

Being an expert rock-climber, Graham possessed fantastic balance. Whatever Falcor lacked in talent, he made up for by being fearless. We approached a wide river-crossing bridged only by a long *blow-down*. The limb-filled tree looked impassable to me. Almost immediately, Falcor began crawling across the 500-armed log on all fours. Weaving in and around branches, he slithered along quickly. He appeared impervious to the raging torrent, which boiled directly beneath the natural bridge. I stared dumbfounded, witnessing the impossible. The blow-down stretched so far, and the whitewater pounded so loudly, that we couldn't communicate between shores.

The far side of the swelling river was guarded by massive downed trees, so when Falcor disappeared, we couldn't tell if he had actually touched land. He appeared to stand on solid ground, and so I began my high-wire act. As I climbed onto the tree, it shifted markedly. I knew immediately that something bad had happened. Unexpectedly, Falcor had still been crawling on the tree, up until that moment. My climbing aboard prematurely had flung him off the tree and had plunged him into the river's edge, where he'd completely submerged. Blocked by the river, we could do nothing for him.

I made the harrowing crossing, and Graham followed hurriedly. We reached a bleeding, drenched, and distraught Falcor. I apologized profusely for my blunder, and he gracefully accepted, seeing right away that I shared his pain. Falcor walked bloody and shivering cold during the next stretch. I felt terrible, and found it hard to forgive myself.

Graham, Falcor, and I often glissaded down steep descents, using our running-shoes as skis. This dangerous practice worried me because we accelerated to high speeds. Besides, if one postholed, a broken ankle or damaged leg seemed imminent. At one nearly-vertical descent, we slid down on our butts. As usual, Graham led the way, and Falcor and I trailed side-by-side. This 600-foot slide played out inside a massive cirque. As we steadily gained speed, a softball-sized rock broke loose and bounced along beside us. While slicing through the air, Falcor asked about the missile, and I shouted, "Rock!" He looked concerned, but we couldn't steer and sped down helpless. Fortunately, the projectile decided not to bounce into the face of one of us.

On this Andes-proportioned slide, our velocity had greatly exceeded a safe speed, and we felt lucky to have completed the vast run-out without getting injured. Graham had shouted at us to stop ourselves using our feet. We'd dug our heels into the crusty snow, and the friction had been just enough to curtail our roller-coaster descent. Loose rocks kept going. Several layers of skin ripped off my rear end on our wild glide. I thought to myself that I'd risked my entire thru-hike while doing this crazy glissade. "Why'd you do that?" I scolded myself. Once more, Lady Luck had watched over me, and I promised her that I wouldn't attempt any more high-speed glissades.

Hiking with Graham and Falcor added spice to my trip, and I enjoyed their company. However, to return to my schedule, I needed to forge ahead. My two companions customarily spent an hour at lunch. I quietly decided that the next day I'd eat quickly and hike ahead. So when noon rolled around, I devoured my ration—a few gigantic spoonfuls of peanut butter, handfuls of Wheat Thins, and a Mounds candy-bar—in five minutes. Falcor prepped to cook, while Graham dipped Oreos into peanut butter. I reluctantly informed my friends that I needed to push north. Although I sincerely thanked them for hiking together, and said how much I'd enjoyed their company, my words couldn't adequately convey my appreciation. We sadly said our good-byes. I felt apprehensive about hiking alone, but keeping my dream alive entailed that necessity.

When I separated from Graham and Falcor, I'd thought that the deep snow lay behind me. In fact, I encountered far more white stuff than anticipated, as I made my way north. Once I'd left my friends, I hiked aggressively. I felt bummed out, but also wanted to gain some time. If they'd hiked past me after taking a long lunch, I would have felt silly because of my record attempt. In the back of my mind, I thought that they might try to surprise me that evening.

While on my own again, I paid close attention to where the trail went. I felt a greater degree of responsibility since I didn't have Graham and Falcor to rely on. Only a single set of eyes guided me now. I initially made decent progress and found the trail pretty well. This good fortune soon ended, though. I reached a point in deep snow where I couldn't determine the trail's course, and after deliberations I decided to veer to the right.

My course led me through abundant snow over difficult terrain. I traveled in an extremely remote area. A raging river blocked my way. The river fell steeply down a mountainside, and the repeated, icy, rocky crossings tested my limits. Drowning on such a crossing seemed distinctly possible. I doubted that many people had ever ventured here previously. Hypothermia worried me, and navigation errors plagued me in the wild landscape.

I continued bushwhacking for several hours, praying against the odds that I would locate the PCT. While desperation arrived, hope departed. I scaled progressively more dangerous rock-faces during my search. My mind raced. One fall. Lost. Life. Death. "Don't quit, Ray!" Eventually, I realized that backtracking held my fate. For hours, though, I'd been telling myself that retracing my steps wasn't possible, since I'd hiked so far over one-way terrain.

I'd violated by hours my rule of going no more than *five* minutes without finding the trail. How the hell did I do that? Why? Earlier I'd promised myself, if lost, to retreat to the last point where I'd stood on trail. Like a cat exploring, I'd just kept going forward, almost endlessly. The consequences built, and I was in a disastrous situation.

During my backtracking attempt, I felt blind-folded. Adrift in a vast snow-covered wilderness, I fought panic. This region seemed bigger than Rhode Island. Thoughts spewed from my alarmed mind. Invisible. Massive mountain forest. Re-find my way. No sense of current location. "Raaaayyyy!!" Dense rugged woods. Trees soaring. Icy rivers. Cliff walls blocking me. "Keep moving!" If anyone else had stood nearby, the striking undulations in these mountains would have shielded him/her from seeing me.

Utterly baffled as to my whereabouts, I expended mammoth amounts of physical and mental energy. I no longer controlled my mind. Remain calm. Keep cool. "You can do this, Ray! Mom. Dad."

Nearly bursting into tears, I screamed "F—!" If any seat had existed, I would have sat, resigning my situation. My problem was the greatest that I'd ever faced. All else became trivial. Live or die?

As on most occasions when I became lost, I was anxious to regain the trail quickly. This necessity to curtail my overwhelming fear resulted in several hairy rock-climbs. While scrambling up a steep hill, I ran head-first into an angled thick tree-trunk. Thud. "Damn!" I'd crashed so violently that I'd knocked myself down. "Pay attention; oh, God." I staggered to my feet. A fleshy lump emerged on my forehead, as I wobbled around. If I'd gone unconscious, my disorientation would have made it impossible to escape.

I gave myself only a small chance of returning from this epic, and that resignation made me very sad. My heart broke. "F—ing idiot!" I yelled. I reluctantly accepted the fact that I would never see anyone again. Would my body be found? When? I thought of friends and loved ones, and I reflected on my life and the things that would be left undone . . . . The whole situation was f—ed! Things had spiraled way out of control.

I snapped back. If I intended to live, I needed to retrace my detour-route and soon. The more snow-covered woods that I walked through, the more similar everything appeared, and I wasn't leaving many foot-prints on the crusty snow. Was I going the right way? Would I find the trail before dark? Surely Graham and Falcor had passed me by now. "Focus! Concentrate!" During the next interval, I repeated this mantra endlessly. "This isn't over yet, Ray! You still have food," I said, trying to implant a modicum of hope.

I remained calm enough to continue searching for the trail—but barely. In extreme danger this time, my life flashed before me. Appalling scenarios troubled me. I cursed pathetically. Again and again, thoughts of family and of friends and their reactions passed through my mind. I needed to deal with reality, though. A survival state swept over me, and I let basic instincts take control of my actions.

The process of sweeping back and forth through the woods restored some hope. My determination grew, and I refused to quit. I possessed the energy and the will-power to persevere. Using dead-reckoning, I guessed which areas I hadn't come from and kept track of which areas I'd already swept. My persistence finally paid off, and, miraculously, I discovered my old footprints in a tiny snow patch. Tears fell. Thoughts of surviving filled me. I repeatedly pumped my fist high in the air, raising goose-bumps on my skin's surface. As I retraced the melting footprints, I occasionally got momentarily off track in places that weren't snow-covered. A long time later I stood on the PCT. While helplessness dissipated, a tremendous joyful feeling warmed me.

How long could I have held out if I had not regained the trail? How would I have perished: exposure, drowning, starvation, or a fall? In my most desperate moment, I'd regretted not having a pen with me. I'd felt an urge to leave a note for family and friends. My letter would have told them how important they'd been, and how strongly I loved them. They fulfilled me, governed my thoughts, and gave my life purpose. I'd miscalculated, not committed suicide. This line of thinking brought more tears. My words fell short. Would such a note be found? I possessed no pen, so I let it be.

Once I rejoined the trail, I detected Graham and Falcor's melting footprints. They'd passed by a couple of hours earlier. If I'd only stayed with them, I would have been six miles farther up trail, would have avoided my harrowing ordeal, and would have had a tremendous amount more remaining energy. The most mentally demanding day of my life would have been avoided. I didn't feel sorry for myself; I felt lucky. At the time I didn't think that I'd ever mention this incident to anyone. A presence guarded me. I pushed forward, following Graham and Falcor's tracks.

At around 7 pm I caught up to Graham and Falcor, who had just stopped for the night and had finished setting up camp. The two said they'd seen my footprints in the snow, but all of a sudden my tracks had just disappeared. They'd wondered with concern what had happened to me. I filled them in on my tale. As they ate dinner, I wolfed down a king-sized MilkyWay and a Hershey milk-chocolate bar. When Graham and Falcor heard me say that I needed to push on, they stared at me in disbelief. I'm sure that they saw the lump protruding from my forehead. They wished me good luck, and I started hiking again. I prayed that I wouldn't get lost again. For a brief moment I speculated on how their conversation unfolded after I left. Having hiked with me for two days, perhaps they'd understood my drive and my determination better than I'd thought. Anyhow, the trail called me, and I needed to give it my full attention.

If I'd continued to hike with Graham and Falcor, I could have stayed on trail and comfortably done 25 miles per day. However, I needed to start hiking closer to 40 miles a day to have a shot at the record. I walked on until 9:30 pm that night, covering another eight miles. This day felt monumental. In darkness, I found a marginal place to pitch the tarptent, but couldn't hang my food. Since I felt worried about bears, I wrote my name on the trail in the dirt, drawing an arrow pointing to where I'd set up the Squall. I felt too exhausted to reflect any further on my day. This day was done. I simply lay down in my shelter and slept as best I could.

Graham and Falcor had told me that four thru-hikers walked north of me on the trail: Fearless, Pacific Beast, Rye Dog, and Tutu. Since snow blanketed the trail, I easily confirmed this information by observing footprints. No other north-bounders hiked ahead of me. If I passed these guys, I'd be on my own. When would that happen? Seeing no footprints would be weird, pristine.

I crossed some hazardous snowfields on my way into Echo Lake, at mile 1,089.4, and arrived there on June 23rd, day 43 of my hike. This moment signified the planned midpoint for my hike in terms of time, yet only 31% of the trail's distance had been covered. Had I properly prepared my schedule? I'd never really contemplated the issue in these terms previously. There's not much I can do about the situation now, I thought.

I'd zigzagged the final descent into Echo Lake without having eaten *anything* for more than 12 hours. The calories that I needed would find their way to my stomach soon. The lakeside store seemed well-stocked, and at the snack bar the staff prepared food. I ordered two sandwiches, and ate them while sitting on the ground out front, where I busily repackaged $100 worth of junk food. For the first time this summer, the midday weather looked ominous with dark clouds forming overhead. The incoming storm disturbed me.

At Echo Lake I contacted the usual suspects via phone. We all felt relieved to chat. Familiar voices encouraged me. Since I worried about navigation during the upcoming stretch, I purchased a compass. I picked up the much-needed shoes that I was supposed to have received 155 miles earlier at Tuolumne Meadows. Taking my custom graphite orthotics out of the tattered shoes and inserting them into the new shoes gave me great pleasure. My orthotics took a serious beating, and I wondered if they'd survive the entire trip. I also acquired *Volume I*. While sorting and recycling my garbage, I happily deposited the unrecognizable worn-out shoes in a green dumpster at Echo Lake. Having trimmed the laces on the new shoes and rearranged my pack, I headed off into a mounting wind and darkening sky. My rest had been brief.

As I started around the lake's perimeter, I encountered a thru-hiker named "Pacific Beast". This red-headed mountain-man hailed from Washington state. He'd been thru-hiking with two other guys, Tutu and Rye Dog, but now, due to extreme foot pain, held over at Echo Lake. We chatted for 10 minutes. Pacific Beast seemed surprised to learn that I'd started the trail three weeks after him. He and his companions had pushed themselves hard.

We agreed how dangerous and difficult crossing the High Sierras had been in the deep snow. Pacific Beast described painful cracks in the bottoms of his feet, and I identified with him, as I possessed a similar crack on one of my feet. Such deep cracks don't heal quickly and cause excruciating pain. Pacific Beast and I had endured much of the same ordeal, but he'd decided to slow down his pace and recover. I attempted to ratchet my pace up another notch. After our brief conversation, I headed out into the brewing storm. Would I ever meet Pacific Beast again? How far north of me were Fearless, Rye Dog, and Tutu? How bad would the storm be? I had no answers.

 7 Blizzard Conditions

The darkening clouds over Echo Lake struck fear in me. I'd been hit by lightning during my AT thru-hike, and thunder still upset me. As I walked the shoreline, a major storm unleashed itself. Wind-effects generated large waves, boat traffic vanished, and tall trees arched. Falcor had warned me that the Desolation Wilderness was a difficult and snowy section of the PCT. Its name worried me. I wanted to be snow-free and out of the storm.

Wearing only my running-shoes, shorts, and T-shirt, and with mounting concern, I hiked past a number of crystal-clear lakes and spotted occasional shelters—NorthFace expedition tents, far warmer and far sturdier than my lightweight tarptent. I never saw anyone emerge from a tent, not even to take a peek at the developing storm; they'd dug in for the evening and likely didn't want to release any precious heat. These campers would have been shocked to see me hiking past in the deteriorating conditions.

My nervous energy helped me to continue walking fast, and eventually I found myself in a thick cloudy mist. My goal that evening was to clear 9,380-foot Dick's Pass, at mile 1,102.7. As expected, the wind grew steadily as I climbed higher. To my distress snow began to fall heavily. While looking for a place to set up my shelter, I bypassed sites not shielded from the wind. For what seemed liked an eternity, as I ascended into the eye of the storm, I found nothing promising. Finally, in near-blizzard conditions I located a questionable triangular spot on the mountainside. Three big trees defined the place's geometry. No one had ever camped here before, and no one would ever camp here again. Jack London's short story "To Build a Fire" came to mind, but I wasn't going to build a fire. I pitched the tarptent, driving the last stake in by using a volley-ball-sized rock. Snow blew in all directions and made its way inside my chapped nostrils. I escaped into the tarptent, laid out my gear, and listened to the howling wind buffet my shelter.

My lightweight down sleeping-bag was rated to only 30°F. After a long day of hiking, I usually had trouble keeping myself warm. While dressed in my inadequate clothing, I crawled into the black mummy bag. I felt cold and began shivering. Walter Bonatti's bivouac on K2 at 27,000 feet on an ice shelf without a shelter nor a sleeping-bag came to mind. The great Italian mountaineer had survived that episode and avoided frostbite, I reminded myself. I tried not to think of the Sherpa who'd accompanied him, and who'd lost all his digits .... If Bonatti didn't come to mind, then Sir Ernest Shackleton did. I never thought of Sir Robert Falcon Scott.

The snow accumulated on the Squall, causing it to sag significantly. My vertical space shrank in half, and the wind thrashed the tarptent. Since I'd no idea how much snow would fall, I became paranoid about the shelter collapsing. If it fell down at night, would I suffocate? I tried to knock the snow off the tarptent by using rapid back-hand flicks on its sides. This technique worked to a degree. The fabric of the tarptent became looser, though, and it made an even more disturbing noise in the wind. The Squall *needed* to live up to its name. I should have gone out and re-staked the shelter, but I felt far too cold to contemplate that action seriously. I just hunkered down, demanded that the tarptent hold, prayed that the storm would stop, and hoped that morning would arrive.

I caught only a few winks during that snowy night. In the morning the wind still blew strongly. When I popped my head outside the Squall, frigid temperatures greeted me. I evicted myself from the lightweight shelter at 6 am. My hands numbed immediately, and I dreaded repacking the tarptent. I tried to break camp quickly; however, the final stake wouldn't come out. In my panic the previous night, I'd pounded the stake deeply into a hard tree root. My white hands became immobile from continued exposure.

Everything lay buried in the freshly-fallen snow, including last night's rock "hammer". I diligently searched for a rock to help me extricate the tent-peg. Pawing through the snow with bare hands, at last I located a suitable rock and tried to bang the stake upward without knocking myself on the side of the face. The peg would not yield. While I struggled to remove the peg, the cold tried to placate me—to make me quit and to lie in the snow. I resisted the appealing temptation.

I worked the stake backward and forward, trying to create a wider sleeve in the root from which to pull the peg free with one butt-planting effort. This strategy didn't work, either. I contemplated leaving the f—ing bent peg behind. Could I get by with just three pegs? For all I knew, snow might fall again later that day, that night, and every day in the weeks ahead. I hadn't seen or heard a weather forecast since leaving Savannah. To stabilize the tarptent in nasty conditions, I needed that peg. My final desperate jerk, which nearly put me on my back, yielded results. The crooked aluminum peg that I held in my hand still appeared usable.

While my core body-temperature plummeted, I attempted to roll up the tarptent. This task caused intense pain and proved virtually impossible. I required hands as strong as Jenny's. With snow increasing the Squall's dimensions, repacking the shelter into its tight-fitting stuff sack became a challenging ordeal. My fingers hurt, yet somehow I managed to store the Squall. I needed to begin moving soon because my entire body shivered. Any additional delay would mean hypothermia, and I didn't want to lapse into a tired euphoria. I scanned my camp area as usual to make sure that nothing remained behind, and swiftly resumed hiking.

As I continued up Dick's Pass, I immediately noticed two things: my running-shoes disappeared in the fresh snow, and all tracks from the hikers ahead of me lay completely buried. Both of these observations troubled me. I trekked on without the aid of my unmet friends' footprints. The fluffy deep powder made uphill walking tough. Early that morning, with much grit and determination, I reached the top of Dick's Pass. Massive drifts and a hidden cornice awaited me at the summit, not the company that I was hoping for. I avoided several deep cracks in the snow, and felt glad that I hadn't traveled through here at night. When would I get a snow-free day?

The trail conditions prevented me from achieving my planned daily mileages. The snowstorm had blanketed many square miles, so I wouldn't be seeing any tracks for awhile, either. I made wrong turns and burned thousands of extra calories because of my faulty navigation. Looking for trail-signs in the snow took all my concentration. A cut branch-end, no matter how small, always signified "trail", and I became adept at discovering such clues. The snow bent over trees which lined the PCT, so in many places no obvious swath existed. I utilized a topo map from *Volume I* and a compass, but in long stretches of deep snow, even with these instruments, I struggled to remain in the PCT's narrow window.

The rugged terrain included many obstacles such as rivers, boulder fields, and cliffs. This complexity made navigation challenging. In only one more week the visual clues hinting where the PCT was located would be sufficient for a hiker to follow the trail easily. I needed just one more clue every quarter-mile, but the signs weren't there, and with the record attempt, I didn't have a week to wait. Since I was hiking the PCT pure, skipping ahead and returning later wasn't an option, either.

One particular incident during this section stands out. While following switchbacks on the PCT, I'd descended a mountain's north face in deep snow. Suddenly, the switchbacks completely disappeared—totally vanished. Switchbacks are inherently difficult to follow in heavy snow because they require constant 180° turns. If a single turn is overshot, the hiker winds up in no man's land, far off trail. Recovery becomes difficult. With compass and *Volume I* in hand, I spent a long time trying to determine where the PCT meandered next. I swept back and forth, up and down, over and around, but simply couldn't find the trail leading north. My worry and frustration built. I could and did retrace my steps several times to the last location where I'd definitely stood on the PCT.

Having no trail-markers pointing the way, after much self-debate, I decided to head directly north. I hiked by *feel* only, since I couldn't find *any* trail indicators. This strategy was dangerous, and as I went ahead, I tried to make sure that I could backtrack, if necessary. On the hard snow, though, I left few footprints. In the forest, maintaining reference points seemed impossible. Throughout this trying time, I tested my faith and my courage. The uncertainty of location, while roaming in a vast wilderness, forced me to confront life's most fundamental questions: What was my life worth? Was there life after death? What had I left undone? Would my spirit go on without my body?

Struggling with deep questions, alone and lost in the wilderness, challenged me unbelievably. Keeping myself together required total commitment, and all my strength. Hours later, when I emerged from the snowy woods onto a logging road, a PCT marker sat staring me in the face. My compass work had been better than I'd suspected, and I'd probably been on the PCT the entire time. What if I hadn't seen that marker, though? I felt immensely relieved and thanked the presence that accompanied me on this trip. Having no time to lose and no one to share my ordeal with, I walked north without further reflection.

For the second time on this hike, I would soon reach a section of the trail, where I had run a race. This knowledge gave me an emotional boost. After all, part of my motivation to hike the PCT had stemmed from my previous experiences on the trail. The first time had been in Southern California, on part of the Angeles Crest 100-mile-run course which coincided with the PCT. Now I would reach part of the Western States 100-mile-run course which coincided with the PCT. I'd run the Western States, the preeminent 100-miler in the world, twice. Seeing that section of trail again would be emotional. I'd been to the edge during both races, pushing myself far into the "red zone".

With great anticipation I finally reached the Western States course. The setting looked different this time because snow covered the area. Memories from my races in these mountains filled my thoughts. Those experiences held special places in my heart. My first 100-miler, a test of courage and of will-power, had been run here. This year's edition of the Western States would take place in two days. The runners would face far more snow than usual, and I wondered how they'd fare. I'd run this course in 22 hours, and had won a silver cougar belt-buckle. Thinking about the incredible effort that I'd put forth years earlier provided me strength. Such runs are defining moments in one's life. I'd learned more about myself in those 22 hours of running than I did in months of the usual day-to-day routine. If time had permitted, I would have loved to have crewed for someone at the race. I wanted to help another runner achieve his/her dream.

Near where the PCT intersects the Tevis Cup Trail, at mile 1,136.2, I could see only the top of a trail-marker protruding from the hard snow.

Unable to dig the sign free, I thought back to my wrong turn at Full Ridge and the partially-buried trail-sign that I'd ignored there. I didn't feel sure how to proceed. While I pondered which way to go, I decided to take a break and eat lunch. The trail had forced me to become more patient in my decision-making. After lunch and some wandering back and forth, I discovered the PCT's direction and continued northward. Lake Tahoe's clear-blue water, size, and proximity to the mountains impressed me during this stretch.

The snow accumulations slowed me down considerably, and I struggled to reach Donner Pass, at mile 1,150.1. Donner Pass was named after the ill-fated and controversial 1846–47 Donner party, which had been pinned down in a blizzard here for an entire winter, resulting in the death of many group members. Several feet of snow could fall in a single day in this region. Hunger dominated my thoughts more than the Donner party did, and I hiked from the mountains into a trailside parking lot feeling ravenous. A fit 45-year-old looking woman stood there adjacent to her RV, and I asked about nearby restaurants and stores. She told me that none existed in this vicinity, but that she and her husband could spare some food.

Rick and Barb Miller lived in Ridgecrest, California, and had traveled here to crew for a Western States runner. They'd just returned from a long training run, so my timing seemed perfect. June 26th was a Thursday, and they confirmed that the Western States 100-miler would be run two days hence, on the coming Saturday. As members of the ultrarunning community, we shared common interests. The Millers told me about their races, including the Western States and the Angeles Crest 100-mile run. Because I'd had little contact with people over the past week, our friendly conversation felt especially important to me. The Millers asked all sorts of questions about my thru-hike. They supported my efforts and identified with my difficult challenges.

Barb kindly offered food, "Would you like a sandwich?"

"Yes, thank you," I replied without hesitation.

"Would you like a soda?"

"Yes."

"Would you like some water? I have a cup."

"Yes."

"How about some fruit? A nectarine?"

"Yes."

I devoured everything they handed me.

"Oh, you already ate that. How about another nectarine?"

"Yes, thank you."

"How about some pudding?"

"Yes."

"How about ice cream?"

"Yes."

"Another sandwich?"

"Yes."

"Turkey jerky?"

"Yes."

"Cherries?"

"Yes."

"Another soda?"

"Yes."

"How about a beer for the road?," said a smiling Rick.

"No, thanks."

"Are you sure?"

"Yes."

"How about wine? Merlot? It's good."

"Yeah, sure. Thanks," I said, as I passed Rick my empty Gatorade bottle.

While Rick filled my water-bottle with Merlot, I asked the Millers if they would take my ice-axe to the Angeles Crest 100-mile trail run in Southern California in late September. They planned to run, and I thought that I might run, too. I hoped that my decision to rid myself of the ice-axe wasn't premature. They happily took my ice-axe, which had saved me more than a few times. I borrowed scissors from Barb and further trimmed the straps on my pack. After a few other minor adjustments, I handed over my trash. The Millers had shown me great generosity and kindness, and exactly when I had needed support the most. I felt fortunate to have encountered these good people. We said our goodbyes, and I hoped that we could reunite at an ultra marathon in the future.

Having just consumed some "real" food, I felt re-energized. Once again, I hiked with spring in my step. Shortly after leaving Donner Pass, I encountered a group of middle-aged women who were enjoying a day-hike. They questioned me about my hike, and I satisfied their curiosity. Trail conditions ranked with the best that I'd seen in a long time, and my feet landed on dirt. For the moment my decision to leave the ice-axe behind seemed like a good one.

Ten miles north of Donner Pass, though, I again walked in deep snow. Now, for sure, I knew that I'd made a big mistake with the ice-axe. I worried about what I'd encounter next. Dammit! Why had I been so desperate to save a pound? Footprints indicated that three people hiked ahead of me. Eventually, one person split off, and I followed the tracks of the other two on the theory that two heads are better than one. Where did the tracks lead? What happened to the lone hiker?

The wind slowly died, and as the sun dropped, the air cooled significantly. This decrease in temperature caused the snow to firm up and become crusty. The hikers' footprints traversed along the top of a snow-covered mountain. Up ahead the PCT descended to a flat valley. In the deep snow the problem was to determine how the trail reached the valley. Repeatedly, the tracks led to a cliff edge and back, tracing the mountain-top's perimeter.

I estimated a 1,000-foot drop to the valley floor. Alternating steep cliff-faces and precipitous snowfields blocked my safe descent. Because of the snow's substantial depth, no clues indicated the PCT's way. I thought about backtracking, but decided to follow a bit farther. Intuition suggested that I turn around, but curiosity provided just enough impetus to go forward, so it won out. In the hardening snow on the steep slopes, long glissade streaks, where the hikers had plunged down the mountainside, disappeared in front of me. Unsure of how to proceed, for the moment I just pushed ahead.

After a brief period of descending, retracing my steps became impossible. The mountain fell away too steeply, and I'd been sliding downhill for awhile. I felt committed. S—! To my amazement I arrived at a section where my two guides had plummeted down a 60° slope. I reached for my ice-axe, but my hand missed. Dammit. I'd given it away too soon. The innocent descent had developed into a dare-devil descent.

The hikers ahead of me were crazy. I was nuts. They probably had ice-axes, and the snow had been softer then. While staring down the mountainside, I realized that a slip here would be costly. Large exposed boulders waited to stop an accelerating hiker. F—. I was upset with myself.

As I descended the black-diamond slope, I carefully kicked in my heels. Each foot placement seemed almost directly underneath me. I stomped hard, but the snow resisted. The minimal purchase that I fought for appalled me. The angle required a steady pace, since without forward momentum, I couldn't have balanced. I stared straight down past my toes, and saw that this face involved the crux of my entire descent and my entire journey. I felt my knees trembling.

Just then, without warning, I lost it. "S—!" I began rocketing downward on my backside, accelerating at close to the speed of gravity. My trajectory pointed straight for a large boulder. If I couldn't somehow stop myself within the next few seconds, the boulder would. I struggled to balance on my rear with my feet facing forward. The f—ing boulder, I needed to see it. The slope tilted so vertically that I felt like I was leaning against a wall. I furiously dug my heels into the snow. The chips that I knocked loose pelted my face, but I forced my eyes to stay open. The boulder got nearer, bigger. Why the hell had I given away my ice-axe less than five hours earlier? "Ray!"

I frantically jammed my hands into the hard snow. Fear overwhelmed me. My mind raced. Feet! Hands! Dig in! Harder! The boulder seemed to call to me. As my prayer time vanished, I stopped just 10 feet shy of the deathtrap. My heart raced wildly. Had I peed my pants? I didn't care. My adrenaline stores had emptied; I felt wiped out. A moment of relief swept over me. Other than my gasping for air, no sounds existed. I felt asphyxiated. "You're f—ing crazy!" I whispered. As my animal instincts subsided and I calmed down, I discovered that my hiking-poles weren't in my hands. "S—! I don't believe this." I began hyperventilating.

My trekking-poles possess leather hand-straps. I would often hold the poles behind me underneath my pack, and lift in order to relieve the strain on my back. With the poles held horizontally against my lower back, the straps couldn't be worn. If there was any chance of dropping a pole and being unable to retrieve it, such as during river crossings or while on questionable slopes, I always tried to remember to put the straps back over my hands. This time I'd forgotten. I turned around, and to my dismay, saw the trekking-poles sitting several hundred feet up the slope. They'd been dropped immediately after I'd slipped.

I couldn't even begin to contemplate the remainder of this descent without the trekking-poles. Furthermore, I had no idea of what lay ahead. If the next stretch involved dangerous fords or snowy-mountain traverses, I would need my trusty poles. With frayed nerves, I began the harrowing climb to retrieve the poles. I jammed my gloveless hands into the snow, as I ascended straight up. The stress of the situation had prevented me from getting out my gloves, another mistake. I worried about a slip and a boulder.

I reached the trekking-poles after the soul-searching ascent. My overworked diaphragm felt tight, and my heart pumped vigorously. I concentrated intensely on my actions, and I grabbed the first pole. The leather strap immediately went over my wrist. The second pole lay farther up the slope and a little way to the side. When I attempted to dislodge the second pole, it began sliding. I grabbed the metal with my frozen hand and breathed a sigh of relief. The trekking-pole had almost escaped from me. I strapped on the second pole, and double-checked my grips. Since I didn't feel capable of kicking steps with my toes because of the hardening snow and the flexible running-shoes, I made a dicey turn to face downward. This move violated basic mountaineering principles, but I accomplished it safely.

Not having grown up in the mountains, I strongly respect heights. Normally, if I was unprotected, just staring at this vertical drop would have sent shivers up my spine. That moment I controlled my fear. Now I faced the exact same predicament as I had failed at 15 minutes earlier. I thought about maintaining balance. Surely Lady Luck couldn't help me avoid that boulder on a second slide down the mountain. I put falling out of my mind and summoned the courage to repeat the vertiginous descent. If I were too cautious, I would likely stumble. I relaxed as best I could, took several deep inhalations, and began the formidable down-climb. The exposure caused by facing outward disturbed me. When I finally reached the boulder safely, I paused for thanks and a brief rest. I felt very fortunate, and happy to be alive.

The remainder of the descent wasn't too difficult, relatively speaking. I started to encounter patches of bare ground. These intermittent open areas made following someone difficult, though. I would see steps leading to a rocky outcropping, but no footprints exiting from the other side. Broader rock fields posed even more difficulty because many possible places to climb off the rocks existed. Eventually I reached the valley floor, which for a long time had been my goal, and crossed directly through dozens of cold streams. With waning energy I worked hard trying to find a trail-marker that night. I worried about sleeping off the PCT, since if I had an incident with a bear or other animal, no one might ever find me.

As darkness settled, I felt no choice but to erect my shelter. This day had been one of extreme highs, since I had reached Donner Pass and had made friends with the Millers, but also one of extreme lows, since I had almost lost my life in an out-of-control descent. I felt disheartened and lonely, and longed to be with people I loved. With the hope that the red wine would help me sleep better, I drank it. Worrying accomplished nothing. I planned to rise with the birds the next morning to continue my northward journey.

The wine had worked, and I had slept like a kitten. My metabolism raced so high that I didn't have the slightest hint of a hangover. In the early morning hours just after setting out, I found a trail-marker right near where I'd camped. Lady Luck had assisted me, again. I felt relieved to face another day of hiking. Shortly thereafter, I discovered the footprints of the guys north of me. The PCT next crossed a small logging road. A frustrated hiker had left a note in a plastic bag there reading, "Do you think you fuckers could put a fucking sign here for the PCT?" Clearly, last night's descent had brought the hiker to the edge. In many places signs read "No bikes" or "No fires above 10,000 feet", but PCT signs themselves are absent. In the deep snow I had walked forward on faith alone.

As I hiked farther north, the snow amounts diminished. I could tell that I was catching up to the hikers ahead of me because their footprints looked much fresher. Their shoe-tread patterns, previously eroded by the time I'd reached them, now showed details. About 10 miles south of Highway 49 at Sierra City, I encountered Fearless—an exceptionally strong thru-hiker who'd done the AT twice and also the

PCT. This 44-year-old man had trail-blazed through the High Sierras in snowshoes this year. When Fearless learned that I was 42, he seemed surprised. He told me that Rye Dog and Tutu, the only two thru-hikers on ahead of him, had gone into Sierra City for resupply. We walked together for awhile. When Fearless stopped to filter water, I hiked ahead of him. At Highway 49, where one turns to reach Sierra City, I became the first thru-hiker heading north. I crossed virgin snowfields alone. Apparently, I would never meet Rye Dog nor Tutu.

When I had departed Echo Lake in a storm, at mile 1,089.4, my original intent had been to resupply in Sierra City, at mile 1,191.5. I'd been planning to hike this 102.1 miles in under three days. The food from the Millers had convinced me that I could stretch my three days of supplies into five, and I'd decided to push on to Belden, at mile 1,283.1, before resupplying. This new plan meant a 193.7-mile hike on just three days of food, plus what the Millers had fed me. To contemplate this distance with less than six days worth of food was unheard of in hiking circles. My all-out assault on the PCT record altered my way of thinking.

On day five of this massive push, I became critically low on food,[1] but the gap to Belden spanned 30 miles. In my weak condition my backpack strained me, even though it probably weighed only 15 pounds. I couldn't move at the desired speed. Yet again, my luck changed for the better. I met Stephanie, a 20-year-old from New Mexico, and her friend "Jill"[2], who lived in this area. These two women hiked alone in the secluded forest, and had appeared so unexpectedly that it seemed to me that they'd been beamed here. The women had obviously just begun a day hike; they were clean, not sweating, and pleasantly perfumed. I surmised that Jill was Stephanie's aunt.

Stephanie appeared worried when she first saw me, and quite frankly, I don't blame her. I hadn't washed, at all, since Vermillion Valley Resort, and that was 350 miles south of here. Dirty, sweaty, and smelly, I must have looked dangerous to the women in this remote situation. Jill could see that I was harmless, though, and she wasn't troubled by my mountain-man appearance. I asked if they'd be willing to take some of my articles and mail them back to Savannah. Their car

---

[1] Duh.

[2] I don't remember her real name.

sat only a half-mile away on a logging road, and they seemed happy to help me.

The PCT led back to their car. After rummaging through my pack, I handed Jill my fleece jacket, gloves, balaclava, and compass. Jill couldn't believe that I planned to finish thru-hiking the PCT without a compass. I said that with the minimal snow ahead, I could negotiate the trail using dead-reckoning. Her concern generated new worries. Was I ditching the compass prematurely? Sending the fleece jacket home bothered me. I possessed *no* backup clothes—in *total* one T-shirt, one pair of shorts, two pairs of socks, and my NorthFace windbreaker.

Jill tore a scrap of paper off a brown-paper grocery bag, and I scribbled my Savannah address on it. I tried to give her twenty dollars to cover mailing-costs, but she would accept only five, at my insistence. Jill found a smashed Tiger bar on the floor of her car. She reluctantly offered me the energy bar, concerned that it was too mashed, but I gladly accepted. Stale lint-covered candy appealed to me at that moment. I thanked my new friends. Their support had meant a lot. While I marched north toward Belden, they headed south to resume their day-hike. I figured that I'd probably altered their conversation for the day.

My pack felt significantly lighter since I'd just unloaded 25% of its weight, and I made better time. My biggest problem involved a lack of food—I possessed only one Tiger bar and one Clif bar. After several hours of asceticism, I ate the Clif bar. The 240 calories helped, but I still ran a huge deficit. I conserved the Tiger bar for as long as possible, but finally ate it 13 miles in advance of Belden. Possessing *no* food felt much worse than possessing a token amount. It was another mental thing, and I dealt with the situation. Since virtually no body fat remained on my paltry body, walking four more hours meant burning muscle, including heart muscle. Using muscle for fuel is painful and unsafe. I set my internal hunger switch to the off position. At that moment I had few options.

I faced a parachute drop into Belden. The last thirteen miles fell 4,500 feet, and 3,600 of that came in the final five miles. Walking in the blistering sun and completely bonked, I felt fortunate to descend. What would I have done if the trail climbed? This snaking downhill consisted of dozens of switchbacks. I dreamed of reaching Belden, eating a gigantic meal, and renting a room with a shower. Sleeping in a bed sounded real good. I needed a rest in the comforts of civilization. Hallucinations danced in my head, as I struggled toward town, walking forward on will-power alone. Dreams blended with reality.

———————————————

The Central California phase of the hike had been far more dangerous than I'd anticipated. The late big snowfalls in the High Sierras had made the trail extremely difficult to find. At one point I'd fallen almost two days behind my schedule, despite hiking much harder than I'd planned. I'd pushed even harder to catch up a day. With kaleidoscope feet consisting of cracks, blisters, cuts, and bruises and more snow lying ahead, I thought that I might have to give up my goal of breaking the record. How many more calculated risks could I survive? I couldn't afford to get lost anymore, nor could I afford many more difficult snowfield crossings—sooner or later, Lady Luck would leave me.

Part III

NORTHERN CALIFORNIA

The Northern California section of the trail winds from Belden to the Oregon state boundary, and covers 409.3 miles. The lowest elevation sits at 1,500 feet, while the highest elevation stands around 7,500 feet. This terrain, although not as rugged as that in Central California, still held lots of snow. Castle Crags State Park, the Trinity Alps, and Mount Shasta loomed ahead. The idea of entering a new state provides a thru-hiker with a huge psychological boost, and I needed one. I'd planned to resupply about five times during this section. The longest distance which I'd planned to hike without resupply stretched 145 miles. The hardest day that I had scheduled measured 38.8 miles. I started this section a day behind schedule on Sunday morning, June 29th, day 49 of the hike, and hoped to complete this stretch on July 9th. Being behind schedule meant that I needed to average 40 miles per day, rather than walking a single longest day of 38.8 miles. This meant 280+-mile weeks, contrasting my originally planned biggest week for the entire trip of an unthinkable 260-plus miles.

8 Mail-Drop Missed

Despite having been lost several times on the way from Echo Lake to Belden, despite having barely survived an out-of-control glissade, and despite having stretched three days of food to five, I'd made the 193.7-mile hike in five days. It was Saturday evening, June 28th, day 48 of my hike. Since I'd fallen behind schedule, perhaps I couldn't achieve my goal of setting a speed record for the PCT. I could still finish the hike, though, and this feat would itself be a major accomplishment. While anticipating picking up my mail-drop at Belden, I thought about getting new socks and new shoes, and enjoying a comfortable night at the Belden Town Resort.

At around 8:30 pm, as I completed the hang-glider descent into Belden, I began to hear loud noises. Hundreds of people talked, and Harleys roared. Was my mind fooling me? I couldn't tell. I thought that I could retrieve my mail-drop at the resort until 9 pm. Having hiked hard on zero calories, I'd arrived on time. Whew! Emerging from the woods, rows of motorcycles greeted me. The army of chrome-polished hogs puzzled me. What was going on? I worked my way through crowds of black-T-shirted bikers and into the small store at the Belden Town Resort, at mile 1,283.1. The cashier told me that the store closed at 8 pm that night, but because of "biker weekend", she would remained open a little while longer.

The cashier informed me that the resort no longer accepted packages from hikers. "She doesn't do that anymore. We stopped in April."

"Really?" I said, feeling shocked. "But I called the store in March, and they assured me that I could send a box here for pickup."

"There are no boxes here," she stated with 100% certainty.

My desperately-needed package had gotten lost. A wave of depression crashed over me. No shoes. No socks. I held the counter to steady myself. Dammit.

As a last-ditch effort, the cashier sent me to the bar, where I queried a young waitress about my package. She provided the leather-clad intoxicated crowd with cheap beers and Jack Daniels shots. Men fixated on her scantily clad body and on her well-positioned tattoos. She seemed perky: bouncing around, serving drinks, and turning heads. My attention returned when she reconfirmed that my box had disappeared. This bad luck sent my mind reeling.

Approaching 9 pm, with darkness imminent, I inquired about a room, but none remained available. In total denial, I asked again—still nothing available. Obviously, no vacant rooms could possibly exist at the small resort with the sea of humanity wandering around that I'd seen, but I couldn't accept this answer. I wanted to shout out, "You're wrong, lady!" But she wasn't. I made a snap decision to resupply and to return to the woods that night. With this night's fate sealed, I hurriedly reprogrammed my switching network to curb my enormous disappointment about missing my mail-drop and civilization's comforts.

I rushed back into the store and asked the woman there if she would stay open awhile longer so that I could resupply. She kept calling me "Hon", as in Honey, and agreed to stay open. While bumping into drunk carefree bikers, I scrambled around the compact store and selected many items. Most of the incoming bikers wanted ice to chill beer, but the supply had emptied long ago. My purchase consisted mainly of candy-bars. As I erected a pyramid of candy on the counter directly in front of the overweight cashier, she informed me of her diet. Her cravings for the pile that I'd built must have been great. I sympathized with her. Chocolate milk, orange juice, root-beer soda, and Gatorade surrounded my stack. While the woman behind the counter rang up the supplies, I ate them. I filled all of my water-containers with Gatorade, and she processed the empty bottles which I'd expeditiously returned to the counter.

When she finished ringing up my sardines, I decided to devour those on the spot. I peeled the outside wrapper and noticed that the tin required a can-opener. The woman offered me a new opener out of a package, so that I could cut the top off. I ate the oily sardines and a co-

conut candy-bar, too. Just prior to departing, I bought and consumed two ice-cream sandwiches—the cheap kind with the outsides that taste like cardboard. Surprisingly, my shrunken stomach complained little.

My mind filled with thoughts about the missed mail-drop. The Savannah box contained gear and food. Where did the package go? Should I wait a day for it? What about shoes and socks? I'd just pushed three consecutive 40+-days mile to get within a day of my schedule, and blowing 24 hours in Belden, hoping that my package would show up intact, wasn't in the cards. I reaffirmed my decision to head north immediately. Despite my cluttered mind, I remembered to grab some toilet paper as I walked away.

This resort, like others along the trail in California, couldn't legally be called a resort in most states. Nevertheless, I'd been gravely disappointed about not getting a bed and a shower that night. Since darkness had swept down, time permitted no phone calls. Besides, back east midnight had struck. Although this crowd was the largest that I'd seen in awhile, I felt totally alone. My frustration with the mail-drop boiled over into other fragile emotional arenas.

Naturally, after the toe-jamming descent into Belden, I faced a big climb to regain the crest. I re-adjusted my switching network so that I could push on farther, and began climbing, carrying a heavy load. These miles belonged to the next day. My eyes adjusted to the darkness, as my pupil diameter maxed out. I hiked for half-an-hour and erected the tarptent on a small patch of flat ground. Setting up camp in complete darkness bothered me for fear of sleeping on an ant hill, snakes, or sharp objects that could rip the Squall, and because of the possibility of dropping and losing a tent peg.

Camp-preparations took only five minutes. I had flossed and had brushed my teeth in the bar's bathroom, so didn't perform that ritual in the darkness. However, unlike when I'm at home, clean teeth didn't discourage me from eating. I opened a large bag of potato chips and crunched a vast quantity. The salt helped balance my unstable chemical system, and would prevent me from cramping the next day. With all the bikers around, I figured that bears wouldn't constitute a problem, so I worried less than usual about dropping crumbs.

At around 10:30 pm a rock-band started jamming loudly to entertain the rowdy bikers. I felt so exhausted that once I had inserted my earplugs and laid my head down, the distant noise didn't bother me. The bikers themselves concerned me little. Whenever I'd hiked a couple of miles away from the nearest road, I felt safe from people. No one else would be hiking up the steep mountainside in the dark that evening.

In the morning I felt rejuvenated by a good night's sleep. My feet hurt and had awakened me a few times, but the Advil had done its job. I'd pitched the tarptent in small bushes and prickly briers, and discovered this fact only as the sun rose. The long days that I'd been pushing and my run-down state made me tired enough to sleep in uncomfortable circumstances. I'd desperately needed this rest, for fatigue had been building. If I could have skipped even a single day of hiking, I would have recovered tremendously, but that option wasn't available.

PopTarts and peanut butter, my heaviest food items, constituted my breakfast. I washed this sticky mass down with warm root-beer soda. Carrying these items up the mountain made no sense, unless they sat in my stomach. While rolling up the tarptent, I thought further about how to handle my mail-drop. I concluded that the package had probably gone to the Belden Post Office, which stood one mile southwest of Belden Town Resort, in the opposite direction of the PCT.

I considered having a friend call the Belden Post Office Monday morning. If I could contact someone, he could have my package overnighted to Hat Creek Resort, at mile 1,371.6. I could thus have my box Tuesday morning, if this plan worked. Since I didn't want to descend to Belden and climb back here, again, I ruled out this possibility. I felt skeptical about the overnight mail service, too. Besides, my package might not even be at the Belden Post Office. I reconfirmed my earlier decision to push north. On Tuesday I'd have to phone the Belden Post Office myself from Hat Creek Resort.

Since the towns along the PCT are so remote, sending mail to them in an efficient manner is difficult. Missing my box at Belden meant that I wouldn't get my critically-needed socks. At that time I carried just one spare pair of socks. I wore the same two pairs of Thorlo socks which I'd been using since Kennedy Meadows, close to 600 miles ago. Across hundreds of miles of snow, through dozens and dozens of rivers, and inside tattered shoes, the poor socks had suffered five growing holes each, and had taken on a mesh-like appearance. The cotton and wool blend no longer felt soft, but instead coarse like sandpaper due to the embedded dirt. This fact didn't bode well for my feet.

Once I no longer needed a *Databook* page, I discarded it in the trash. My stack of pages grew tiny. Why hadn't I noticed this situation earlier? S—! I only now remembered that in order to save weight, I'd been carrying *Databook* pages just through mile 1,450. The second half of the book was in the Belden mail-drop. The *Databook* provided me critical mileages and water-stop information. Thinking about hiking by Braille for a couple hundred miles troubled me.

I developed a two-pronged contingency plan to solve the *Databook* fiasco. The first prong involved asking all southbound hikers for their *Databooks*. This option probably wouldn't bear fruit since I hardly ever encountered people hiking south. The second prong involved requesting that a new *Databook* be overnighted to Burney Falls State Park (mile 1,417.5) from Hat Creek Resort (mile 1,376.1). This idea probably wouldn't work, either, since I'd arrive at Burney Falls just a day-and-a-half after leaving Hat Creek Resort. The expressed *Databook* would arrive a day or two later. In any case I'd probably hike without the *Databook* for awhile. My logistical mistake bothered me, as did the fact that I had no real solution to the problem.

Every day challenged me significantly at this phase of the hike, since I cranked over 40 miles. This distance is a long way to hike in rugged mountains in one day. For most backpackers 40 miles would constitute a four-to-five-day trip, from which they'd spend a week recovering. Hiking 40 miles daily, without any chance to recover, is exceptionally difficult. Each succeeding day felt more difficult than the preceding day, due to cumulative fatigue. Aches and pains built; they didn't go away. I didn't know if my body could endure much more punishment.

During the next stretch, I carried plenty of food and encountered only minimal snow. The one significant problem that I faced, other than mileage itself, was the number of blow-downs on the trail. Due to the late snowfalls, no trail crews could yet access the PCT in Northern California to clear it. In fact, many parts of the PCT in this region appeared not to have been cleared for years. I climbed over, crawled under, ducked around, or slid between thousands of blow-downs. Lots of the trees exceeded three feet in diameter. Why did they fall? Who'd clear them? When? If I made it through the summer, I wanted to volunteer and help re-establish the PCT here.

No matter how carefully I maneuvered around blow-downs, I often cut my legs or my arms on branches and on rough bark. The piles of dead trees stacked up in impassable configurations. My arms and my legs became bloody scabs with hundreds of abrasions. The miles passed slowly, and I could have measured distance by the number of cuts I'd sustained. I hoped that the trail would be clearer for those thru-hikers coming behind me, as I was just beginning to see a few logging-crews arriving. These volunteers faced a daunting task. I thanked them all.

In the sandy red trail just before Hat Creek Resort I'd made a wrong turn. It cost me a mile. I'd missed a closed gate in a fence that had sat directly in front of me. Upon returning to the spot, the gate practically grabbed me. How had I missed it originally? A second set of eyes would have helped me to avoid such demoralizing wrong turns. Having a partner to commiserate with after such a blunder would have reduced my stress and my loneliness. Although I tried hard to dismiss such mistakes, I found it tough to do so. Until I reached deep into Oregon, I hadn't expected to be the first hiker going north. I'd thought that the hikers who'd left Campo in early April would be blazing the trail and leaving footprints to follow, but I was wrong.

Two-and-a-half days after leaving Belden, I hiked into Hat Creek Resort at lunchtime on July 1st. Hat Creek seemed like every other California PCT resort which I'd visited—a rustic hiker camp with limited electricity. Staying at Hat Creek Resort had never crossed my mind, as I certainly couldn't afford to waste the bulk of a day there. I needed to be hiking during *all* daylight hours. Phone calls caught me up with people who'd expected to hear from me when I'd reached Belden. I allayed their fears. They were happy to hear that I was already 90 miles north of Belden, and past the halfway point on the PCT.

I called the Belden Post Office. The friendly woman on the phone searched for my box. While she did, I kept my fingers crossed. She located my missing mail-drop. Yes! Since overnight postal service involving Belden couldn't be guaranteed by any stretch of the imagination and since July Fourth was that Friday, I decided to have the package sent all the way to Seiad Valley, at mile 1,657.0. I shuddered to think of wearing my decrepit socks for another 300 miles. On the other hand, at the speed with which I was now hiking, this distance would entail only one more week. Besides, no satisfactory place near the PCT existed to ship my mail-drop to prior to reaching Seiad Valley. I knew of no store along the way to buy socks at, either. If I wanted to go after the record, I needed to sacrifice my feet and hike north with pitiful socks. I intended to do just that.

Because I hiked bigger and bigger miles, I'd been getting into camp later and later at night. This fact came as no surprise since my pace remained steady. My nighttime arrivals necessitated a headlamp. I had more trouble waking up in the morning due to cumulative fatigue. Preparations required additional time, as my increasing stiffness resulted in slower movements. This meant later starts and contributed to later arrivals. The tiny child's watch that I'd been using possessed no light, nor alarm. So that I could read the watch at night and wake up on time, these two features now became necessary.

From Hat Creek Resort I called my friend Jimbo and asked him to send me a Petzl micro headlamp with spare batteries, a Timex Ironman watch with five alarms and a light, four pairs of socks, *Volume II*, and a *Databook*. I requested that he send all these items to Seiad Valley, the same destination as my Belden package. Although we suspected that it wouldn't arrive on time, Jimbo also planned to overnight a second *Databook* to Burney Falls State Park, at mile 1,417.5. Jimbo and I handled the mailing addresses carefully to ensure that we didn't make a mistake. I'd made enough already.

I'd asked Jimbo to send the *Databook* and socks to Seiad Valley in case my package from Belden didn't arrive. Redundancy became part of my planning, and I figured that if we sent two separate packages to Seiad Valley, at least one would arrive. Because the PCT is so poorly marked, it had become abundantly clear to me that a thru-hiker needs both *Volumes I* and *II* to minimize the number of times that he/she gets lost. For this reason I'd asked Jimbo to send me *Volume II*, which I'd never planned on using during my hike.

The extra weight which would be caused by carrying the Washington PCT pages through Oregon bothered me little since I didn't want to risk not having the Washington pages on hand when I really did need them. As my investment in the hike increased, I became more cautious and planned better. Jimbo was very supportive and immediately got to work locating all the items which I'd requested. Thank goodness he lived in Southern California. There he'd have a good chance of finding all these items and shipping them to me on time. If my request could be met, Jimbo would deliver.

If a *Databook* arrived at Burney Falls for me, I would need neither the *Databook* at Seiad Valley that Jimbo was sending nor the second half of the one that I'd forwarded from Belden. Time permitting, I would simply mail those home. I would need a fresh *Databook* post-trip to assist me in writing a book about my journey. In any case I hoped that at Seiad Valley, my gear situation would be resolved for the remainder of the trip. Obtaining the items that I needed at Seiad Valley would give me great relief.

Having completed all my phone calls, I cruised into the 30-seat restaurant at Hat Creek Resort. The waitress seemed kind, but to my surprise a cook said, "I smelled you the minute you walked in the door. We make hikers shower before coming here." Although I felt angry, I let the comment roll off me, and felt glad that I'd ordered already. Obviously I smelled, but the tone of his impolite remark insulted me. I needed a hot meal more than I needed to lash back at this man. If I'd had the time, I would have loved to have showered. The bowl of minestrone, cheeseburger, and French fries disappeared quickly, as did several sodas and glasses of ice water. Rather than the pleasant relaxing meal that I'd hoped for, I'd rushed through my lunch, paid, and felt glad to exit the restaurant.

When resupplying at small stores, I would have to stack my order up on the counter while other people maneuvered around me. None of the stores where I'd resupplied provided shopping-baskets. Hat Creek Resort's tiny market fit the pattern, and when I'd finished shopping, a laundry-load-sized pile of junk-food sat on the counter. After signing my credit-card receipt, I lugged my bags outside and plunked down on the ground to repackage my supplies. Never more so than at times like these did it become apparent why we need recycling in order to save the environment.

Two chainsaw artists cut busily at logs. They had obstructed my hearing during the earlier phone calls. I unwrapped candy-bars, filled my water-bottles with Gatorade, and placed assorted items into plastic bags with dueling chainsaws for background music. The chainsaw artists drew a small group of onlookers despite the extreme heat, sawdust, and illegal multi-decibel-level noise. Thoughts about chainsaw artists, their art, and their customers flashed through my mind. Some day I figured a psychology PhD student would do the analysis required to answer the questions that I had posed to myself while there. I finally completed repacking and headed back toward the PCT. The entire re-supply process, phone calls, and restaurant meal had taken me only an hour-and-a-half. The stop didn't qualify as a good rest.

I left Hat Creek Resort, at mile 1,371.6, well-hydrated and with plentiful food. The weather felt toasty and dry. Two miles past Hat Creek Resort the *Databook* listed a 29.4-mile water alert, meaning no accessible water for this distance. Because I was by now accustomed to traveling long distances without water, this stretch didn't worry me. Whatever our link to camels, it was closer than I'd thought. Knowing the locations where I could find water helped me to ration it properly. I planned to hike to Hat Creek Rim Fire-Lookout, at mile 1,389.7, that night, climb the tower, and camp in it. For the next day's push, I'd go 16 miles to Rock Spring Creek. I would satisfy a great thirst there, but nothing would ever compare to my Mission Creek thirst.

While heading to the Fire-Lookout, I hiked on a slightly uphill grade at a fast pace. I was spacing out and feeling relaxed, as the sun dropped lower in the cloudless blue sky. All of a sudden I rammed my big toe into a protruding rock, as though kicking a 50-yard field-goal. I accelerated from four miles per hour to ten while running to avoid a face plant. My chin dropped toward the ground; my legs spun like the Road Runner's.

When I finally stopped, my pack had vanished. The *G4* wasn't on my back. "What the hell?" I became worried. Where's my pack? Then 10 feet farther up the trail, I noticed my pack. Without a waist strap, the G4 had simply flipped off and flown over my head during the toe-stub impact and my sprinting forward. Unrestrained laughter hurt my abs. "Do toes have funny bones?" I laughed hysterically. On the AT, Fish and I would belt out Steppenwolf's "Born to be Wild" when the other guy stubbed his toe, "Get your motor running, head out on the highway, ..." Since my feet felt numb from nerve damage, the toe never really bothered me from the violent crash. I have no idea why my toe didn't break.

I re-established my rhythm, as a spectacular night for hiking un-folded. While I was powering uphill full bore, two hikers startled me.

A father-and-daughter team had appeared out of the blue. I surprised them as well. We chatted for awhile, and I learned that they were section-hiking. I couldn't gauge the daughter's enthusiasm-level for hiking, because she remained very quiet. Her silence said something. I ascertained that the father felt a responsibility to introduce his teenage daughter to the wilderness. She seemed to be holding her own and making the best of the experience. I figured that some day this time with her dad would mean a lot more to her than it did then.

The father questioned me regarding my trip, and when he finished, I learned of a water-cache near Road 22, at mile 1,392.5. This good news meant water the next morning. I told the duo that I planned to camp at the Hat Creek Rim Fire-Lookout that night. From his expression I could tell that the father didn't believe me. The gap to the Fire-Lookout measured eight miles, and the Casio read 7:30 pm. I assured him that even without a light I could hike there before darkness fell. He still seemed dubious. We wished each other good luck, said goodbye, and I shoved off, employing a quick gait.

Another lovely sunset descended on the mountains. As dark replaced the light, I arrived at the Hat Creek Rim Fire-Lookout. It had been transformed into an inaccessible communications tower. I'd really wanted to sleep in the tower and prowled around the fenced-off area, which was posted with ominous "Do Not Enter" and "Warning" signs. Entry seemed infeasible, so I perched the Squall on the lip of a nearby plateau that overlooked a wide valley. The lava-covered ground felt uncomfortable as hell, but I slept well.

In the morning I reached a large water-cache at 7:30 am. I never counted on caches, but finding this one fully stocked lifted my spirits. I enjoyed a couple of liters of warm water and signed the register there:

7/2/2003

Wall here at 7:30 am.

Pushed into Hat Creek Rim Fire-Lookout last night at around 9:30. Missed my mail-drop at Belden. My socks feel like strainers.

Hi to Falcor and Graham.

Heading to Burney Falls State Park today.

This cache is a God-send.

It's been good to be out of the snow. The weather has been exceptional.

Thanks for the water. Good luck to all thru-hikers.

If all goes well, I hope to finish the trail in about four weeks.

Only 25 miles separated me from Burney Falls State Park. I wanted to arrive there by mid-afternoon, so I continued at a good clip. The sun felt hot, but the hiking felt easy. I made excellent time.

 9 Hiking by Braille

As I approached Burney Falls State Park, at mile 1,417.5, I encountered a middle-aged, blond-headed ranger. She was walking south on the trail. When the ranger discovered that I was thru-hiking the PCT, her eyes lit up, and she said, "You must meet Shirley." This information planted hope that I'd soon meet another trail angel. I asked the woman directions to the Burney Falls store. Her hand-waving explanation involved several turns. The ranger could see that I felt unclear about the store's location, so she kindly volunteered to walk me over to the park. I could already tell that I would like Burney Falls State Park.

The blond-haired woman and I hiked to the state park together at an easy pace. Since we got along well and since I hadn't hiked with anyone for a long time, her company felt good. The G4 weighed next to nothing, as Burney Falls marked a resupply point. My new friend paused at the entry booth and asked one of the women working there if she knew Shirley's whereabouts. We learned that Shirley had passed by recently, but couldn't be located at the moment. That day seemed busy at Burney Falls State Park, as the Fourth of July crowd assembled for the coming weekend. In anticipation of a late arrival at my next resupply stop, I asked the state park employees in the entrance booth about the store hours in Castella, at mile 1,499.7. They phoned Castella, and informed me that the store there closed at 9 pm. This detail was important to me, and I thanked the booth attendants. I also thanked the ranger for her help.

As I headed to resupply at the Burney Falls' store, I encountered Shirley. This vibrant woman appeared to be in her late forties, although

I guessed that she was probably older. Shirley cared deeply about the welfare of thru-hikers. Her personality, clarity, and directness created an instant bond between us. She inquired about my journey with deep feeling. This kindness warmed me. We enjoyed each other's company. I learned that Shirley intended to buy a home computer. Never before had I been so happy to share my knowledge about PCs, and I fielded her questions regarding RAM, CPU speed, and peripherals.

Since I'd read email only once on the PCT, I asked Shirley if I could borrow a PC at the ranger station. I felt an urgent need to communicate with more people. Shirley indicated that her machine would be free in an hour. The Casio displayed 4 pm, and I felt extremely hungry. I suggested to Shirley that I go resupply and return to use her computer at around 5 pm. This plan seemed like a good idea to her. I hoped that Shirley would be there when I returned.

I hurriedly walked down to the park's store, hoping by some miracle that the new *Databook* which Jimbo had overnighted would be there. My anticipation grew, but, unfortunately, the cashier told me that the book hadn't arrived. This disappointment meant that I'd be hiking by Braille for a spell, as the pages of the *Databook* which I carried extended only a little farther up the PCT. I'd prepared myself mentally for this inevitability, so I didn't stress too much.

The store had seemed pretty well-stocked until I'd finished shopping. I'd piled a jumbo-sized stack of food on the counter. The woman working there instructed a teenage girl in cash-register procedures. Since I'd selected 50 items, I could see that checkout would eat up time. A take-out, snack-bar window adjacent to the store caught my eye. I informed the cashiers that I'd return in a few minutes, as I decided to put in a parallel order at the snack bar.

When I saw the snack-bar menu, juices in my mouth began flowing, and my hunger pangs increased. I wanted to buy at least one of everything. I ordered a veggie burger with double bacon, French fries, a grilled-cheese sandwich, and two milkshakes. Observing that the busy lone employee would take an eternity to prepare my food, I drifted back to the store. Luckily for my feet, the two operations stood only 75 feet apart. My stomach begged for food. I would appease it soon.

Passing by a few tourists, I re-entered the store, and the trainee was just ringing up my last item—excellent timing. I paid the bill with a credit card, which naturally required more instruction. After moving the whole kit-and-caboodle outside, I nibbled and repackaged everything. As soon as I'd finished this tedious process, I returned to the snack bar where my order had just appeared. I seemed to be in sync with the two, independent, food operations.

I devoured my much-needed meal. Time elapsed quickly, as it always did during resupply stops. I made several phone calls, as I finished my refreshing fast-melting milkshakes. If Shirley's offer to use her computer still held, everything regarding this break would have gone to perfection. I rushed back to the ranger station, showing up 20 minutes later than originally planned. Shirley met me and indicated that my timing was great. She'd just finished her work and said that I could use the PC.

While I logged onto the computer, Shirley picked my brain about my thru-hike. I let her know that I was attempting to break the speed record for the PCT. Shirley had met Flyin' Brian Robinson in his record-setting year. I could see her pondering whether or not I might break the record. Having already come through many extreme challenges, I told Shirley that unless I broke some bones, I would go faster than the old record. She stared into my eyes, and I could tell that she believed in me. Talking to Shirley made me realize how much I'd grown over the past weeks. I opened up much more to people, shared my thoughts, and felt more comfortable with myself. My mental strength had expanded immensely, having been through many high highs and many low lows.

When Shirley learned my age, she seemed dumbfounded. Her questions led to my showing her my Web page, and she asked to see pictures from some of my other adventures, including the climbs of four of the Seven Summits—that is, the highest peaks on each continent. We spent time Web-browsing together, and I wrote down my URL for her. She indicated that she'd check my "PCT Updates Web-Page" to see how my hike progressed. I felt glad to know that she'd be following along and supporting me for the remainder of the trip.

I told Shirley about the *Databook* which Jimbo had sent me and that it would probably arrive the next day. Shirley suggested that she fax the pages which I needed to the Castella store. This thoughtful gesture touched me. The pages that I needed covered the route from

Castella to Seiad Valley, and I specified a rough mileage interval to Shirley. Since they didn't have a copy of the *Databook* at the Burney Falls ranger station, I told her to keep this one whenever it arrived.

Shirley needed to get home, and I needed to process my email. So my new best friend departed after a pleasant goodbye. In our brief encounter, I'd learned enough about Shirley to know that she was a beautiful caring person. Several times she'd gone out of her way to help me; she was extremely gentle and splendidly positive. Although our meeting was brief, our goodbye left me feeling sad. I'd detected a deep yearning in Shirley for hiking the PCT herself, and I felt sure that in another life she would have succeeded in grand style.

From the computer at the ranger station I telneted into my Linux-box at home. One thousand email messages awaited me. Time had advanced to 5:45 pm, and I needed to return to the trail as soon as possible, since I planned to hike another nine miles on that day. I began processing the messages triage-style, responding to only those that seemed absolutely necessary. Many business-related emails got forwarded to my assistants at work. A dozen emails went out to family and friends. My typing skills had degraded significantly, due to lack of use and the unfamiliar keyboard, so I couldn't work as efficiently as usual. Having finally read everything to the extent that I'd deemed necessary, I left the building at 6:30 pm.

The fully stocked G4 weighed me down, but I easily retraced my steps to the PCT. My next resupply point was the Castella store, at mile 1,499.7. I planned a 9 pm arrival there on the Fourth of July. Independence Day wasn't foremost on my mind, but I did know that my feelings about my country had strengthened over the summer. A lot of great people who willingly helped out hikers had inspired me. Meeting them, rather than reading newspaper sensationalism, had generated good feelings and a genuine sense of rediscovery. The beauty of America stunned me, too. My faith in the United States grew, and I felt proud to be an American.

From Burney Falls State Park to my next resupply point, I needed to hike 82.2 trail miles, plus two miles to reach the Castella store, plus two miles back to the PCT, plus a mile farther to find a suitable campsite. Since I wanted to cover these 87 miles in just two days, I couldn't afford to lose any time. The trail always held surprises for me, and I never knew what loomed around the next bend. Given this fact, I worried about reaching the Castella store before it closed. Thanks to the women at Burney Falls State Park, I at least knew when the store closed. Getting there on time was my responsibility.

Two miles from Burney Falls State Park, I reached Lake Britton's dam. Panning right-to-left, I observed a large reservoir, a 150-foot-drop down a concrete face, and a rocky gorge containing a meandering river. Intuition suggested that the PCT crossed the dam, but I detected no trail-markings. While applying my five-minute rule, I walked halfway out on the broad dam, spotted no trail-signs, and retraced my steps.

I descended metal steps and followed footprints there to river-level, soon realizing that I'd been following day-time fisherman's footprints, not those of thru-hikers. S—. After climbing the 150 feet back up the steep steps, I walked to the middle of the dam, again. I had seen a PCT marker at the southern end of the dam, but no other trail-markers. A single trail-marker mid-dam would have made my day, and saved lots of hikers considerable time and uncertainty. Why wasn't one there?

Eventually, I crossed the dam and walked along by Braille for awhile. Sure enough, this direction was the PCT. I felt happy about that fact, but still frustrated by the uncertainty that I'd faced. At least I'd reached this point in daylight. Getting through unmarked sections in the dark, even with a light (and I didn't have one), would have been nearly impossible. The lost time at the dam meant that I could hike only six miles that night. This glitch left a long distance to Castella over the next two days. If there were any more snafus, I probably couldn't reach the store before it closed. I hoped that luck was on my side.

The next day I hiked at around 5,500 feet most of the time, and snow played no role. I easily stayed on trail, and tried to make good miles so that I'd be well-positioned to arrive in Castella the following evening. The sharply angled mountain-side prevented me from locating a suitable campsite. When I'd begun my searching at around 9 pm, it soon became clear that I'd waited too long. The darkness and the undulating landscape created a difficult situation. Rather than spending the night stumbling in the darkness, risking injury, and getting lost, I accepted a poor spot in the vicinity of Deer Creek, at mile 1,461.7. This location measured 40 miles from the Castella store. My Fourth of July would be spent trying to reach the store, not at a barbecue, mixing alcohol and fireworks, as is customary in the United States. I needed to arrive at the market before 9 pm in order to eat that night.

I broke camp early on Independence Day, and started my extensive trek to Castella. When the sun peaked for the day, I could tell that I'd reach Castella at 7:30 pm, assuming that no wrong turns thwarted me. When I possessed a high-energy level, as I did that day, I could gauge and adjust my pace to arrive at a destination within five minutes of the desired time. An hour past noon I began hiking along beautiful Beartrap Creek. I encountered many excellent swimming-holes. These pristine blue pools contained sandy bottoms, and I saw meal-sized trout in them. Little waterfalls cascaded into the circular hide-aways. The sun shining through the symmetric fir trees created interesting starbursts and reflections. I felt tempted to join the trout, relax, and enjoy nature at its finest. However, such a break would mean a delay and foot work, since my bandages would need re-doing if I soaked in a pool.

I knew that I was passing up something very special, so the decision to hike on required discipline. Nothing tempted me more at this particular moment than a refreshing dip. My commitment to break the PCT record involved many sacrifices—this skip included. To me life wasn't always about just enjoying the moment. I sought a greater overall joy. Completing the PCT in record time would constitute an accomplishment which I'd never forget and always treasure. I didn't jump into the water, but instead promised myself that I would return here someday. My will-power had prevailed.

During this section, the trail was in great condition. No blowdowns, no roots, and no rocks hindered me. The lack of obstacles meant that I paid less attention to details and truly enjoyed the hiking. My mind entered a deep-meditative state—no worries, just blissful freedom. Suddenly, I reached a dead end. This fact alarmed me; it interrupted my peaceful afternoon. Only now did I recall that I hadn't seen any PCT markers for a long, long time. Was I off the PCT? For how long? My mind rocketed out of "lotus position". I hunted around to see where the trail went, and after some bushwhacking, concluded that this path couldn't be the PCT. But where was the damn PCT, then? I'd encountered no other turns.

After going through my usual denial phase, I realized that I'd missed a turn three miles earlier. The six-mile detour plus bushwhacking plus deliberations would put me close to two hours behind schedule. A beautiful possible day of hiking had become an ugly impossible day of hiking, but no, I wouldn't let it. That day was too beautiful to become ugly. My ETA for Castella was 9:30 pm now. This option wasn't acceptable. I needed more food, and I needed it that night. A pathetic burst of profane words ending with "Raaaaaaayyyyyyyyy!" filled the air, as I released my frustration.

Using my hyper-alert mind, I carefully reconfirmed my mistake, and raced back along the creek. Its swimming-holes were the best that I'd seen all summer, yet I needed to pass them by again. I accepted this revisit as a second chance to admire their beauty, and a fulfillment of my promise to return. Two lovers swam in a gorgeous blue pool, and I asked them the PCT's whereabouts. They had no idea, but, then again, neither had I. I felt angry at myself for disturbing them. When I got farther up trail, I scolded myself, "You idiot!"

After 50 minutes I found where the PCT branched to the left up a steep hill. The intersection itself stood unmarked, but 30 yards farther a sign was stuck in the ground. Approaching from the southerly direction of the PCT, this turn was a right-hander at five o'clock with no signage; while looking straight ahead, it was, in fact, impossible to see from the PCT. I repeated the usual sequence of four-letter words, and then stopped feeling sorry for myself. It would take an all-out effort to reach Castella by 9 pm. My only consolation was viewing the spectacular series of unforgettable swimming-holes a second time. What should have been an easy 40-mile day (if there is such a thing) had turned into a difficult 46-mile day, of which only 40 would "count".

I rejoined the PCT at 3 pm. Nineteen trail miles and two road miles separated me from the Castella store. I couldn't make up the lost time all at once, but rather needed a strong, sustained, five-to-six-hour effort. After four hours of hard hiking, I realized that I wasn't going to make it, if I kept walking. This emergency necessitated running. I felt in shape to stride out, and aerobically, even felt comfortable running. However, the possibility of developing shin splints or a more serious injury gave me great concern. Throughout my 30+ years of running, I've experienced nearly every conceivable leg problem. My taxed body felt close to its breaking-point, and I knew that running with my pack could easily result in an injury.

Good running and Lady Luck's assistance brought me to the Castella store at 8:40 pm. To say the least, I felt greatly relieved. That day had been another Herculean effort. My revised plan called for hiking 160 miles to Seiad Valley over the next four days. While the market approached closing time, I bought the usual fare for four days. The heap weighed 20 pounds. The store also sold burritos, and I ordered two of them. The young tattooed woman behind the counter heated the burritos, while I sat on the ground outside repackaging my supplies. She brought the microwaved food to me, and I ate a bean burrito during the reloading process. If this plastic-wrapped burrito qualified as Mexican food, it was the first that I'd eaten since Idyllwild. I stored the second burrito in the mesh compartment of my pack.

A two-mile return to the PCT faced me; this effort would be followed by finding a camping-spot. Fireworks exploded in the distance, momentarily distracting me. The store's owner arrived to complete the last 10 minutes of the teenage girl's shift, as she left to watch fireworks at Mt. Shasta. Neither the store owner nor the departing girl possessed any knowledge of my fax from Burney Falls State Park. Shirley had no doubt sent the *Databook* pages, so I figured that the fax had been mishandled. This fact bothered me little (at that moment) because I'd already endured a rough day.

During my packing time, an old Volkswagen Beetle had parked directly in front of the store. The tan-colored Bug appeared similar to the Bug that Ted Bundy had driven. A vicious-looking dog occupied the back seat, and a suspicious-looking, middle-aged fellow drove. Out of the blue, the man asked if I needed a ride. This unexpected invitation troubled me, but I sure could have used a lift back to the PCT. I masked my concern, hesitated slightly, and suggested that he wait for me, while I made a last-second purchase. At the cash register I quietly asked the owner if he knew this fellow. The owner indicated that this guy lived nearby, and was completely harmless, allaying my fear. With my extra pouch of beef jerky in hand, I took the store owner's word and accepted the ride.

The dog and his master seemed friendly. I felt bad that I hadn't accepted their ride more freely, but attributed this reluctance to society's conditioning. This excuse didn't satisfy me, though. If anyone should have been worried about someone's appearance, the driver should have been worried about mine. We enjoyed a good chat during the five-minute ride back to the PCT. I had answered many questions about the PCT, and the Vietnam veteran had answered many questions about trench foot. The well-behaved dog brought my dogs, Julie and Dottie, to mind. I said goodbye to my new friends, and wished them well. While setting off into total darkness, I thanked the driver one final time. He'd saved me a tough road-walk.

The traffic sounded surprisingly loud and consistent for the Fourth of July, but I was near one of the busiest freeways in the world, I-5. I decided to hike up the trail a way, both for quiet and for safety. Within a half-mile of walking, I couldn't tell where the PCT went. The trail seemed to branch into two separate paths. In the pitch blackness who knew which one was the PCT? I couldn't afford to make another wrong turn, so decided that I needed to camp soon. This move would minimize any error. I bushwhacked into one area, searching for flat ground, only to embed my face in a table-cloth-sized spider web. S—! I thought I might get bitten by a spider. Jeff, a thru-hiker whom Fish and I had encountered just south of Kennedy Meadows, had told us that a spider had bitten him and that he'd spent three days off the trail recovering. The web freaked me out, and I pawed at the "cotton-candy" in my beard.

The land tilted at 20° or more. I hiked on without any light, constantly tripping over branches and battling frustration. At the junction with the Kettlebelly Trail, at mile 1,500.9, I found a tiny flat spot. There I set up camp in total darkness. I crawled into the tarptent, ate the second burrito, and drank a can of warm root-beer soda. The spider web had given me the willies, and I repeatedly felt spiders crawling all over me. I brushed my face and arms over and over. Spiders had taken over my thoughts, as only creepy arthropods can. Bears also occupied my mind. After all, the tarptent was now full of burrito tidbits and a food wrapper.

Fireworks blared in the distance, as did I-5's automobiles. The 1,500-mile barrier was significant to me, and I felt happy to have reached this milestone. I set each remaining 100-mile increment as a subgoal. If I could make it to 1,600, then I could make it to 1,700, and so on. Since I'd hiked close to 50 miles that day, I felt exhausted. I scrunched in my earplugs and blocked out my worries. Feeling at peace with myself and the world, I slept well.

My camp at the Kettlebelly Trail sat at a mere 2,420 feet. Joyfully out of the snow, I believed that smooth sailing awaited me. All I wanted to do was stay on trail and avoid getting lost. Route-finding and orienteering didn't interest me. I loved walking north and knowing that I was on the PCT. If I'd been on a relaxed schedule, I wouldn't have minded a few detours, but now each mistake cost me time and precious energy. Mentally, I didn't know how many more wrong turns I could handle; I knew only that the number was small.

Castle Crags State Park and the Trinity Alps looked spectacular with jagged rocky outcroppings and spires. In this region I filed away many images and sounds into my library. Snow blanketed the distant mountains, and this winter scene distressed me. I climbed thousands of feet in the next few days, and whenever I entered the 7,000-foot range, I encountered snow. The PCT became hard to follow, again, and I didn't see any footprints ahead of me, as I was the first thru-hiker going north. I half expected to encounter other hikers who had bypassed the Sierras all together, but these meetings didn't happen. If people had skipped the Sierras, they had probably jumped to a point that lay south of me.

In snow-free areas pine-cones fascinated me. They ranged from half-an-inch to greater than 24 inches in length and came in a variety of shapes. Some were easy to pick up, while others felt too sharp. Under the canopies of some trees lay thousands of pine-cones, and no cones remained on the trees. Other trees held thousands of cones, yet no cones lay on the ground nearby. Occasionally, I'd see a pine-cone fall, watch it tumble through space, and bounce on impact. I'd also notice pine-cones at a great distance from the nearest pine tree. Questions about the travels of a typical pine-cone and its lifespan circulated in my head. Although such wonderings puzzled me, I could merely speculate on their answers. I wished that a couple of the huge cones could adorn my fireplace mantle, but decided that here is where they belonged. They gave me far greater enjoyment in nature than in an artificial environment. Besides, I possessed no means to get a cone home.

As I approached Highway 3 at Scott Mountain Summit, I felt hungry. The reliable Casio said 12:30 pm on July 6th, day 56 of my hike. I decided not to eat lunch until after I'd reached the road. Usually, when a hiker experiences "trail magic", the encounter happens at a road crossing, where trail angels can access the PCT more easily. I was hoping to get lucky that day. After crossing Highway 3, I entered a parking lot on its north side. This rest-area is where I encountered two trail angels.

A man and a woman in their late forties were resting in the lot. Upon reaching their pickup truck, I learned that their names were Diane and Dan. Their friendly laid-back demeanor made me immediately feel comfortable. Dan asked me if I wanted a cold beer. The beer felt tempting in the heat, but I could see that one would quickly lead to six. Since I still wanted to hike a long way that day, I politely declined the brew and asked if they could spare a soda. Dan sipped on his Corona, while Diane retrieved a pop for me.

I removed the G4 and laid it up against the rear tire of their truck. It felt good just to lean against their vehicle for support. While in this position, I noticed that the pickup's bed housed a variety of suitcases and boxes. They must have been on a major road trip or moving. Fortunately for me, this meant that they carried plenty of supplies. Dan suggested that we move out of the hot sun, and I seconded his motion. We ducked under some trees and felt noticeably cooler. The high temperatures at this altitude amazed me. I'd never expected so many hot sunny days.

Diane offered me a slice of cold pizza, which I gladly accepted. The meat-lovers slice disappeared into my stomach. My emaciated body preferred meat to veggies, and I craved fat. This pizza slice was the first that I'd eaten since my memorable feast at Agua Dulce. Diane offered me another soda as well as a handful of dried fruit. They gave me powdered milk, which Dan didn't drink, and a 16-ounce package of trail mix. Diane and Dan seemed happy to share with me, and to help me. Diane kept providing me with additional items, and I happily consumed them. My decision to delay my own lunch had been an excellent one.

With genuine curiosity Diane and Dan asked me detailed questions concerning my thru-hike, and I told them that I'd been on the trail since

May 12th. They couldn't comprehend the fact that I'd already walked nearly 1,600 miles. I let them know that I would reach Seiad Valley in a couple of days. Diane and Dan planned to drive to Southern Oregon. They gave me their phone numbers, and offered to meet me on the PCT near Dead Indian Road. I'd actually lived on Indian Road in Riverside, Rhode Island, for 18 years, and I hoped this naming coincidence was a good omen. If possible, I would try to call them. I said a heartfelt thanks, and we said our goodbyes. Feeling replenished, I pushed north in the bright sunshine and clear-blue skies, wondering what mysteries the PCT next held for me.

Diane and Dan had fed me well, and now I felt adequately nourished and supplied to hike comfortably into Seiad Valley in two days. I passed the 1,600-mile mark at 5,960-feet Etna Summit and pumped my fist in the air. This victory motion always gave me goose bumps. I approached the 1,000-miles-to-go barrier! This target marked another significant milestone which I'd set. Everything seemed to be going well. I felt confident and relaxed.

Suddenly, directly ahead of me, I spotted a huge Black Bear on the PCT. He, too, walked north, but he had not yet detected me. Instinctively I banged my trekking-poles together overhead to get his attention. The clanking worked. The Black Bear stopped dead in his tracks, spun around, and stood up on his hind legs assessing me. He balanced effortlessly, while fully demonstrating his massive size. I wondered why my natural reaction had been to attract his attention. For a full five seconds I froze while this gigantic animal contemplated his next move. Would he charge and kill me? Look large, I thought, as I held my poles overhead. Don't run, Ray. Very luckily, the Black Bear sauntered off into the woods. His slow pace proved that he was king of this forest. Minutes later, I zoomed past the point on the trail where the bear had exited. The claw marks at the ends of his wide footprints prompted me to say, "What were you thinking?" No answer came.

The hiking progressed well, thanks to my recent adrenaline surge and the limited snow. These conditions were short-lived, though. When I reached the Kidder Lake Trail vicinity near mile 1,615, I encountered vast amounts of snow. The PCT averaged 7,000 feet there, and I simply couldn't escape the snow. When in deep snow, I needed to rely more heavily on *Volume I*. This book usually frustrated me. My stress level escalated, as I removed *Volume I* from my pack.

The material in *Volume I* describing the Kidder Lake area was horribly convoluted, and the PCT itself was poorly marked. *Volume I* talked about the old PCT route, alternate routes, the new route, side routes, and so on. It never became more clear than then that *Volume I* wasn't a book designed for thru-hikers, but a book written for section-hikers. Thru-hikers needed the book, as I'd discovered, but they constituted only a small portion of its market, so naturally the author and the publisher geared the publication to section-hikers.

Volume I warned of a dangerous and snowbound trail in this region, and in that regard it was correct. I performed yet another dangerous snowfield crossing. If the snow had been any firmer, I couldn't have traversed it successfully. Later that night in darkness, having descended thousands of feet, I hiked through leafy overhanging plants into an area called Marble Valley. In the yellow moonlight the white rocks glowed. I didn't know the hours of the Seiad Valley Post Office, but figured that I should push into Seiad Valley by 4:30 pm just in case they closed early. In order to improve my chances of reaching Seiad Valley on time, I walked late that evening. My campsite, set up using only moonlight, left me 33 miles shy of Seiad Valley, at mile 1,657.0. If I'd had even a single cloudy night, I couldn't have hiked without a light as late as I did. I was grateful that the weather held.

With wrong turns included, I'd walked over 45 miles per day for the past three days. Waking to another pleasant morning, I planned to hike 33 miles by 4:30 pm. My starting elevation of 5,800 feet meant that I'd be hiking predominantly downhill to Seiad Valley, which sat at an elevation of 1,371 feet. The hiking felt easy, since the trail was smooth and well graded. One couple whom I encountered walked with two German Shepards, and those playful dogs made me think of mine. The hikers told me that it was an easy trail all the way to Seiad Valley, but they didn't know at what time the post office closed. Footbridges repeatedly crisscrossed the clear-flowing, trout-infested Grider Creek, so I didn't have to get my feet wet. The dense canopied forest provided excellent shade. I flew and felt free.

The last stretch into Seiad Valley involved mainly road-walking on either gravel or paved roads. Along one portion of unmarked road, I asked some farmers for directions. They happily assisted me, and gave me precise directions to town. The farmers said that I was the first thru-hiker whom they'd seen this season and wished me luck for the remainder of my journey. They cheered for me, as we departed company. I thanked them and continued down the road feeling good. Since I hiked near sea-level, carried a light pack, and walked over relatively flat ground, I made great time and arrived at Seiad Valley around 3:30 pm, almost an hour earlier than I'd anticipated. This infrequent occurrence of an early arrival kept my spirits high.

I expected two packages at Seiad Valley—the one that I'd forwarded ages ago from Belden and Jimbo's. To prepare myself for one or both of the packages not being there, I adjusted my internal switching network. Luckily, I found the post office open and both packages there. While the postal worker retrieved my packages, I got a terrible cramp in my left hand. I bent over in agony and used my right hand to try to straighten my unnaturally-curled fingers on my left hand. The woman cried "Help!" because she thought that I was having a heart attack. When I told her that it was just a bad cramp, she seemed greatly relieved. I apologized for giving her a scare, and continued working on my fingers.

Since I'd forwarded the Belden box first class, I owed substantial postage. Given my great need for the contents of these packages, I was more than happy to pay the fee. While struggling with my potassium-starved body, I successfully dug out my cash and settled my bill. I learned that the post office stayed open until 5 pm. After I stacked the boxes, I thanked the woman and let her know that I'd be back in an hour with a package to send. She would be there.

I purchased a couple of imitation-juice beverages at the store adjacent to the post office, pulled up a cheap white-plastic chair alongside my boxes, and plopped down near a trash can to prepare my pack for another quick departure. My plan was to hike to mile 1,664.1, at the Darkey Creek Trail. This point rose to an elevation of 5,170 feet, and I currently sat at only 1,371 feet. I faced a whopping 3,800-foot climb after this resupply. In my cramping state, this ascent with a heavy pack would take awhile.

Excitedly I tore open the package from Jimbo to find a Petzl micro headlamp. Since I'd been setting up camp in the dark on most nights, this light brought me great relief. My risk of getting lost or breaking an ankle decreased significantly with the Petzl light. I was still behind schedule, and would have to do more night hiking. Jimbo sent four pairs of socks. He'd also found the Timex Ironman watch that I wanted, so I'd be able to tell time at night and use an alarm. He'd included the batteries that I'd requested, too. A *Databook* and the latest edition of *Volume II* rounded out his shipment. Jimbo had delivered everything, and I felt delighted. My emotions were so rocked that I almost cried.

I ripped into the infamous Belden box, relieving stress in the process. This Savannah-mailed package had traveled thousands of miles, but would travel no more. I'd wondered about who had handled this box. Since I wanted to mail a box to the Seattle area, I processed the contents quickly. The Seiad Valley Post Office would close in an hour. The Belden box contained shoes, socks, and food. I desperately needed Compeed, which I used to bandage deep cuts and foot cracks, but I'd overlooked including a supply of it in this box. I felt disappointed and angry with myself.

As I sorted through my goods, re-hydrated, and planned for my departure, I made friends with two hikers—Coach and Just Jane. The PCT brought people close together. Just Jane was about my age, and Coach was about 20 years older. This former football coach instructed me regarding my trekking-pole grip. I illustrated my technique for him per his instructions, and he shook his head from side-to-side in disbelief. Coach took one of my poles and demonstrated the type of grip that cross-country skiers use. For the remainder of the trip I planned to adopt the method that he'd showed me. It would help me get more power on big climbs yet stay relaxed. Coach had been given the correct trail name.

I gathered that Coach had attempted a thru-hike the previous year. He'd been one of the first hikers into the Sierras then, but had contracted a bad case of giardia. This year he would finish the trail. Coach said that if he'd met me last year, he probably would have killed himself trying to hike with me. Much wiser from his time on the PCT, Coach hiked his own hike this time around. Coach planned to overnight at Seiad Valley. In a week he would temporarily leave the trail to join the wedding party of a former football player. I felt sure that Coach had played an important role in the lives of many young people.

Coach had lost his watch. Having acquired the Timex Ironman, I offered him my bandless Casio, which he gratefully accepted. The Casio required a complex set of instructions for setting the time: push Button One eight times, Button Two four times, Button One six more times, Button Three to advance the hour, and so on. When I'd inadvertently pushed a button at the start of my trip, these directions had been indispensable. Pre-trip I'd trimmed the nine non-English languages from the directions. As I handed the instructions to Coach, he and Just Jane smiled when they saw that I'd taken scissors to the paper. My little gift made Coach's day, and mine, too.

I learned that Just Jane lived in Vermont and that she was section-hiking. We spoke about my hiking partner in the High Sierras, Fish, who also lived in Vermont. Just Jane and I had some mutual friends. She asked me about my other adventures, and I asked about hers. Just Jane wanted to hear more regarding my Seven Summits climbs. We chatted for awhile longer. While I was finishing my resupply organizing, Just Jane and Coach departed to the neighboring campground.

I finally assembled everything and prepared a box to send to Seattle. The package contained spare socks, shoe inserts, shoe-laces, Jim's *Databook* (I would go with the trimmed second half from my Belden-box.), and miscellaneous items. After successfully mailing the goods, I returned to the store, and bought a few sports drinks and a box of 100 Band-Aids. I grabbed 60 of the Band-Aids and left the remainder in the Seiad Valley hiker's box. The store's proprietor, who is well-known in hiking circles for his famous "Pancake Challenge", tried to sell me a roasted chicken, but I declined the good-smelling bird. I wanted to grab a shower and then eat dinner at the adjacent restaurant.

Time passed quickly, and I'd already been in town an hour-and-a-half. I rented a towel and purchased soap at the campground near the Seiad Valley store, and there changed currency so that I could operate the shower. Except for standing barefoot on the concrete floor, the eight-quarters rinse felt great. This shower was the first shower that I'd taken since Vermillion Valley Resort, where I'd stayed over three weeks earlier! Grime and dirt poured off me, producing a brackish-looking water, but I couldn't get clean. I brushed, flossed, and rinsed my bite-guard. As I was leaving the shower facility, I saw Coach and Just Jane at the campground. They barely recognized me. I penguined my way over to them with sore and improperly taped feet. Re-bandaging my feet was my top priority.

Coach and Just Jane sipped beers and kindly offered me one. I felt tempted to stay at the campground with them. However, I couldn't afford to lose three hours of hiking time that night, and I knew that I'd lose more time in the morning trying to eat a colossal-sized stack of pancakes. After chatting briefly, I suggested that we have dinner together. I planned to push north immediately after eating a big meal.

Unfortunately, the restaurant served only lunch. Thoughts of the skipped chicken flew around in my head. I'd missed my opportunity to get a meal at Seiad Valley and to talk more with my new friends. The Timex had advanced to 6 pm. I said goodbye to Just Jane and Coach, and felt sad to leave them. Even though we'd met only briefly, we'd shared good times. I wished that I had been able to get to know them better.

I returned to the phone booth outside the Seiad Valley store and made the usual calls. While I updated friends on my progress, a local man in his early twenties came by with a T-shirt that he wanted me to autograph. He'd heard that I planned to set a record for the fastest thru-hike and wanted my signature.

"Are you sure you want me to sign it?"

"Yes," he stated emphatically.

I smiled and signed the shirt. My signature read "(His name) Best wishes and happy trails, Ray 'Wall' Greenlaw." We talked a bit, and I learned that he designed computer games. He asked about my background in computers, and I told him that I'd once worked for the co-founder of Microsoft, Paul Allen. The local man seemed interested and attentive. He requested my email address. I wished him the best, and I hoped that his dreams of creating a "killer game" would come true. While leaving several new friends behind, I walked north at 6:30 pm.

I passed several trailers on the road-walk leaving Seiad Valley and wondered what the lives of the people living there were like. Although not financially well off, they seemed to have a small piece of paradise. I climbed steeply uphill after leaving the pavement. The beautiful night soothed me, and I had a marvelous view of Seiad Valley from up high. I'd hoped to camp near Lookout Spring, at mile 1,663.3, but even by my low standards, no viable options there presented themselves. As usual, I'd hiked past a perfect campsite earlier, but it hadn't been stopping time yet.

The mile-high rocky ridge which I'd attained offered no opportunities for camping. Since I was too exhausted to continue searching, I ended up erecting the tarptent on rocky ground. This image would not have made the on-line Squall gallery. With the use of my newly acquired headlamp, pitching the tarptent in the dark seemed much easier. I'd probably use the headlamp every night now. Despite having spent three hours at Seiad Valley, I'd hiked another 40 miles that day. On that evening of July 8th, I camped only 15 miles behind schedule. Having the comfort of my headlamp, my new shoes, and, most critically, my new socks made my spirits soar, again.

I'd shared a poor night's rest with many ant visitors. Despite my groggy state, I felt excited because the gap to the Oregon boundary measured only 30 miles. Finishing California would give me an extraordinary psychological boost. Only 457.9 miles of the PCT existed in Oregon, and I would set the Washington State boundary as a short-term goal. My feet hurt, but the record was within reach. This thought motivated me further. I motored ahead at full throttle.

On July 9th, with the sun's rays penetrating to the evergreen-forest's floor, I reached the California/Oregon boundary alone. "Yippee!" I shouted. "Ray, S—, yeah!" I'd greatly anticipated this moment. My sole focus had been walking the full length of the immense state of California; my realization that I'd done it left me drained. I'd been dreaming about this instant for years, and cried tears of elation. My loneliness was temporarily forgotten. A great joy and relief overwhelmed me. Less than 1,000 miles remained!

I'd covered the 409.3 miles from Belden to the Oregon boundary from June 29th to early afternoon on July 9th, or just over 10 days. I'd averaged 40 trail-miles per day and probably closer to 42 miles per day including wrong turns and road-walks. The longest day that I'd planned to hike during this stretch measured "just" 38.8 miles. In order to reintegrate the schedule, I'd *averaged* more than my biggest planned day. Recent 280-mile weeks eclipsed my originally-planned, biggest, trip week by a full marathon. My largest week on the AT had measured an "unthinkable" 215 miles. I hiked 10 miles per day farther now. These unheard-of miles were hard for me to fathom, but mentally and physically, I'd gone way past my old limits.

I'd encountered more snow than I'd expected, but other than having worsening feet, I felt strong. My internal switching network was in full utilization, and many items were being checked out of and checked into my internal library. Reintegrating my schedule and getting back on record pace seemed inevitable. I'd heard from many hikers, including Fearless, that Oregon provided easier terrain. Fearless had told me that previously he had hiked Oregon in 14 days, and he had said that I could do it in 10. I sure hoped so.

Part IV

OREGON

The Oregon section of the PCT extends 457.9 miles from the northern California boundary to the southern Washington boundary. The lowest elevation rests near sea-level at 200 feet; the highest elevation reaches skyward to 7,500 feet. The terrain is remote with an astonishing variety. Some of the trail segments are dotted by many lakes; others are desert-like and extremely dry; still others are lava rock or deep pumice. The volcanic peaks in Oregon dominate the trail. Due to the considerable horse traffic, blow-downs don't litter the trail. Due to the weight of a horse and rider, the trail is sandy powder. Many deer, as well as Black Bears and Mountain Lions, roam the trail in Oregon. I had planned to resupply about six times during this section. My longest gap without resupply spanned 100 miles. The biggest day that I had scheduled stretched 41.5 miles. My third and final mail-drop waited at Elk Lake Resort. I entered Oregon on July 9th, day 59 of the trip, a mere 10 miles behind schedule. My initial schedule had been developed with the thought that a friend would join me near Crater Lake. This week was "soft", since I'd scheduled it at 222.4 miles—nearly impossible for someone coming in "off the couch", but a week that I could now easily exceed by 60 to 70 miles. I thought that I could not only reintegrate my schedule but also surpass it.

 10 New State

I had hoped to find a trail-register at the California/Oregon boundary so that I could jot down my thoughts. Since my loneliness bothered me, I felt it was important for me to make some sort of communication. Many solo hikers carry a journal, which in addition to providing a place to record memorable events also provides therapy sessions, but I possessed no means to express myself. At the line dividing the two states, I found a beat-up old notebook housed in a raised metal box. The register was nothing more than some tired paper, but it meant a lot to me. After rummaging through loose-leaf pages, I felt relieved to locate a ballpoint pen that wrote marginally well. If I hadn't found something to write with, I would have been very upset.

I had been thinking about my upcoming sign-in continually for the past days, and what I had written went roughly as follows:

7/9/03 2pm

Wall here.

I love this trail!

Glad to have made it through California. What an incredible state. This day is a big milestone for me. I am delighted to be here and am almost back on schedule.

I plan to push through Oregon in about 10 days. Weather has been perfect. I need something that ends in "dane" or "done" for my feet.

Coach, thanks for the tips. It was great meeting you and Just Jane, and I hope your hikes go well.

I am glad to be out of the snow ... for now.

I read my sign-in aloud and reflected. Although I truly loved the PCT, the PCT also hurt me. Physically and mentally, I was beat-up. The trail challenged me; it forced me to change and to grow. Walking through this process alone was a hard struggle. However, I never wanted to take an easy path. If I needed to suffer to gain insights, to learn, and to grow, I was willing. I'd evolved so far in so little time. My cupped hands slipped off my face, and I walked north.

My first resupply in Oregon was planned for mile 1,745.1, at Hyatt Lake Resort. I hoped that resorts in Oregon would be nicer than those in California. Although the desert-like heat and the paucity of water took me by surprise, the hiking in Oregon felt easy, since the trail was well-graded and didn't involve lung-bursting climbs. Hiking in the PCT's middle state was a genesis. California became a memory, and I concerned myself exclusively with the next 10 days.

During difficult times, I willed my inner strength to the surface. As I walked north, my desire to reach the end of the trail increased. The positive aspects of hiking and the beautiful scenery kept me motivated, as did the thoughts of completing the PCT and setting a record. Other than my aching feet, I was in top-notch physical condition. Improper rest meant that I was susceptible to injury, though. Pain switches remained in the off position only briefly because of my fear of causing permanent physical damage. If I didn't periodically listen to my body, I'd hurt myself. I couldn't always ignore my symptoms.

While singing my way north, I noticed that the louder I sang, the less foot pain I felt. I turned the volume on high. Indefatigable as a Nepalese Sherpa, my legs could grind out any rhythm for any duration. Endorphins provided me highs. Foot pain caused me lows. My emotions swung back and forth. I worried about myself.

My foot pain was excruciating in Oregon: general trauma, an infected big toe, a mashed big toenail, deep cracks in the heels and balls of both feet, athlete's foot, and cut-up little toes. Foot-focused thoughts overwhelmed me when internal switches below the ankle were flipped to the on position. I recalled a song that Fish and I had composed and had sung on our AT thru-hike. Our ditty went as follows:

This little piggy had blister.
This little piggy had a ton.
This little piggy had toenail.
This little piggy had none.
This little piggy bled all the way home.

It was a sick song, but my mind was infected. This tune mildly reduced my suffering because it conjured happy memories of Fish. Simon and Garfunkel's more eloquent "Bridge Over Troubled Water" provided me with additional relief when I sang, "When pain is all around, like a bridge over troubled water, I will lay me down." Garfunkel's beautiful voice soothed me regardless of how much pain I felt. If I could control my mind, then I could control my body. I sang an off-key "Bridge" over and over. The process kept me going.

On July 10th I pushed 45 miles to reach the road to Hyatt Lake Resort. It was only 6:45 pm. For the past 13 hours, including stops, I'd averaged three-and-a-half miles per hour. Oregon provided far easier terrain than California did. I needed this decrease in difficulty, and I felt encouraged by my recent progress. My schedule called for me to spend the evening at the junction to Soda Creek, at mile 1,751.9. To return to schedule that night would require another seven trail miles. The *Databook* indicated that the Hyatt Lake store was a three-quarter-mile road-walk from where I stood. Since I was resupplying at Hyatt Lake, I faced another one-and-a-half miles of road-walking, too. It would have been a huge boost to return to schedule, but I wasn't worried about it happening that night. The return to my itinerary would happen eventually; I now firmly believed that.

Thus far, the trail in Oregon was well-marked. Like a lost child with approaching parents, I always felt extremely relieved to know my whereabouts. My most desperate and discouraging moments had occurred when I was lost, and those emotions had settled little. Before leaving the trail at any road-crossing, I always tried to ensure that I knew where the trail continued north. Many intersections were not marked at all. Others had small rock *cairns* consisting of only two or three Big-Mac-sized stones.

Upon reaching pavement near Hyatt Lake, I could see that the PCT crossed the road, as a well-placed sign opposite me protruded from the tall dry grass. In a couple of hours I might return here in pitch darkness, so I felt glad to scout the route successfully. I wondered what I'd find at the Hyatt Lake store. Would it be open? Could I hitch a ride to it? Was there a nearby restaurant? I was getting ahead of myself, though. First, I needed to determine the store's location.

My frustrations with *Volume II* continued from where those with *Volume I* had ended. The street names in the book didn't agree with those on the roads, and I couldn't tell for sure which road to take to reach the Hyatt Lake store. The description would have been much more helpful if it read something like:

> You reach a paved road; go left on this road for 50 feet; there
> you reach an intersecting road, turn left; head downhill on
> the asphalt road and walk three-quarters of a mile; you will
> see the store 30 feet off to your left.

Instead, a convoluted ambiguous description presented itself, complicating matters further; embedded throughout the text were notes on side routes, alternate routes, the main route, and the old PCT route. I wanted to hike the real PCT. The book was hard for thru-hikers to use as a reference.[1]

I began the road-walk hoping that I was proceeding in the right direction. Having no means to verify my surmise, I walked because I needed to explore some route. Since I'd traveled what seemed like over three-quarters of a mile, doubts filled my vulnerable mind. Cars ignored my extended thumb. A white cargo van sped by with a young red-headed man behind the wheel, and he passed me, too. He probably saw me cursing in his rear-view mirror, as he cruised ahead. My choice words with lips quivering helped release emotional tension; I couldn't fault anyone for bypassing a hitch-hiker, never mind one having my scruffy appearance.

Within two minutes the large van, which had obviously done a U-turn, was coming back. I figured that I'd get my ass kicked for mouthing

---

[1] Note: the latest releases of these books are significantly improved and use highlighting, a variety of fonts, and gray boxes to distinguish different parts of the descriptions.

off. The young man pulled over and offered me a ride. I climbed in, stepping up high, and my driver did another U-turn to head toward what I hoped was the Hyatt Lake store. We accelerated quickly. My sense of distance on trails was accurate, but my sense of distance on roads was unreliable. We drove for awhile.

The fellow who'd picked me up was a delivery man. Wes[2] brought fresh meat and other sundries to the Hyatt Lake store. Earlier he'd dropped off a large delivery, so the company van was practically empty. Wes told me that he lived in the nearby valley. I didn't know which valley that might be, but let it go. I found out that Wes was a college sophomore at a small, private, liberal-arts school in Oregon. He achieved good grades and had not yet chosen a major. His two older brothers had gone on missions, so I assumed that Wes was a Mormon. I strongly recommended that he do a semester abroad, if possible. Wes drove me directly to the store, and we entered the rustic wooden building together. The drive had felt like a roller-coaster ride, but I am sure that the van had traveled at only the speed limit.

I'd already come 45 miles on the PCT that day and another three-quarters of a mile on the road. I faced another mile on the road and then another couple of trail miles to find a campsite. In my tired state I thought that it would be good idea to secure a ride back to the PCT. I asked Wes if he wanted to dine with me. We enjoyed each other's company, and I wanted to treat Wes for his kindness. Since this stop was his last delivery for the day, Wes was able to accept my dinner invitation.

Wes and I sat down at a four-chaired table in the cozy restaurant. My young driver knew the menu by heart and didn't bother to consult it; I took a quick look at the worn laminated sheet and ordered. The waitress repeated the order twice, but she didn't convince me that we would get what we had requested. While Wes waited for our food to arrive, I purchased groceries at a nearby counter.

The selection at the store was poor, but not as bad as when I left it. They normally charged 75 cents per candy-bar, but the proprietor discounted it to 50 cents, since I bought the whole lot. I hoped that no thru-hikers would arrive right after me and find the store completely empty. It would be a few more days before Wes would return with

---

[2] I don't remember his real name.

another delivery. I returned to the table with my goods and began repackaging. While waiting for our food, Wes and I got to know each other better. The waitress finally delivered the hot meal, and we devoured it. Wes possessed a thru-hiker's appetite. I offered to pick up the tab, but Wes wouldn't allow this gesture, so I paid only for my meal and left a generous tip.

After our satisfying meal and good conversation, Wes and I walked to the van. I noticed that no one else had come or gone, when we'd been in the restaurant. If it hadn't been for Wes, I'd have been forced to hike back to the PCT. I climbed into the van and placed my pack between my legs, leaving the seat-belt unfastened. Once I spotted my trekking-poles, I felt relaxed.

My red-haired friend asked me many questions about the PCT on our uphill drive. I piqued his interest in the trail, and felt sure that one day he'd attempt a thru-hike. Wes dropped me off at the PCT road-crossing at around 8:20 pm. We shook hands firmly and made direct eye-contact. I gave Wes my sincere thanks for the rides and his company, and disappeared into the darkening woods. As the van pulled away, I didn't look back. I never did visit the Hyatt Lake Resort, so I still don't know how it compared to California's resorts.

With the additional weight in the G4, the large quantity of food sloshing in my stomach, and the late hour, it became clear that I wasn't going to align with my schedule that night. I hiked another three miles, though, so by day's end, I found myself only three miles behind schedule. This decreasing gap gave me a positive feeling. I quickly finished camp preparations. The next day called for me to walk 36.4 miles, and, barring unforeseen circumstances, I would be back on schedule.

I looked forward to being even with and then ahead of my ambitious schedule. Originally, the PCT record had meant nothing to me; it had merely provided me a challenging goal. However, that goal's importance had grown over the past two months. I admitted this fact to myself. The thought of hiking the PCT in 85 days or less had motivated me and had kept me going. My eyes closed involuntarily as such thoughts circulated in my mind. I fell into a deep sleep seconds later.

I loved the beautiful PCT in Oregon. It was well-marked, devoid of roots, isolated, and relatively flat. No giant snowfields or blown-down forests beleaguered me. I saw more equestrian traffic in Oregon.

Without the horses, the trail never would have been as clear of dead wood nor as well marked as it was. Although the horses created a sandy trail and sometimes a smelly trail, these facts bothered me little compared to blow-downs and getting lost. In addition, I made friends with many trail angels who were on horseback. Many hikers oppose sharing the PCT with horses, but this joint usage never bothered me.

As I sang my way north, at around mile 1,760 near the Rogue River National Forest boundary I encountered two middle-aged women on horse-back. They were enjoying themselves and the outstanding weather. When I'd encountered the two ladies, they were heading south on their mounts at a slow trot. We talked for awhile, and they learned that I was thru-hiking the PCT. One woman immediately felt comfortable with me, but the other seemed apprehensive, and perhaps rightly so, given our remote location. The friendlier woman offered me an apple, which I gladly accepted. I'd no doubt taken an apple intended for her hungry horse. The horse shot me a dirty look, confirming my suspicion. As I started to push north, the same woman offered me a bag of ripe red cherries. I happily accepted those, thanked her profusely, and said goodbye. Nice lady, I thought.

While hiking north, I enjoyed the delicious apple. No core or stem remained to be discarded because I ate everything. Eating while walking gave me great pleasure. I'm not sure why. Did it have something to do with my breathing? My guess was some primitive instinct, but I didn't care. I knew it felt good.

For the next mile or so, I hiked the trail, spitting cherry pits great distances, alternating between trail sides. I used rings on cut-off blow-downs as targets. The closer I hit to the tree's younger years, the more points I accumulated. Its birth year signified a bulls-eye. I kept score between the left and right "sides". My mind was occupied, summing and remembering numbers.

The juicy cherries tasted good. The woman on horseback had intuited correctly that I hadn't eaten fresh fruit for ages, and seeing my broad smile upon receipt of her gifts had given her pleasure. I continued northward, feeling happy. My confidence soared, and Lady Luck blessed me. Hiking in the wilderness seemed to be my calling. I felt free and was flying. My superb fitness level made me think that this high was what world-class athletes felt like—powerful, self-assured, never breathing hard, at peace, and relaxed. Positive thoughts filled me. I stored these feelings in my library for later use.

A while later, I crossed Dead Indian Road, at mile 1,764.0, near where Diane and Dan had suggested that I could call them. I didn't see a phone in either direction. Had they driven by looking for me? Disappointed that I'd missed these two trail angels, I hiked onward. A mile-and-a-half farther north on the soft pine-needled trail, I came to a junction for the South Branch Mountain Shelter. The sign indicated that the shelter sat one-tenth of a mile away. At this point in my thru-hike I rarely went off trail, if ever. Since the *Databook* noted that water was available at the shelter and I needed water, I decided to make the short side-trip.

At the speed at which I was now walking, a two-tenths-of-a-mile detour consumed at most three minutes. I quickly came upon the rustic log shelter at around 12:30 pm. A heavy-duty picnic table provided me a comfortable lunch spot. I stepped over the cutout door into the rugged winter shelter and found a trail-register. This dusty notebook and a pen returned to the sturdy table with me. The water-source, an old-fashioned hand-pump, sat nearby on a concrete platform. With swarms of bees circling me, I went over to the platform, pumped for awhile, and filled my water-containers with cool water. I splashed the refreshing water onto my sweaty head with my dirty hands. This small pleasure provided a big relief.

Large piles of firewood surrounded the perimeter of the shelter, and I imagined that the winter wonderland received many visits from cross-country skiers and snow-mobilers. As I consumed my mediocre lunch, warm Spam and Oreo cookies, I thumbed through the weathered trail-register. I flipped through a few pages of entries from day-hikers. The last sign-in was an inane comment to the effect that people who don't love hunters are idiots. "Live and let live", I said.

The trail isolated me from society's problems. Small differences among people, which often escalate into unpleasant situations, didn't plague me in the woods. I wished that everyone could have an experience that gave them deep perspective, and helped them to understand and accept all people as equals. I penned an entry that read something like this:

7/11/2003

Wall here at noon.

Came into Oregon a couple of days ago. Everything is going great, and the weather is perfect. Feet are hurting, and I have been pushing 40+-mile days. I hiked 48 miles yesterday.

Heading to Crater Lake tomorrow. Can't wait to see the lake again. It's been years.

I am a four-year-old Tanzanian girl.

I love this trail.

P.S. Should we be concerned about the number of ants in California?

I returned the trail-register to the dark and dirty shelf in the shelter, double-checked my water-supply, and began my return to the PCT. At that very second my two horse-back-riding friends emerged on the spur trail. Both women perked up when they saw me. We three shared a pleasant conversation. I learned that one woman worked part-time doing arts-and-crafts-type stuff; picture-framing was her specialty.

The artsy lady and her husband had moved to Oregon to escape the rat-race. Wages weren't competitive here, but one could make do with less income since the cost of living was lower and fewer items needed to be purchased. Nature provided enrichment. Entertainment could be found outside the back door. The woman seemed truly content, and on days like that day, I could tell that the wilderness was her domain and her happiness. Riding gave her freedom, and she loved her horse. I admired her decision to move here.

I said goodbye, again sorry to be departing so soon. As I headed toward the spur trail, the woman who'd initially been cautious toward me offered me the apple intended for her horse. I went back for it, and thanked her with a friendly smile. She could see that her gift had made me happy, and I think that this gave her a great deal of satisfaction. I received the anticipated dirty look from the second horse. The two horses communicated with each other; one gesturing "I warned you" and the other simply nodding foolishly. I turned to the short spur trail, and this time I kept going.

In less than two minutes I had rejoined the PCT and had finished the last bite of the apple. The woman's remark that her family couldn't afford horses in most other parts of the country stuck with me. I couldn't help but wonder if someday I'd return to this idyllic place. Would I ever see these two women again? I wondered if they'd changed directions to catch me or if they were merely riding further because it was such a beautiful day. I walked northward, grinning.

 11 Mosquitoes

During the next stretch in the Sky Lake Wilderness area, I noticed that my Deet supply was getting low. Until this point of my trip, the bugs had hardly been noticeable—that is, to a thru-hiker, who is used to enduring an inordinate amount of discomfort. Hundreds of blue mountain lakes sandwiched the PCT, and coupled with the melting snow, a great volume of water stood near the trail. When I saw the number of lakes shown on the topo maps in *Volume II* for this area, I shuddered at the jigsaw-puzzle appearance. The mosquitoes whined loudly, confirming my fear.

I'd been stingily rationing my Deet for hours. When the final precious drops disappeared, I sank to a low point. I had made a grave mistake. My thoughts turned to the impending crisis. In denial I squeezed and squeezed the tiny Uncle Ben's bottle, but only a puff of air came out of it. I *was* without Deet. The mosquitoes created dark clouds near me. "How can I be without f—ing Deet?" When I'd opened my mouth, a dozen mosquitoes flew in—I said no more. The temperature hovered around 90°F, so I didn't want to wear my NorthFace jacket, but I donned it anyway to protect my already pin-cushioned arms and neck. My legs, hands, and face remained exposed. I was sweating like a body-wrapped dieter. Fragments of thoughts flashed through my mind. Rough ride. Strap yourself in. Hang in there. The bugs wouldn't allow me to complete a thought.

Mosquitoes chewed me. During this period, I saw no one else in the woods. A thru-hiker would be the only person in such maddening conditions, and perhaps due to my early arrival, I would be the only thru-hiker this season to experience peak mosquitoes in Oregon. I wished these conditions on no creature. If I encountered some other crazy person in the woods, I planned to beg him/her for insect repellent. This hope felt important. To think (even unrealistically) that someone else shared my predicament provided comfort.

The horrible swarms followed me. At each snow-melt area, pond, or lake, another 200 mosquitoes joined the pursuit. The bugs buzzed, hissed, and whined. They craved my blood. I suffered and endured alone. The mosquitoes pushed me to the edge. I knew that nightmares about these days would haunt me endlessly. Evolution had made a mistake in creating the mosquito. I was paying for that mistake.

Stopping for a bathroom break was impossible, so I had to go while walking. Taking a moving pee still resulted in a dozen bites, despite using my hands as cymbals. A walking "number two" resulted in even more bites. Pausing to glance at a map was also out of the question; if performed at all, this task had to be done while walking and without slowing. The complicated descriptions in *Volume II* were even harder to parse while hiking. I tried to elevate my pace, but even at five miles per hour the bugs swarmed me. They flew faster than I could hike.

Between expletives, I recalled the video "Walking the West" that Fish had loaned me pre-trip. One scene in this PCT-hikers documentary takes place in Yosemite, where the main characters run out of Deet. I saw the film twice and both times thought how stupid they had been to run out of Deet. The movie scene showed mosquitoes flying into their mouths, eyes, and ears, and in general, being a huge blood-sucking nuisance. Now, *I* was out of f—ing Deet. In a disgusted and angry voice, I could still hear one hiker saying, "Well, we're out of Deet." He shared his frustrations with friends, but I dealt with this catastrophe alone. Despite the deplorable situation, I laughed at both him and me. (Incidentally, he had quit the PCT just 70 miles south of Manning Park.) As the tiny Kamikaze pilots ravaged me, "Everybody plays the fool, sometime, no exception to the rule" cycled through my mind repeatedly.

My hope of obtaining Deet from a day-hiker didn't materialize. Who else would be out in these conditions? No one who had any option, that is for sure. Eventually, I tired of killing mosquitoes. I realized that a single mosquito-bite, in and of itself, didn't really hurt too much. I decided that it was okay to get bitten 1,000 times but not

1,001. So, for the most part, I stopped killing the hated pests and let them fill up on my blood.

I suffered 20 bites on each eyelid, 20 bites on each eyebrow, 50 bites on each ear, 20 bites on each hand, 100 bites on other parts of my face, 250 bites on each leg, and 75 miscellaneous bites. Another 100-plus bites, and I'd be over my limit. I killed the nasty needle-noses only when I could get 20 or more with one swipe. A palm with 20, smashed, blood-filled mosquitoes wasn't a pretty sight, but I had neither means nor time to clean my hand. Stopping for anything required intense concentration. I did what I needed to do mentally to survive and threw all itch-switches to "off". Pain-switches to the face, ears, eyes, legs, and hands got switched off, too. My difficult predicament nearly broke me.

Mosquitoes carry hundreds of different viral diseases, including encephalitis, dengue fever, West Nile, malaria, and yellow fever. My chances of contracting something seemed pretty good given the number of bites that I'd sustained. I wondered, too, if I would have an allergic reaction from the sheer trauma of close to 1,000 bites. Perhaps after crossing some threshold, my body would simply shut down. I really had no idea if my system could handle this situation. My exposed skin resembled an inverted Chinese Checkers board. The mosquito density in the air must have been over three bugs per cubic inch.

I looked forward to getting my camp erected that night, but not to stopping to set the Squall up. This upcoming ordeal required mental preparation. While continuing quickly northward, I carefully visualized and rehearsed the steps involved in set-up. Once I stood still, I would be overwhelmed by mosquitoes. Films of baby Caribou in northern Alaska came to mind. The poor things often died of blood loss before their lives got underway. If I cracked, I would be a cow in a school of piranhas.

I ran to a flat spot, dropped my pack, and began setting up camp. Mosquitoes flew at me from all angles. I focused on getting the tarptent erected in record time. While mosquitoes bit me unchecked, I worked on the mission at hand. As fast as possible, I unzipped the front fly, tossed in my pack, climbed in, and zipped the door shut. The next half-hour was spent killing the mosquitoes that had flown in during the 30 seconds when the fly had remained open.

I failed to kill all the mosquitoes that had entered the Squall because of their sheer numbers. Toggling the itch-switches to obtain an overall reading, I thought that it would be okay to sustain more bites during the night. I wondered how swollen I would be in the morning, though. Leaving the Squall wasn't an option that night, so I placed my "pee bottle" near the edge of my sleeping-bag. I lay down and curled up inside my bag.

Even with my dirty earplugs inserted deeply, I could still hear a loud humming noise most of the night. I slept little. The anticipation of facing the enemy that morning troubled me. Since I was whisper thin, my blood seemed to flow closer to my skin's surface. The mosquitoes sensed this fact. After breaking down this horror-movie set as quickly as possible, I performed a moving bathroom-stop and hustled up the trail. I marveled at how many mosquitoes flew in the same airspace with no apparent mid-air collisions. They seemed to defy the Laws of Physics.

I'd already endured a full day without Deet. My mind couldn't handle much more. A half-day later I encountered a young couple by a mosquito-infested lake. They'd stacked a small pyramid of gear on the ground, so I knew that their SUV was nearby. I hustled over and asked if I could borrow some insect spray. They handed me a full spray bottle, so I figured that they'd just used up the last of another. While half emptying the container, I drenched myself with the poisonous liquid. This application would probably cause health problems, if not that day, then at some future date.

The infatuated newlyweds offered me a cinnamon-raisin bagel from their stash. As I ate my first bread-product in ages, I ingested a substantial quantity of Deet that had been absorbed by the spongy bagel from my hands. Since the chemical juice was already diluting my blood and saliva, I ignored the extra. Protected by my liquid shield, I strode down to the lake shore to gather water. The mosquitoes hovered in clouds a mere 6-to-12 inches above the water's surface, forming an unfriendly fog. My hand had left an oily diffusing splotch near where I'd submerged the Platypus. Minutes later, with the clear-blue alpine lake disappearing behind me, my single thought was that of reapplying insect repellent to my right hand, which I'd carelessly dipped into the lake.

On returning to the couple's gear mound, to my chagrin, the bug-spray bottle had been put away. I'd used more bug juice than I should have during my first application, so I didn't ask for the bottle again. Despite the natural beauty of this location, the two told me that they couldn't camp here because the bugs were too bad. I merely nodded at this foregone conclusion. The young bride looked distressed, as her summer vacation had become an unpleasant struggle. It seemed unlikely to me that she'd ever return to the woods after this experience, her first wilderness outing.

I had survived a full day-and-a-half without repellent through horrible mosquitoes. The Sky Lakes Wilderness's mosquitoes topped those of the other 49 United States and 53 countries where I'd traveled. My timing had been completely off, and I'd caught the blood-thirsty insects at their peak. I pitied any hikers entering this area during that time. Surviving such an experience wasn't easy. I prayed that the worst was over.

One evening during this stretch, at about 9 pm, I heard a big cat nearby. The animal made an eerie whistling noise, causing the hair on the back of my neck to stand up and shivers to run down my spine. Right away I could tell that the sound emanated from a sizable predator. My worry was immense. Suddenly, I heard another raspy growl on the opposite side of me. As my fear built, I walked faster, periodically clanking my trekking-poles together overhead. If one of these Mountain Lions grabs me, it's all over, I thought. The moment of silence that I'd spent at the Western States 100-miler one year, remembering a runner killed by a Panther, stirred buried emotions.

The growls kept pace with me, as the large animals moved through the woods parallel to me. One followed on my left and another on my right. Panic beset me. Was their behavior normal? The raspy growls sounded like those of large house cats. I became exceptionally stressed, and felt droplets wetting my shorts. This fact didn't concern me. Visions of a Mountain Lion snagging me and dragging my mosquito-tenderized body off for a paltry meal filled my thoughts. Would my body ever be found?

The growls accompanied me alongside the narrow rutty trail. My fear peaked as darkness fell. I decided to stop hiking immediately and found a camping spot. While trying to remain upright and look large,

I set up the Squall and crawled into it. Another minute of walking might have been my last. A few more growls sounded, but gradually the cries subsided. My mind had the Cougars killing me over and over. The animals belonged here, and I didn't. I put in my earplugs.

Nothing I could do would slow an attacking Mountain Lion. Worrying merely wasted energy, but I had trouble conquering my fear. Larry and his buck knife came to mind. I wouldn't have had the courage to face these animals with a spear, never mind a small jackknife; I wasn't a Masai. The next morning I bolted from the area. Happily, I never heard the cats again, although they were always on my mind at dusk. I didn't like being stalked.

The following day I encountered a 21-year-old woman along with two young male admirers. Betty[1] planned to section-hike the entire state of Oregon. In their mosquito netting the two men looked like beekeepers. They sustained few mosquito bites, though. Betty didn't wear netting, so I spoke mostly with her rather than talking through a veil. She was obviously a strong and tough hiker. When Betty observed how eaten alive I was, she offered me a bottle of Deet. I didn't accept her gift at first, but when she told me that this bottle was an extra, I gratefully accepted it. Acquiring this Deet made my day.

Betty and the guys told me that I was the first thru-hiker whom they'd met. I said that I didn't think they'd encounter another for at least a week. Since the mosquitoes still swarmed, I needed to continue north. I wished Betty the best of luck in achieving her goal, thanked the trio, and headed on my way. Although I speculated for awhile, I reached no conclusion as to whether Betty would complete the PCT's middle state. I hoped that she would be successful.

On my approach to Crater Lake, the deepest lake in the United States at 1,932 feet, four items dominated my thoughts: Deet, food, my feet, and the lake itself. To ward off mosquitoes and to preserve my sanity, I needed more Deet. I couldn't afford to go through another blood-loss of the magnitude that I'd just endured. Although Betty had given me a small bottle, I wanted to make 100% certain that I possessed extra. Mosquitoes, quite simply, now disturbed me mentally.

Food always filled my dreams. I wasn't running particularly low at that moment, but contemplated the quantity that I would need to

---

[1] I never caught her real name.

purchase at the upcoming store. The gap from Crater Lake (at mile 1,829.8) to Elk Lake Resort (at mile 1,953.2) measured 123.4 miles. Being a numbers freak, I noticed the consecutively increasing four digits in this distance, and computed the probability of that happening again. My original schedule had called for me to hike this stretch in four days, but now I would walk it in under three. Thus I needed to purchase only 15 pounds of supplies. The *Databook* indicated via an 'M' that meals could be obtained at Crater Lake, so there I anticipated eating meats, vegetables, and fruits. A real meal would provide a psychological boost, but also help to balance my improperly-nourished system.

My feet hurt me. These gross ankle attachments were badly torn up and deteriorating. I couldn't keep my feet or my socks clean. With the horrific mosquitoes, I'd never even contemplated going to a lake shore to wash. Although I'd developed a mental framework for coping with pain, I couldn't completely ignore it. My feet demanded, and often got, my utmost attention. I worried about permanent nerve damage.

The last time that I'd been to Crater Lake its beauty had inspired me. My spirit needed a lift, and I relied on those fond memories. I arrived at Crater Lake Rim Village on July 12th at 6:30 pm, having hiked another 40-mile day. The wind whipped. The cold would affect me that evening. My limited clothing, my depleted state, my insufficiently-rated sleeping-bag, the high elevation, and the snow on the ground all hammered home this point. Any one of these facts alone would have made me cold, but I faced a quintuple whammy.

I entered the small store at Crater Lake and inquired about a phone and a restaurant. The cafeteria housed a phone, but it had closed at 5 pm. No! I politely asked if I could use the store's phone, but this possibility was out of the question. What? After asking a second and third time, I gave up and felt disheartened. This meant at least three more days without being able to communicate with friends and family.

The closest public phone was at Crater Lake Lodge, described as only a quarter-of-a-mile away. The woman who provided me with this distressing information suggested that it was a short walk for me, since I'd already come from Mexico. In fact, my feet throbbed so painfully that under no circumstances was I going to detour off trail. Her logic was totally flawed to me, but I didn't point out this fact, since she genuinely tried to be helpful. The cafeteria was the only restaurant nearby, so the meal that I'd been looking forward to didn't happen, either.

The Crater Lake Rim Village store caters to tourists. For my resupply the only viable option was candy. I looked at the salmon and other real food items, but these gift packages sold for exorbitant prices. A six-ounce piece of salmon cost twenty dollars. It came in a pretty box and all, but I needed thirty-two ounces, not six. The selection forced me to purchase gobs of candy-bars, Skittles, M&Ms, and potato-chips. I bought a six-pack of root-beer soda and several quarts of Gatorade, too.

Although I searched furiously, I didn't make out much better with the insect repellent than I'd done with the "groceries". The store didn't carry concentrated Deet in one-ounce bottles as I'd been hoping, so I ended up buying a six-ounce, bright-orange-topped spray-can of Off. The additional bug-spray helped my psyche. I hurriedly used the restroom in the store, performing my standard rituals. While I was repacking my pathetic supplies in front of the store, the chilly ground made me shiver.

As I sat outside the store, I encountered a thru-hiker named Strider who had skipped the High Sierras. Since he possessed little mountaineering experience, I told him that his decision to bypass the High Sierras was a good one. My remarks put his mind at ease. It had obviously been a difficult decision for him to jump over part of the PCT. I learned that Strider was staying at the Mazama Campground that night. Although I felt tempted to join him, I decided to push north.

While the wind continued to build, the temperature dropped steadily at my 7,000-foot bench. My body felt cold. I finished packing and hiked over to see Crater Lake. Strider headed off in the other direction saying, "Take care, brother." I waved goodbye, smiling. Would I encounter Strider again? Did he plan to make up the section that he'd skipped? Whatever his plans were, I hoped that they worked out well.

My Timex displayed 7:30 pm, so I still planned to hike several more miles that night. I was now shivering, but when the lake came into view, I felt an inner warmth. Mother Nature had outdone herself. The magnificently-colored blue water looked as I'd remembered it. The crater itself with its rugged meandering edge also impressed me, and, other than the mounting wind, a stunningly-beautiful evening unfolded. I filed away many images of the lake. Two women sat chatting on a rock wall with Wizard Island positioned directly behind them. "Would you like me to take your picture with Wizard Island in the background?" I inquired.

These two tourists spelled road-trip. Liz handed me her digital camera, and I snapped a picture of them, being careful not to obstruct the camera's aperture with my baseball cap or my fingers. Liz and Karen had attended college together in Mississippi. In part because of our southern connection, we immediately befriended each other. This day culminated their one-week vacation out west. I detected a sadness in their delivery of this information. They'd just arrived at Crater Lake from a long day of driving, and hadn't known the island's name.

Liz and Karen were each 36 years old. Liz designed television show and movie sets; she resided in Southern California. Karen taught elementary school and adult yoga classes in north Georgia. The two had become friends in college and annually took extensive road-trips together. They'd stayed close over the years, and enjoyed a "Fish and Wall"-type friendship. Liz snapped a close-up at arm's length of all three of us. She planned to email me the pictures.

Liz and Karen enjoyed healthy lifestyles. This fact became obvious from our conversation, but I had also sensed it from their dress. They kindly offered me food from their over-packed car. I assumed that they'd taken pity on me initially because I looked like a man whose life was on the slide. Their vehicle seemed to burst at the seams from all their gear.

I'd packed 10 pounds for 12 weeks, whereas they'd packed 300 pounds for one week. Their pounds-to-week ratio was over 300 times greater than mine! I ate a couple of scones and drank a can of organic mango juice. This treat rated high above Skittles and iodized water in both nutritional value and taste. While I'd been sitting outside the Crater Lake Rim Village store, I had polished off a bag of potato chips and had super-hydrated on Gatorade and soda, so I couldn't take full advantage of their southern hospitality. I glanced at my watch and realized that I needed to push on, or I'd be sleeping higher than I intended that night, in cold and blustery conditions.

Liz and Karen had cheered me up. Although we'd spent only a brief period of time together, we became good friends. They had taken an interest in my hike and had happily supported me. We shared mutual interests, and I felt sad when we parted company. As they drove away in their home of the past week, I turned back and waved, returning to my home of the past two months. They both smiled and waved, and shouted "Good luck!" I hoped that Liz would email me the pictures that we'd taken.

Mile 1,860.6 measured the highest point in all of Oregon and Washington, reaching to 7,560 feet. I'd encountered snow in the vicinity of Crater Lake and wondered what I would find at the high point 30 miles ahead. As I hiked north, I hoped that Liz and Karen would have a safe journey back to California, where Liz would resume work and Karen would catch a flight home. My spirits had improved in their company, but now I felt lonely. Foot pain once again dominated my thoughts.

The following day, when I reached the Mt. Thielsen Trail, at mile 1,853.6, I encountered five people. On weekends I would usually see day-hikers, and that July day was a Sunday. Outstanding weather always brought people into the mountains. I greeted two young couples and a seven-year-old girl. Everyone wore comfortable shorts and T-shirts, and displayed interesting tattoos, including the little girl, whose decorations I assumed were temporary. Like everyone that I'd encountered in Oregon, these people treated me well. They seemed to be environmentally conscientious and nature-lovers. I sat down to talk after unshouldering the G4.

The group offered me food, which I gladly accepted. Since each adult carried a small backpack, they had plenty of supplies to spare. I ate a dripping-ripe nectarine, a bag of gourmet potato-chips, and slices of smoked sausage. To a hungry thru-hiker, these items tasted like the meal of a lifetime. I learned that they all lived in the Portland area. The previous day they'd car-camped, and this day the foursome introduced the young girl to hiking. They commented on how great the weather had been in Oregon that summer. There had been almost no rain, so the fire danger was extremely high. I worried about myself and other thru-hikers completing the trail in the event of a large fire. If the PCT caught on fire north of me, I would need to abandon my record attempt and leave the woods. This thought upset me.

While sitting on a small rock trailside, admiring distant lake and mountain views, my rear became sore. I noticed that one of the Portlanders carried a camera, and I offered to take a group shot. This idea went over well with everyone, except the little girl, who didn't want any part of the picture. She may have been frightened by my appearance or was merely too shy. I tried to coax her into the scene but to no avail, so I took the shot with just the four adults. Through the viewfinder, they had looked happy and carefree.

Once on my feet, I decided to push north again. The acts of standing up and sitting down hurt, and emphasized my stiffness. I didn't really want to go through that difficult process another time. Additionally, the snow depths that I would encounter remained unknowns. If I got delayed, lost, or sustained any other problems, I would need to hike longer hours. For these reasons, too, I felt my schedule calling me. I thanked everyone for their kindness and said goodbye. They wished me good luck, and I trekked north through another snowfield with my legs bare.

Over the next few days, I passed hundreds more ponds and lakes. In this stretch dozens of deer grazed along the PCT. They seemed healthy and bounded away, gliding effortlessly, as they detected my presence. I felt privileged to see them run straight downhill, directly uphill, and across mountains with ballet-like precision. If they hadn't yet seen me, their movements were all the more rhythmic and beautiful. Their grace inspired me.

During this period I plowed through, what seemed to me, a surprising amount of snow. My timing with most of the snow was good, though; I usually encountered snowfields between 10 am and 7 pm, which is when the snow wasn't completely frozen. This timing had been pure luck. If my timing had been off, I would have crossed anyway, thus assuming an even-greater risk. I did fall once on an icy patch that I'd reached too early one morning. Luckily, I'd stopped myself just before sliding headfirst into a partially-buried, evergreen-tree trunk. That incident had happened in a flash and had shaken me up. Afterwards I'd shouted, "Be more careful, Ray!"

In places where the snow was deep, I walked near the tops of strong-scented evergreens. Sometimes I tree-grabbed to maintain my balance, and this swinging reminded me of traversing monkey-bars as a child.

Each tree that poked up through the snow exhibited a different melt-pattern around its trunk. Many trees had jacuzzi-sized depressions near them. Although I didn't really care, I figured these bowls formed because the heat radiating from the tree melted the snow more quickly. I took care not to fall through or slip on the mogul-covered ground. In these types of forests, while ignoring the inherent dangers, I enjoyed 5-to-10-foot glissades, zooming through and around the maze of trees and branches.

One day, out of the blue, I sang John Denver's "Annie's Song". "You fill up my senses, like a night in the forest, ..." This tune made me think of my father. He had passed away three years ago. Tears flowed from my eyes. I missed my dad tremendously, and I'd thought of him often during my hike. He would have loved to have heard about this journey, but only after the fact. I released deep sorrows.

I felt happy that I had shared so much with my father. We'd gotten along well, and I believed that I'd been a good son. My friend Paul (whose trail name is "Superman") once said to me, "Ray, you made your father proud", and that remark meant the world to me. My dad was a man of few words, but I knew that he'd cared about me deeply. I finished the song and kept walking.

When my heart broke or when I felt overburdened with grief, I cried freely, many times getting things back together just moments before encountering other hikers, then resuming my crying once they'd passed south of me. I didn't mind people seeing me crying, but I didn't want anyone asking me what was troubling me. I didn't want to burden them with an honest answer. Walking gave me time to think and to sort things out. The PCT provided an excellent outlet for me.

In the vicinity of Elk Lake a large fire had consumed the forest in recent years. The fire had thoroughly charred everything on both sides of the PCT plus the trail itself. Tree remnants stood only 20 feet high, and many looked like "widow-makers". I'd been worried about coming to an unmarked intersection, and during this stretch, my fear came true. I arrived at several forks in the PCT that *Volume II* had neglected to mention. If there'd been trail-markers at these junctions, they were burnt and gone now.

Like Peter Lorre contemplating a crime, I turned over the charred remains of anything that could possibly have been a sign. This effort blackened my hands further, yet provided no real clues as to which direction the PCT headed. Numerous times I made best guesses and traveled by Braille. Occasionally, I needed to backtrack. This area slowed me down, but my faith and my endurance saw me through.

At last I came to a side trail that descended to Elk Lake. The route lay in a burned-out area. Later that night I would have to walk up this hill with a much-heavier load in order to return to the PCT. I detoured on the spur trail and walked a mile downhill to reach Elk Lake Resort. This resort held my last mail-drop, or so I hoped. If I could catch their restaurant open, that would be a plus. A hot meal with meat and veggies sounded wonderful, and I needed to get off my throbbing feet for an hour.

 12. Failing Feet

As my energy waned, I emerged from the dusty spur trail near Elk Lake and entered an empty parking lot, at mile 1,953.2. The open space sharply contrasted with the narrow confining trail. I noticed that my breathing felt less constrained in the airy lot. There I encountered a man walking a small leashed dog. I asked him where Elk Lake Resort was located. He told me to follow the dirt road around the corner and downhill. "It's just a little ways", he said snappily in a tone which indicated that I should have known this fact. I smiled and hiked away.

In their declining condition my throbbing feet hurt terribly on any road-walk. Although it was probably only half-a-mile, this pavement ouch-ouch-ouch lasted longer than the unfriendly man had indicated and longer than I'd hoped. I crossed a more-developed road, reminded myself of a pre-hike habit to watch for vehicles, and flagged down two women in a car to inquire about Elk Lake Resort. They kindly informed me that the resort was just a little farther. To confirm that I was following in the correct direction always meant a great deal. At this stage of my hike, to learn that I was headed the wrong way nearly shattered my spirit. I reached the so-called resort at 8 pm on July 15th, day 65. If I was going to retrieve my resupply package, make phone calls, and enjoy a hot meal, I needed to take care of business quickly. The falling sun never waited for me, and I would need to return to the trail and establish camp that night.

My utmost concern involved the retrieval of my final mail-drop. Thank goodness I found it intact. I'd packed this box three months earlier, and laying my hands on it again brought a sense of relief. I'd done extensive mental homework to cope with a missing Savannahoriginating box. This planning involved developing a recovery strategy, including contingency plans for replacing gear and for acquiring food, plus deciding on additional phone calls. Since I possessed nothing to write notes with, I kept long to-do lists in my head.

More significant than devising a course of action to replace the box's contents, though, was preparing for the disappointment of a missing box. If I had been caught off guard, I would be very upset. Already my Belden package had been mishandled. To miss two of only three mail-drops would have been maddening. My breaking point neared the surface, and bad news could have been the final hike-ending straw. When I'd retrieved the Elk Lake package in good shape, I'd enjoyed a greater high than seemed reasonable. My pendulum-like mood-swings crested and troughed. Since this mail-drop was my last, I felt relieved not to have to go through contingency planning again.

No other customers occupied the resort's restaurant, which was inside the store itself, so I sat down with my mail-drop right at one of the wooden dinner tables. Since the rickety table could accommodate four, I had adequate room to spread out my equipment. Normally, a lack of customers signals poor-quality food, inferior service, or some other issue of concern, but that night I felt grateful to have the place to myself—regardless of those factors. I was glad not to be imposing on somebody's summer vacation.

The waitress looked to be in her early twenties and sported a leafy-rose tattoo in the small of her back. This artwork was etched precisely between her low-cut jeans and her midriff-exposing tank-top. Whenever she moved away, my eyes fixated on the red flower. She brought me a folded-paper menu, and while informing me of the daily special, she tested her recall. I ordered a rice stir-fry, a salad with ranch dressing, a classic Coke, and two milkshakes. Shortly after the cook put down his newspaper, my server began bringing me food.

As the food continued to arrive, I struggled stiff-legged to the store's podium-sized counter to purchase Advil and Deet. They sold painkillers in tiny two-packs for two dollars. I'd hoped to buy 200 Advil, but this quantity would have cost 200 dollars. Feeling discouraged, I returned to my table. My feet hurt, and I allowed myself to ignore them only part of the time. For some reason I hadn't put any Advil in the Elk Lake mail-drop. This omission was a bad oversight. In denial I riffled through my box again—still no Advil. How the hell could I not have put Advil in this box? No satisfactory answer came to mind, so I let the omission pass without berating myself endlessly. The store didn't sell Deet, either, which also disappointed me.

I ate my salad and drank the ice-filled Coke. Whenever I drained my soda glass, my friendly waitress refilled it. The store didn't sell adhesive bandages, either. I asked the waitress if she had a bottle of Advil or any Band-Aids. Unfortunately, her purse search turned up bad news. She willingly raided the store's first-aid kit, though, to provide me with 20 Band-Aids. This gesture meant a lot. I couldn't accept the fact that I would depart here without any painkillers. This thought scared me.

I ate the mediocre stir-fry as I repacked. During the meal, I had re-taped my feet, had pulled on fresh socks, and had laced up my new shoes, having thrown away their generic inserts and replaced them with my tired graphite orthotics. Seeing my feet during dinner did nothing to stimulate my appetite. Occasionally, I would get up from the table to perform a bathroom chore such as washing out my mildewed water-containers. When I'd eaten all my solid dinner food, I flossed and brushed my teeth.

The waitress got off work at 8:30 pm, and I asked her if she could give me a ride to the trailhead, when she finished her shift. She agreed to this suggestion, but let me know that she might be running a little late. I made a couple of phone calls from the resort's phone. They charged me a whopping $56 for one of them. I planned to have a package with Advil and Deet waiting for me at the Olallie Lake Ranger Station, at mile 2,047.8.

When I sat back down at the table and began drinking my by-now-melted chocolate and vanilla milkshakes, a man arrived at the restaurant and angrily declared that he wasn't going to stay at the resort as planned. Apparently, he'd paid $35 for a room and was later asked to pay another $10 for his wife and him to shower. This fee struck him as outrageous, and, using a longshoreman's vocabulary, he blasted the proprietor in front of our small audience. The waitress cringed and seemed embarrassed by the distraught man's outburst. I sympathized with the resort's three employees. They returned the fellow's money, and he stormed away.

Deet, Advil, Deet, Advil. I couldn't prevent these words from reverberating through my mind. The similarities between these two words and "Dead" and "Alive" are remarkable. Substituting an 'a' for the 't' created a perfect jumble. The wall clock read 8:40 pm, but the waitress still didn't appear ready to leave. I handed her a shoe box full of spare items. Included in the New Balance box were two pairs of socks, my recently-discarded shoes that I'd been wearing for only 300 miles, powdered milk, and various sundry food-items. No female community-college student would have ordered the care-package's contents, but she graciously accepted. I told her that I needed to continue my journey. If she passed me on the road, she would pick me up.

I returned to the trail at 8:50 pm, thinking that I'd probably seen the last of the rose. During the half-mile on blacktop with my heavy pack, I didn't see any cars, so I assumed that the waitress had been further delayed. My missed ride didn't matter in terms of time, but those 10 minutes on the road caused me mind-boggling amounts of foot pain. I wished that I could have avoided this pain.

When I arrived at the deserted trailhead parking lot, I now saw two trails exiting. One, which led to the right, would reach the PCT a mile-and-a-half north of where I'd left it. The other, which led to the left, would take me back to where I'd actually departed the PCT. I could see why any non-purist would have chosen the right-hand trail. After all, the burned-out, brown-powdered trail that I'd come down wasn't worth seeing a second time. Nevertheless, I wanted as pure a thru-hike as possible, so while staring at my old 806 footprints, I retraced my steps.

Eventually I rejoined the PCT. I turned north at the PCT junction, being very careful not to miss it. With the sunlight dying out, the thought of a wrong turn had worried me. In the dimming light it would have been easy to have gone south accidentally because the right-hander wasn't well-marked. Darkness and animals had started to overwrite my earlier tracks, too.

I pushed on another couple of undulating miles. Sunset came and went on another spectacularly-clear evening. I set up the Squall just as the night became really dark. The "campsite" that I'd settled on was a dirt spot in the middle of 50-year-old evergreens, about 30 yards off the PCT. In the morning I'd forgotten whether I'd set up on the east side or the west side of the trail. In a dense forest such a memory lapse can lead to a dangerous situation. This incident wasn't the first time that I'd found myself in such a predicament. I wandered back and forth in the morning, mumbled a few choice words, and finally discovered the PCT, where I'd left it. Such incidents troubled me, and I cautioned myself, "Ray, you need to be more careful, really; pay attention!"

My feet deteriorated daily. While hiking over 40 miles per day, I couldn't keep them clean. In the mornings standing up barefoot was impossible. I felt arthritic. My muscle flexibility had all but disappeared. Simply emerging from the Squall became difficult and felt like crawling out of a cave. I executed my Methuselah-like risings with Swiss precision, though, since I always needed to relieve myself at the exact same time just shortly after stirring. Mother Nature gave me no buffer, and normal bladder-control had vanished. Throughout the summer, I had methodically taken the following steps before answering the "call".

I would first take out my crusty earplugs, grab the plastic ziplock that contained my cut-off tooth-brush, and deposit the earplugs in the foggy malodorous bag. Hungry mosquitoes and unfamiliar birds welcomed me sans earplugs. I would remove my plaque-covered bite-guard that I'd been chomping on all night. This device went into its floss container. I would then deposit the plastic bag and the Petzl headlamp in my yellow stuff-sack.

Five minutes after waking, I would usually eat a package of smashed PopTarts and a previously-melted candy-bar. I always woke up hungry, and I always felt relieved to get in the first calories of the day. If any liquid remained in my bottles, I would wash down breakfast. If not, my mouth would be coated with sugar and my teeth sticky for the first part of the day. In the latter case I would have dry lips until I reached water. In the beginning of the trip, I always had water with me at night, but as the trip progressed, I usually didn't have water at night. Having eaten something and woken up a bit, I would tear out the day's *Databook* pages. From my green food-bag, I'd remove the snacks for the first six hours of the day. They consisted of eight candy-bars, pumpkin and/or sunflower seeds, beef jerky, Fritos, and powdered Gatorade.

The weight-saving, Z-rest sleeping-pad that came with my G4 pack was only three-quarters body length. I used the G4 itself as a pad under my legs. It provided only the equivalent padding of about four layers of paper-thin nylon, but felt better than nothing. I always emptied the G4 at night, so that I could sleep a little more comfortably. The Z-rest itself looked like a container for hundreds of hummingbird eggs and had acquired many black ground-in dirt-splotches.

When repacking, I would first put the sleeping-pad back in its place in the G4. This material served as the "frame". I always performed this task with great care, since I didn't want to tear the lightweight mesh fabric that held the pad in place. Next I would insert the two empty Platypus containers and empty Gatorade bottle back into the G4's sleeves. Having ripped out the book pages needed for the day, I also stashed them in one of the sleeves. This positioning gave me easy access to information throughout the day.

Next, I would remove my Speedo sleep-ware and dress in my shorts. Removing the Speedo required hopping on my butt a few times in synchronization with quick arm pulls. Dressing in my shorts entailed threading the feet and a single, rapid, high-elevation, butt jump. I would then take off my polypro shirt and put on my hiking T-shirt. In cold weather this move caused my body temperature to drop. The shorts and the T-shirt served as part of my pillow, as did my Goretex jacket. All of my clothing was filthy and smelly, but I ignored these facts and didn't think about hygiene.

I carried a small white garbage bag into which I would put the Speedo and polypro shirt, and then sealed the bag with a tiny piece of wire (a bread tie) to waterproof it. Next I would cram the sleeping-bag into its little black stuff-sack. During this repacking phase, I needed to keep my head low, as the tarptent stood only about three-and-a-half-feet high. I always placed the sleeping-bag and minuscule clothes-bag in the bottom of the G4. This material served as the pack's interior anchor and gave the G4 a little more stability. If I wasn't going to wear the NorthFace jacket, I would also cram it into the bottom of the pack. Next I put in my food bag. If I had resupplied recently, this job involved a struggle.

My attention then would turn to my feet. At night I took off all Band-Aids, *Compeed*, and tape to let my cracks, cuts, and blisters heal. Pulling off these sticky items required courage, since this process often entailed ripping off loose bloody skin. Lots of breath-holding, teeth-gritting, and 'ouches' and 'ahs' happened in total isolation. I dreaded this torture each night, but felt that my feet healed better if they remained uncovered for a spell. In the morning I always re-bandaged everything.

Another plastic bag held Band-Aids, Compeed, adhesive tape, and sometimes dabs of Neosporine. I would carefully put two to three Band-Aids, or a piece of Compeed on each little toe. Next I would put two Band-Aids on each big toe. Then I would tape each little toe. Sometimes the toes next to the little toes would require a Band-Aid simply to protect them from the friction caused by the bandages on the little toes. Fortunately, this problem never propagated to the middle toes.

Whenever my heels became really painful and cracked, I needed to bandage them. Band-Aids lined the sides of my feet, too. I would often fiddle with my shoe inserts. Sometimes I modified them and supplemented my orthotics with an extra heel-cup. Other times I would add more padding in the front of the shoe. The key was to be flexible and willing to try out new things. Any innovation that reduced my pain was good. Lastly, I inspected my feet for any additional trauma. If I found any, I continued to play doctor, nurse, and patient.

Continuing my morning routine, I deposited the unused Band-Aids in the yellow stuff-sack. Next I put this small stuff-sack in the backpack, so that it rested on top. Then I loaded the backpack's open mesh pocket with my snack food, Deet (if I had it), the small brown iodine water-purification bottle, a spare pair of socks (if they needed drying out), and toilet paper. I kept a sandwich-sized plastic bag there, too, for garbage. All bandage trash and food wrappers went into the little garbage bag.

The most difficult step of the day was pulling on my trail-running shoes. This event generated pain waves that radiated throughout my being. The shoes always contained dirt, leaf and grass matter, and a few small twigs. I usually needed to take out my orthotics and bang on the heels of the shoes to eliminate these items. Many thru-hikers use gaiters, but I didn't. My swollen and flattened feet barely continued to fit into the 11 2E shoes.

I would often experiment with different shoe-lacing tensions, sometimes lacing very tightly and at other times loosely. The lacings on the left and right shoes weren't balanced; I listened to my feet individually. Depending on how swollen my feet were, proper lacing could bring me from excruciating blacking-out-type pain to a level that felt tolerable with only a handful of Advil. If I got my feet into the shoes without shedding a tear, I considered that an accomplishment. Using my bare hand, I would then sweep the pile of dirt and twig matter toward the door of the tarptent.

Once I'd double-checked that all preparations were made correctly, I unzipped the tarptent and brushed out the dirt pile. Over the course of the summer, I encountered many hikers who had lost items, including cameras, trekking-poles, and food bags. My routine was designed to prevent me from losing anything. At night I always brought my second pole inside the tarptent so that I wouldn't accidentally step on it in the next morning's darkness. In the morning I would toss this lone trekking-pole out of the Squall. Next I pushed my pack up near the opening of the tarptent. I would then toss out the Squall's stuff-sack and tent pegs. While moving stiffly, I would make my way out of my summer home and stand up. My feet usually began to hurt much worse as soon as I stood on them. On many mornings it initially felt difficult to balance.

I would pull the G4 out of the tarptent, zip up the empty tent, and next take toilet paper from the mesh pocket of the G4. After hobbling to a restroom site, I'd return to disassemble the Squall. This procedure took only a couple of minutes. I would then push the Squall into the G4, vertically away from my back. This action helped position the food bag closer to me. Since the food bag weighed the most, this move in turn reduced the stress on my back.

My next step was to transfer four or five candy-bars from the mesh pocket of the G4 to my shorts' pockets. I rarely applied insect repellent in the mornings. After having sealed the G4's top compartment, I would hoist it and start hiking. When slinging the pack over my shoulders at any time of day, the Platypus tube often became tangled, but eventually I worked out an effective system for the tube automatically situating near my mouth. Once back on the trail, I could relax my busy mind.

Late in the day on July 16th, I crossed Highway 242 near McKenzie Pass, at mile 1,984.5. I'd already traversed several lava fields on this grueling day, and now as the time approached 7:15 pm, up ahead I saw a lava field of infinite proportions. The wind blew steadily at 30 miles per hour. Since my feet were putting me through purgatory, I felt concerned. As I left the last stand of 40-foot evergreen trees, I walked onto black lava stretching to the horizon.

I hiked at only two-and-a-half miles per hour on the lava. This speed was only two-thirds of my usual pace. The field consisted of dark rocks mainly between the size of a baseball and that of a soccer ball. With each step my ankle rolled and cracked. Through a lifetime of training, my strong ankles held. In low-cut sneakers like those I wore, weak ankles would have fared worse. I used my trekking-poles to maintain my balance and as canes. Each step hurt significantly; each succeeding step hurt worse. I absorbed the pain and continued north. As I proceeded, this lava field became even more desolate. *Volume II* read something like "The observant hiker will notice plants and even small animals in the lava field." I saw neither, and I looked, hard. No macroscopic life existed here. No way.

The strong wind, slow pace, and falling sun forced me to put on my NorthFace jacket to stay moderately warm. Although the lava field rolled, the wind never seemed to be blocked and always struck me with full force. I hadn't eaten dinner yet, and felt completely ravenous. Time flew by, but progress was slow, and now from my stance, rather disturbingly, I could see nothing but lava in all directions. "S—!" I really didn't know if this field went on for three more miles, ten more miles, or even farther. Letting my fate unfold as the PCT desired, I *never* looked ahead in *Volume II*. At around 8:30 pm, I decided to stop for dinner. This place qualified as a minus-five-star restaurant.

Sitting down on the lava pile made me feel exceptionally uncomfortable. My rear felt like I'd just watched *Gone with the Wind* from a bench. This lava field seemed unfriendly. No one could have sat down here and been happy. For a moment I wondered about how powerful the blast must have been that created this inhospitable landscape. A similar blast now would take me out of my misery.

I ate a packet of tuna fish, some crackers, and several candy-bars. After a few swigs from my Platypus, I was alarmed to find it empty.

In addition to the ensuing cotton mouth which I would experience, I thought about the possibility of having to spend a water-free evening in the lava field. Darkness would arrive in one hour, and I couldn't risk hiking at night in this leg-breaking trap. Sprawling out on this uneven surface for the night would test anyone. At that moment I didn't feel up to such a test.

I quickly finished dinner and attempted to rise to my feet. "Get up, Ray! You can do it, Wall," I encouraged myself. Once I'd stopped for even five minutes, my legs became so stiff that I struggled to walk normally. When my muscles started to function properly, I hiked on with a sense of urgency. Twenty minutes later I felt relieved to see another stand of trees in the distance. This other-worldly area would soon be but another memory.

I now saw a beauty in the lava field that I'd missed in my state of worry about sleeping there. Nevertheless, I sure felt glad when I exited the rugged moonscape. The ground beyond the lava field wasn't sleeper-friendly either, though, and probably rated eight on Moh's scale of hardness. I pushed on as far as I could, while the light lasted. Eventually, I found a niche on a gradually-sloped hillside and set up the tarptent there. My feet seemed happy when their punishment ended for that evening.

After Highway 242 a 16.5-mile water-alert existed. During dinner the previous night, I'd run out of water. That next morning I was making poor time, since my feet had continued to degenerate. As I became badly dehydrated, my thirst grew. This fact only exacerbated my foot problems. Dehydration seemed to reduce foot padding. My fortune changed, though, when in the Cold Springs area, at mile 1,994.2, I met a male Outward Bound instructor. He was heading south. I was sitting on an uncomfortable black porous rock, retaping my feet. I wasn't crying, but tears had welled in my eyes from pain. He could tell right away that I was thru-hiking.

The instructor stood at about my height, but his towering pack made him appear much taller. He struggled under its weight. The load would have flattened me. His legs were well-muscled, and he sported over-developed calves. His dark tan matched the color of his hair. I could tell from his odor that he'd been in the woods, but only for a couple of days. He stopped, and we exchanged thoughts, sharing in each other's trials and tribulations.

My foot pain peaked on that day. When the Outward Bound instructor saw my bare feet being re-taped, he cringed. I inquired with not-so-subtle concern about the next water-source. He could see white globules on my lips and generously offered me a liter of his iodized water. As an instructor with group responsibilities, he carried extra for uncomfortable students. In giving me water, he'd reduced his pack weight by two pounds, so this gesture seemed like a win-win situation. He explained to me that his feet hurt, too, but not compared to mine. "I don't do more than twelve miles a day anymore," the 25-year-old wilderness man added. I thanked him for the water, and he motored south.

After several more minutes of taping, I hobbled down the trail, where the remainder of the instructor's group passed me, while heading in the opposite direction. I heard comments like: "Did you see how dirty that guy was?" and "He must be a thru-hiker." The word "thru-hiker" was spoken with great reverence. I struggled during that time without any Advil. I plodded, all day, everyday. The fact that I was about to pass the 2,000-mile mark gave me encouragement. When I crossed the Santiam Highway a short time later, at mile 2,001.6, I almost broke down. A smile came to my cracked lips. This trip marked only the second time in my life that I'd been over the 2,000-mile barrier on a single trail.

On July 17th my feet spoke volumes, and I struggled significantly. I could walk 40 miles per day regardless of the shape my feet were in, but with all the nerves in my feet which weren't numb screaming "Stop!", hiking wasn't much fun. My internal pain switches remained off, but were being overridden. I told myself that a "wiring problem" existed in my switching network. Current leaked, and I tried to "repair" the faulty circuits. While thinking about my next steps, I caught up to a middle-aged guy, who seemed lost. He and his friend had become separated while day-hiking. We hiked north for a mile and encountered his concerned friend. During this stretch, any company made me feel better and distracted my mind.

I learned that the taller man taught at Portland State University. Fitting the stereotype of an academic in the northwest, he had shoulder-length hair which made him seem laid back. From my uneven gait, the professor could tell that I was hurting. He wore a Walkman and asked me if I'd ever heard of the Pearlmen.[1] I told him "No". He put his earphones on me, and I listened to a Motown-sounding group performing the Beatles' "Nowhere Man"—"Making all his nowhere plans for nobody ... ." I enjoy the Beatles, and the familiar lyrics momentarily transported me to a comfortable place. The professor's remedy cured me, if only for a while.

The guys offered me a plastic two-liter jug of lukewarm water that was half full. They expected me to walk off with the container. I downed the water in one shot, handed the vessel back, and thanked them. They questioned me about my hike. After our discussion, they wanted to take my picture. They kindly asked me to join them for a steak dinner later that evening. I regretfully declined, given my time constraints. Steak dinner! How did I pass that up? At the next fork in the trail, we separated. On that gorgeous day they had found a spur trail to a lake, and had planned to spend the remainder of the day swimming and sunning. I felt sad to be alone, again. Walking with them for even just a short time had meant a lot to me.

I felt tired as evening enveloped me. My mind wandered, and I enjoyed the sunset and the towering evergreens in that beautiful forest. I was hiking surprisingly fast, as I often did at the end of an endless day. During the latter part of the trip, I required about 20 miles or around 6 hours of hiking just to loosen up. With little but walking on my mind, I came around a tight unprotected corner and slipped right off the PCT. As I was free-falling, my flailing hands grabbed a cooler-sized rock. The solitary rock sprang up to a 45° angle. While staring at the rock and exerting a downward force, I stopped it. As I exhaled deeply toward the rock, it slowly settled back into place.

My feet dangled in space. The muscles in my back, my arms, and my neck tightened. My heart transported maximum quantities of blood to these tense areas via bulging arteries. Using a horse-mounting technique, I dragged myself up onto the trail. From the narrow lip I looked down behind me and saw sharp rocks 35 feet below. If the soil had been any softer, the entire gray stone would have ripped loose, and I would have sailed 35 feet vertically with the rock clutched to my chest. The brown-dirt trough that I'd seen underneath the stone looked like a hole dug to bury a house cat. The well-formed hole with criss-crossing wormy lines at its base was nearly the last thing that I ever saw.

---

[1] I don't remember the group's real name.

Pain emanated from my left hand. I glimpsed down only to discover that blood was squirting from its palm. A gaping wound the size of a silver dollar had been torn open. My shredded skin caused intense pain, but only for two minutes. My foot pain overwhelmed the pain in my hand alarmingly fast. Using Coach's grip on my trekking-poles, I hiked on. The hand no longer bothered me much. If I'd not sacrificed the hand with this incredibly lucky save, I would have been lying on my back for a few days. I figured that a bear probably would have come by before I passed out. Who knows how that end game would have played out? While paying closer attention to the trail, I walked north.

On July 18th I caught up to a hiker named Bruce.[2] He worked as a handy-man, and did carpentry odds and ends. I learned that he'd seriously injured his back in an accident several years earlier. His two hiking companions, a father-and-son team with whom he occasionally camped, were in a rush to leave the woods on that day. The trio had planned a three-day trip, but were leaving after just one. Bruce seemed upset about this change in plans. His friends had made an early start and pushed ahead, even before Bruce had really woken up. He was trying to catch them.

Bruce hiked with a medium-weight, full-grown Dalmatian, and I joined them. The white-dotted-black dog made me think of my German Shepards—Dottie and Julie. I missed them. I prayed that my 13-year old pets would make it through the summer. Bruce's and my pace seemed far slower than my usual speed, but on that day, with ailing feet, it felt fine.

Bruce possessed a great sense of humor. His extensive repertoire of jokes and sayings sustained me. I assumed that he'd acquired them while working construction. As a teenager, for three years I'd been in construction, working at a fencing company with Bobby, Frank, Louie, and Vinnie. I knew where such expressions originated in America. My sense was that Bruce worked just often enough to pay the bills, but not one second more.

My feet hurt so badly that I asked Bruce if he had any painkillers. With his ongoing severe back-pain, I felt hopeful. He produced several, elongated, gel Advils that were a lime-green in color. Since Bruce

---

[2] I am less than 100% sure that Bruce was his actual name.

had taken so many Advil over the years, he needed the gel form to protect his scarred stomach-lining. From a secret container, he carefully removed an ominous-looking cylindrical pill. Handing it to me, Bruce warned, "Take this baby only when you are in extreme pain." I didn't really catch the name of the painkiller, but immediately popped it into my mouth and swallowed. Bruce stared in disbelief; I guess he'd assumed that I would take it that night, if at all. I felt pain-free for two hours, during which time we made excellent progress. Since Bruce had only one "emergency" pill, relief wouldn't be coming again.

We finally caught Bruce's two friends on the top of a rocky ridge. The son looked to be in his late teens and fit. The father seemed to be in his late forties and far less energetic than the son. Bruce introduced me and relayed my story to his companions. My being there eased their tension, and Bruce had already calmed down substantially. We moved on together and crossed a number of snow patches, glissading down them. "Sparky" the dog kept going ahead, falling behind, and then bolting ahead again. He enjoyed this beautiful sunny summer day more than anyone else. Once or twice, the Dalmatian actually fell through fast-melting snow bridges. We would have broken an ankle, but he recovered instantly.

The father trailed us and proceeded cautiously on the descents. I asked Bruce if he knew anything about Olallie Lake Ranger Station, where I planned to resupply next. He told me that he'd been there several times. "Nice piece of eye-candy behind the counter, but she isn't very friendly," he relayed with shifting eyes. He indicated that the small store had a decent selection. When Bruce traveled in this locale, he always stopped by to "visit" the store clerk.

At last we emerged onto a dirt road. My new friends would split off here to a nearby trailhead to retrieve their car. Bruce gave me his remaining energy bars, beef jerky, and Band-Aids. These supplies were substantial since he'd left the woods a couple of days early. I felt grateful. We parted company with a firm handshake and heart-felt goodbye. Bruce planned to follow the remainder of my thru-hike via the Web. Knowing that I had his continued support would help me get through some tough times.

My thirst grew as I pushed on alone. I paused for water at the next creek. Once I'd drunk my fill, I dipped my smelly T-shirt. A soaking shirt helped to cool me on hot cloudless days. I hiked on with tolerable foot-pain and reached a two-lane dirt road. After querying a group of day-hikers, I walked a tenth-of-a-mile on the road and arrived at Olallie Lake Ranger Station, at mile 2,047.8.

Bruce and his gang had planned to stop here as well, but obviously they'd already come and gone. On that early afternoon of July 18th, I didn't see the attractive blonde there, but I did find a cozy store with the customary bait-shop taxidermy on the walls, and the exorbitant prices that Bruce had promised. A small package, which had been sent in response to my phone call from Elk Lake Resort, had arrived, so I felt relieved. Retrieving the envelope cost five dollars; I was so glad to see it that they could have charged me any amount. I bought drinks with which to super-hydrate and went outside to open the package. An eight-ounce bottle of perfumed Off insect-repellent in a pump-spray container fell out first. The liquid contained Deet, but not concentrated. I felt delighted to find 250 pills of Advil. This number decreased rapidly. Compeed for torn-up feet rounded out the small stash. Whew!

Having discovered the contents of my package, I dodged the swing-ing screen door and re-entered the store to resupply. The ranger-station market sold the usual fare. While I grabbed dozens of candy-bars, sev-eral tourists arrived. A couple of brothers whom I talked to told me that they made an annual pilgrimage with their father to fish here. My dad and I had spent many hours fishing together. I'm sure fishing in Olallie Lake would have made him smile.

While I stood in line reminiscing about my father, a nine-year-old girl arrived with her dad and a big lake trout. I saw them weigh the 14-pound, beautifully-colored trout. The massive fish reminded me of my steelheading days in Washington state. The girl smiled ecstatically since this fish marked her first catch ever. I wondered if she'd ever top this monster; I doubted that I would. The father beamed, extremely proud.

I was stunned by the size of the trout and forgot about my feet for a brief moment. Fish stories would circulate in her life forever. I could see her 70 years from now explaining to her great-grand-kids about the day when she landed the big one, "... children, I remember a real-smelly bearded man named Wall, who saw us weigh the fish, but for the life of me can't recall if your great, great grandpa caught anything that day."

I paid my enormous food bill and asked if there was a public phone. A portable phone could be rented, but in order to get any reception one needed to walk off shore on a long dock. I carried the rented cell in my damaged but fast-healing hand, and my supplies in a red basket in the other. I left the crowded store and sat down on a wooden porch bench overlooking the lake. While enjoying the time off my feet, I began to prepare for my departure.

I was busily unwrapping various items and placing them into plastic bags when a section-hiker came by to visit. Her long, straight, dark hair blew in the breeze. She penetrated my world with her attentive brown eyes. We shared our thoughts of late. After I'd sprayed the outside of my pack, I gave her the bulky bottle of Off since I had enough Deet in my possession. She planned to overnight at Olallie. My master called me north that afternoon, though, and for a moment my new friend seemed disappointed. She had plans to hook up with her sister and another girlfriend. I asked if she could spare any Band-Aids, and she dug out a few large ones. We enjoyed our brief conversation. I headed off to make a couple of phone calls.

I carefully negotiated the narrow dock, which rocked back and forth, as I walked out over the lake. I became a wave-machine disturbing the calm water. The sun blazed down on Olallie Lake, which threw the rays onto my dark-brown skin. The evergreen-covered shore entrapped the lake, and mirror images of trees glistened beautifully. The sky possessed a warm blue. Where the wood ended, I dropped the G4 and sat down to reduce the pressure on my feet. I dialed a complex series of digits, but failed to reach anyone back east.

After those unsuccessful attempts, I made a last-ditch effort and called Jimbo in Southern California. Amazingly, that call went through. We had a good talk, and he provided me with much-needed support. Jimbo always listened to what I had to say and always offered support. "Let me know if there is anything you need," he would say. Knowing that I had such a good friend, who was willing to help out, comforted me immensely.

Mentally, I'd struggled as of late and dropped to an all-time low. Without Jimbo, who knows where I would have been. I needed to pull myself together. By breaking the hike into smaller parts, I was able to cope with my roller-coaster emotions. Reach Washington state, and you will get a boost. Walk to Snoqualmie Pass, and you're halfway across Washington. Then meet Paul. He will bring you home. "Paul *will* bring you home!" Superman could get me to the end. I just concentrated on reaching Snoqualmie Pass. The last 260-plus miles never worried me. Superman will be waiting for you at Snoqualmie, so don't let him down, I told myself. This thought kept me going.

I tried to place a few more calls but failed. While I sat on the dock, two girls drifted by in a slow-moving paddle-boat. They smiled on that sunny day, and I borrowed what pleasure I could from their delight. Several tourists walked out on the dock and boarded their rental motor boat. They rocked the dock, and shook me up pretty good. I'd already been on my rear for 20 minutes and felt dehydrated in the intense sunlight.

During my last communication, the phone died mid-call, "Are you there? Can you hear me now? Hey! F—!" The phone quit. No way would I walk back out on this dock again, so my calls ended for that day. I returned to the store, bought a chocolate ice-cream bar, and paid my massive phone bill, which amounted to about five cents per syllable.

I'd started to return to the trail when I saw the brown-eyed section-hiker busily scribbling in her journal. She sat alone at a wooden picnic table. After a very sincere good luck to me and a warm smile, she continued updating. I told her goodbye and good luck, and headed back to the gravelly road leading to the trail. Fully resupplied, I'd soon be back on the PCT.

I accessed my library repeatedly during this time-period, pulling up inspirational images. They included a cap-wearing Joan Benoit winning the first women's Olympic marathon in Los Angeles, a struggling Mark Allen passing Dave Scott on the last uphill at the Hawaiian Ironman, a courageous and cancer-filled Jim Valvano saying, "Never, ever give up", …. I sang "God Bless America" from "The Deer Hunter", and the lyric "You can do anything, the opportunities on …" from "Harold and Maude". I smelled evergreen forests and replayed conversations with friends. I brought myself back with enough strength to continue the dream, at least for that day.

 13. Dreams Don't Die

On July 18th, day 68 of my hike, I walked 43 miles to reach Timberline Lodge at 8:15 pm. Although I hadn't planned to stay at the lodge originally, my extreme fatigue changed my mind. Each morning when I woke up, I felt as though an 18-wheel, tractor-trailer truck had driven over me. Every single day seemed harder than an Ironman triathlon. I was wasted. Mine was a fatigue that perhaps only sleep-deprived, special-forces, military troops and a handful of others knew. This tired was a multi-month exhaustion. My mind and my body played tricks on me.

A shower and a bed sounded nice. I'd hiked through six inches of pumice in the Mount Hood vicinity, and that difficult surface had burned all my remaining energy. It had further dirtied my feet and my legs. Walking in the fine gray powder had stressed my feet even worse than asphalt had done. While pushing off with my feet disappearing in the sand, it was difficult to get any purchase. This stretch felt akin to dune walking. I experimented with the angle of my foot placements, but nothing worked.

I detoured down a steep paved trail to reach the expansive Timberline Lodge. Groups of lively tourists played in the snow patches. The wind whipped at 25 miles per hour, blowing up shovelfuls of volcanic ash. Dust irritated my eyes, ears, nose, and mouth. Every opening filled with dirt. I entered a parking lot and asked the first person whom I encountered where the lodge entrance was. The fellow directed me around the building. While passing through another larger lot, I noticed some expensive cars. Near the stone entrance to the lodge stood a trash-can. I emptied my pack of all garbage, as a young teenager paced back and forth talking to her boyfriend via cell phone. Paved ground, intrusive devices, and loud chatter—I didn't miss these things.

The Timberline Lodge looked like a reasonable place to stay and may have been the best hotel along the PCT. I inquired about a room but learned that the lodge was full. This fact upset me. I discovered that their store had already closed. This situation further upset me. My empty pack needed resupplying. The only place to obtain food for the road was a coin-operated vending-machine. What? Not possible, I thought. But it *was* possible. A barmaid changed bills for me, and I began a five-minute period of pumping coins into the metal box. I didn't worry if my selection became stuck, as the next selection of the same item would drop both purchases. An abysmal set of choices poured from the cursed machine. I would feed on high-calorie candy for the next day's 47-mile hike.

Having completed my poorest resupply of the trip, I asked about a room for the second time—still none available. I gave up hope for a room. Giving up hope hurt. A large wedding's attendees had depleted the room supply. Many people who would be sleeping in beds that night sauntered around in formal dress. They looked at me askance. I located a restroom, gathered toilet paper, brushed and flossed, rinsed and refilled my water-containers, and splashed water on my dirty face. My routines kept me going.

A phone tucked underneath a stairway provided me a chance to make a few calls. While I placed my calls, a well-endowed young woman in a pink evening-gown came up to me and asked if I knew how to pin a corsage. She held a beautiful flower arrangement in her hand. I told her that I did but that she probably didn't want me touching her lovely dress, given how filthy I was. She agreed and found someone else to perform the task. While I talked on the phone, I watched the successful pinning operation.

The lodge had a restaurant upstairs, and I decided to grab a meal. I walked gingerly up a lengthy flight of stairs. If stairs hurt so much, how the hell was I tackling massive mountains? My waitress appeared to be in her early twenties. From her I ordered a Coke, burger, French fries, salad, and chocolate cake. She knew that I needed to return to the trail before dark. I mentioned that the lodge had no vacancies, and she told me that weekend nights filled quickly.

The restaurant seemed busy and understaffed. My waitress moved methodically from table to table. Never did she rush. She seemed poised and unflappable. I chatted with her, and she would sneak questions to me, while passing by to another table. She refilled my Coke between serving other customers. My gigantic meal disappeared quickly. The bill came, and I left a generous tip, unloading all my ones and the unused vending-machine change. While departing the warmth of the lodge, her image passed through my mind one final time. I felt glad that we had become friends.

Time had ticked rapidly, as it always did during resupplies. The driving wind necessitated zippering all openings on my NorthFace jacket. I marched uphill and rejoined the PCT where I'd left it. By now the tourists had returned to their comfortable rooms. Temperatures plummeted. I wanted to get away from the lodge before dark and walked quickly to prevent hypothermia. Shortly after leaving the lodge, I entered a ski area where a number of significant ups and downs greeted me. The downs led to glacial-river crossings, while the ups led out of them to high points from which the next silty river-crossing became visible.

In the dark on a descent to a ford, I bumped into a woman. Maybe I should have had my headlamp on, I thought to myself. The lady had obviously been drinking heavily. I had no clue as to where she had spent the day or would spend that night. She reached out with both arms as if to hug me, but I dodged her, knocking loose rocks onto the narrow trail. I said, "The lodge is just another half-mile farther. Keep going." Without looking back or breaking stride, I proceeded, hoping that she didn't fall face-down into one of the icy torrents. I felt bad that I didn't have time to escort her to the lodge.

Wearing every stitch of my clothing, I pressed on vigorously, but still felt cold. Shorts, T-shirt, and my NorthFace jacket didn't cut these conditions. I eventually found a spot to camp near Hidden Lake Trail 778, at mile 2,103.5. I'd passed the 2,100-mile mark, and this realization provided me a huge psychological boost. I set up the Squall, climbed in, arranged gear, put in my earplugs, and lay down to sleep. The wind howled loudly, but my earplugs reduced the sound to an almost pleasant level. Violent winds made me nervous; peaceful winds soothed me. The earplugs converted most winds to soothing winds.

I started to nod off. Amazingly, in the dark I then saw two groups of hikers without lights pass me that night, heading toward the lodge. They must have misjudged their return times. I hoped that they would make it safely back to warm beds that evening and would take care of the intoxicated woman, if she'd fallen.

Early the next morning, I headed north. That day was one of the most emotional days of my life. My plan required hiking 46.8 miles to mile-marker 2,150.3 at the Oregon/Washington boundary. While a graduate student in computer science at the University of Washington, I had lived in Washington state for six years. These years had set the tone for my life. I knew that simply gazing across the Columbia River Gorge on the way into Washington would cause emotions to flow. Forever, I was a Washington Husky. Many fond images from my library surfaced.

On July 20th, exactly one week before my birthday, the weather bordered on perfect again, with deep-blue skies. Although my feet suffered unspeakable pain, the thought of being in Washington the next day gave me a great sense of joy and relief. Reaching Washington would constitute a tremendous accomplishment. I would have completed two of the three states on the PCT, and I would have exceeded the entire distance of the 2,159.2-mile Appalachian Trail in just 70 days. In 1995 I'd hiked the AT "pure" in 97 days total, with six of those being rest-days. Eight years later I'd shaved 27 days off that mark. Granted that the two trails are different, but to me the AT seemed like a walk to the corner store compared with the PCT. This trek was already the greatest athletic accomplishment of my life, and if I continued at this pace, it would undoubtedly be my biggest physical achievement ever. Soon I would be in new territory. Each step beyond the AT's length would be the farthest that I'd ever hiked.

My schedule was nothing more than a 30-kilobyte Excel document that I'd dumped onto an 8.5-by-11 sheet of paper. I'd duplexed the schedule and trimmed the paper to 6-by-10. The decreased size increased its value. This sheet of paper got folded into quarters. Tea-like stains, from pocket crud and from being held by dirty hands, decorated the paper, but other than the stains, the schedule appeared an almost uniform light-brown color. My fingerprints covered the record-breaking schedule, which I'd consulted hundreds of time over the past two-plus months. The schedule meant nothing to me, yet meant everything to me.

I'd prepared the 85-day schedule based on grocery-store locations. Later that day I'd arrive at one of these unfamiliar stores to buy my fill. Store hours, exact location, and selections were unknowns to me. If a place was on my schedule, I planned to go there and resupply. I never knew what I'd find.

My schedule was my foe and my friend. To be behind my schedule hurt and worried me. To be ahead of my schedule uplifted and encouraged me. To be behind meant pushing to catch up. To be ahead meant pushing to stay ahead. The schedule dictated my pace. It became my master, my religion. If the schedule had read differently, I would have followed it. If it had been more than two days more ambitious, I would have been behind. If it had been less ambitious, I probably still would have been two days ahead. Two days seemed like a good margin. If I hurt myself or had equipment problems, though, this cushion would vanish instantly. This night I would be two full days ahead for the first time on the trip. A deep satisfaction would accompany this achievement.

I had great expectations for the town of Cascade Locks, Oregon, which is the boundary town on the south side of the powerful Columbia River. The usual town-approaching urgency built in my steps, since I wanted to reach Cascade Locks before 9 pm. Overnighting here would provide the opportunity to get a shower, do laundry, and check fire danger. Such hotel and resupply plans had fallen through in the past. I put the necessary psychological structures in place so that in the event things went awry, I wouldn't be too distraught.

The day's hiking progressed well. The miles and hours clicked off in a 3.5:1 ratio. At the start of each day, I would tell myself that I had to hike for only 15 hours. The first daily milestone happened at 2 pm, when my day was half over. Periodically, I would glance at my watch and, for example, at 4:00 pm say to myself, "Only five more hours to go." Five hours of hard exercising now felt easy, plus I always looked forward to seeing pretty sunsets. The latter hours of the day often transpired the most quickly, especially if I wanted to reach a town before its store closed, like that night.

As I began a long quad-busting descent, the first views of the gorge appeared. With each downward step the temperature and humidity rose dramatically. For most of the summer the warm air had been vacuum-dry, but now the sun beating down on the big river caused moisture to enter the atmosphere in great quantities. Being from Savannah, I regarded anything less than 75% humidity as comfortable, so I wasn't seriously affected. Gravity assisted me, and I occasionally enjoyed views of the impressive river, looking around for people on boards in this wind-surfing mecca. Due to the late hour, however, I didn't see any wind-surfers.

Years earlier I'd visited the Columbia River on a number of occasions. None seemed as special as this visit, though. The milestones which I'd accomplished that night overjoyed me. However, I still faced a hard hike. No day was over until it was truly over; no destination was reached until I stood there. I would arrive in town just before darkness, barring any adverse incidents. The switchbacks were long, and as I weaved back and forth across the mountain-side, stealing glimpses at the grand river, I became pensive about how I was weaving my way through life. I'd formed many patterns in my life, but this summer many of them had come unraveled. I went back to the basics, to a primitive ancestral lifestyle. This approach helped me to see which things in my life are meaningful. With the orangy sky brightening and darkening, as can happen only at sunset, my thoughts meandered downstream.

From my dream-state I woke and focused on the trail again. More hours had been subtracted from my pool, but these ones counted; they felt significant. I traded dirt for pavement at 8:30 pm, walking gradually downhill toward town. Having plummeted 4,000 feet in the last 10 miles, I neared the PCT's lowest point. I contrasted this dip with Fish's and my ascension to the PCT's highest point at Forester Pass, nearly two-and-a-half miles higher. While I thought about Fish, the Bridge of the Gods, which spans the mighty Columbia, suddenly came into view. Washington lay just on the other side. In my excited state I felt tempted to dash across the metal structure, but my feet abruptly and definitively said "No!" I proceeded directly to the first person whom I saw. She worked in the lane-dividing toll-booth on the bridge.

"Hi. Where's the nearest hotel?"

The woman in the tiny booth looked at me strangely and pointing said, "There's a Best Western right there."

She wound up to deliver several other options, but I said, "Great, thanks," in the nick of time to stop her short. I pivoted, flew down a flight of stairs, crossed the road, and strode into the Best Western's front office.

It was 9:10 pm. Feeling greatly relieved to have made it to Cascade Locks, I let out a massive sigh.

"Do you have a single nonsmoking king?"

"Yes; it's $99 per night. Are you hiking the trail?" the clerk asked.

She had volunteered the rate information, perhaps suspecting that for those used to paying zero, the cost might be too steep.

"Yes. I'll take the room."

"AMEX. Okay. There's a market down the street that's open until 10 pm."

"Are any restaurants open now?"

While handing me the bill to sign, she said, "Char Burger is next door. Good burgers."

This check-in contrasted starkly to the Mojave check-in. I felt thankful.

The registration clerk phoned Char Burger, and let me know that they closed at 10 pm. The hotel's laundry facilities were situated near my room's entrance. She'd thoughtfully put me in a handicap-accessible room because of the manner in which I'd struggled in. I made mundane inquiries about change and laundry soap. She communicated about check-out and the free continental breakfast. I thanked her after obtaining my card-key and took the elevator one flight down to my ground-floor room.

The room felt spacious compared to the Squall. The bright bath had a tiled floor, large mirror, shower, and wide toilet area with metal handrails. When I passed by the mirror, while reaching for a hand-towel, I saw a stranger. "Who are you?" My appearance stunned me, and I froze to do a double take—a bushy beard, thin face, matted hair, ripped arms and legs—my God, I'd been transformed. I hadn't looked in a mirror for weeks. Physical changes had accompanied the mental changes.

Moving farther into the room, I tossed my pack onto the bed and flipped on the TV. I walked over to the window and realized that I had a waterfront view. Parting the curtains further, I enjoyed the view, but only for a brief moment. I filed away the image to withdraw it later. Time escaped, so I decided to go directly to the store. I would return and then head to Char Burger. A juicy burger would be that night's reward for hiking through Oregon in record time. I treasured the thought of eating a fatty burger with greasy French fries. My lean body craved fat, an item it no longer possessed.

Being careful while crossing a road was no longer instinct, and at the last second I avoided getting hit by a car. I walked downhill one-quarter of a mile to the Cascade Locks Market. It felt great to walk without a pack. In the market I grabbed a cart and began a major shopping expedition. This spree exemplified binge-buying. The store rivaled the one in Idyllwild for the best resupply point on the PCT. I purchased $120 worth of food for three days. The stash included nectarines, grapes, and bananas. I planned to eat these heavy items in the room. At the market check-out, I asked if there was an area Internet Café open. The hyena-like response shocked me, "In this town, are you kidding?" The largest software company in the world was just "up the street". Oh well. The cashier loaded my groceries into plastic bags. When I left the store, it was already 9:35 pm.

The thin-plastic handles on the bags cut into my hands. The bags felt heavy. Momentarily, my feet weren't the overriding concern. I'd bought four liters of Gatorade plus many other weighty items. I realized then that I should have brought the G4 with me. For once my pack would have been a comfort. Without stopping to rest and with my fingers devoid of blood, I reached my room. I dropped the bags on the floor and blood surged back into my white fingers, restoring their natural color. Immediately, I high-tailed it to Char Burger in search of a fast-food meal.

I arrived at Char Burger at 9:45 pm—perfect timing. Perfect timing except that the boss had made an executive decision and closed up early that Sunday night due to lack of business. My persuasiveness wasn't prime that night; I couldn't convince them to reopen. I'd been salivating over a humongous burger with all the trimmings, but instead I'd be eating the usual cold fare. I felt disappointed.

With my head hanging just a bit lower, I returned to the motel. A nectarine disappeared as I readied my laundry. This washing would mark the first and only washing of my sleeping-bag this summer, and the first time that I'd done laundry since Vermillion Valley Resort, an unfathomable 1,180 miles earlier. I popped into the hallway wearing only a towel, and sped directly across to the laundry facility. After loading the dirty clothes into the top-loading machine, I jetted back to my comfortable room.

I eased my way into the bath-tub. Why did feet have so many pressure-points? So many nerves? Standing barefoot always hurt; standing barefoot in a curved tub hurt terribly. I scrubbed for awhile, blackened the water, and removed all tape and bandages. When I reached the point of being merely filthy, I called that good. Trimming toenails caused intense pain. While monitoring my watch, I performed the other customary chores.

Returning to the laundry-room, I encountered a young mother on holiday with her little daughter. The two were vacationing from nearby Portland. The hard-breathing daughter had obviously been running around. When I entered the room, the girl found a chair and sat down. This cute child wouldn't be moving or talking again until I left. We shared close quarters. The mother looked me over and smiled. While I unloaded my washer in front of the motionless daughter, her mom and I talked. The mother asked, and I answered, many questions about my journey.

My sleeping-bag, which according to the manufacturer is never supposed to be washed in a top-loading machine, was now clean but ruined. The down seemed full of tumors. The drying-cycle held my hopes for restoring some loft to the cancerous bag. I moved the remainder of my load into the dryer under the watchful eyes of the two, and then returned to my room. After I left, the little girl probably asked her mother many questions about "the man" wearing no clothes.

I devoured more food, repackaged supplies, and laid out all gear. The tarptent aired over a chair. I ripped out unnecessary *Volume II* and *Databook* pages and hydrated on my-favorite beverage—blue-ice Gatorade. While loading food into my green stuff-sack, I saw that I'd significantly over-bought. I erected a pile of Hershey bars, Tang, cookies, grapes, and nectarines.

Using the bedside pad and pen, I wrote a note for the maid:

Please enjoy this food. I am hiking the Pacific Crest Trail and bought too much in my starvation state. The orange powder in the bag is Tang. I can't carry all this.

If the maid had expected a tip, I'm sure that this stash wasn't it. I hoped that he/she would take the groceries the next day. As I began nodding off, my clothes needed attention.

I wrapped a damp towel around my waist and slipped next door. The clothes felt dry enough. My sleeping-bag's loft hadn't improved nor had the clumping. The mashed bag would no longer keep me as warm as it had. I brought the tiny load of clothes and sorry bag to my room. Nothing needed folding, since I had only clothes to wear. My NorthFace jacket definitely fared the best, going from black to its original red. I looked forward to wearing clean socks that next morning.

After grabbing a trash-can and the ice-bucket from the by-now-filthy bathroom, I hobbled down the hall in my towel and loaded these containers with ice. I lay down in bed at 11 pm, glad to be resting finally. My feet disappeared beneath gallon ice-packs. The cold hurt, but I iced for 45 minutes anyway. The treatment dramatically reduced the swelling in my feet. I switched off the TV, which I hadn't even looked at.

Superman would meet me at Snoqualmie Pass on my birthday in one week. We'd leave there exactly two days ahead of schedule. Thus, for the next week, I needed to hike only at the pace of my schedule for the penultimate week. I'd planned 260-plus miles, which had originally seemed huge, but now would actually feel easy—at least I thought so. With no reason to wake up until 6:30 am, I looked forward to sleeping late. My dream was still alive. I lapsed into a deep sleep.

Part V

WASHINGTON

The Washington section of the PCT extends from the Oregon state boundary to the southern Canadian border. The trail snakes through 508.4 miles of challenging mountains. The lowest elevation sits at about 200 feet and the highest elevation stands at over 7,000 feet. This terrain is remote and rugged. The beautiful old-growth forests with their towering giants contrast with the clear-cuts full of slash and overturned stumps. Goat Rocks Wilderness, Mount Rainier, Mount St. Helens, and North Cascades National Park highlight this section with their alpine lakes and glacial peaks. Hundreds of Elk graze near the trail in Washington. Black Bears and Mountain Goats wander close to the PCT, too. I'd planned to resupply about four times during this section. The longest segment without resupply stretched 150 miles. I'd scheduled a biggest day of 44.8 miles.

 14. Emotions Flow

This special Monday, July 21st, day 71 of my trip, found me in good spirits. I didn't sing the Boomtown Rats lyric "Tell me why, I don't like Mondays", as I'd done on several other Mondays during the course of the summer. Soon I'd be in Washington state. My feet felt bad; beaten. Trauma and nerve damage plagued them, but the recent icing had helped. It would have been wonderful to have iced my battered feet every night. I'd slept better with less foot pain, so I felt well-rested that day. The soft king-sized bed hadn't hurt, either.

I'd eaten my fill at the complimentary continental breakfast by 6:45 am. Reflective thoughts bombarded me. This summer I'd been through a lot. The extreme challenges and isolation had accelerated normal development. I grew spiritually. My perspective broadened. Armed with new abilities, courage, and understanding, I wondered which path would I follow next? Would I ever pass this way again? I doubted it.

Thinking about all the good times that summer put a smile on my face. The friends whom I had made, and the PCT itself, had inspired me. The sacrifices required to reach my new spiritual and physical levels felt rewarded. In fact, the sacrifices were necessary. The more I put into this effort, the more meaningful the trip became, and the greater my personal transformation. I never would consider trading that summer's experiences.

When I returned to my room, reality returned to me. I lacked the energy for a second shower. Dirt and sweat would soon cover me, anyway. I called my older brother Bob back east before departing. His voice-mail answered; just hearing his voice lifted my spirits. Then, as

I began to leave a message, I fell apart crying. What the hell? My unexpected collapse made me realize how strained my emotions were.

Many factors contributed to my mental state, and one was the return to my former home state. Loneliness acompanied me, too. I had been teetering on the edge for weeks, pushing myself to the breaking-point. The effects of improper nutrition and poor sleep throughout the summer took hold. As I choked back tears, I said a few words to Bob. My update filled him in on my journey's progress. I relayed to him that it looked like I would set a new record and achieve my goal. He would be incredibly proud of me.

I sobbed between each sentence, as I spoke to Bob's machine. What was really on my mind? While trying to regroup, I exhaled deeply. I told Bob that I would be okay, not to worry. He'd heard me cry only once in the past 25 years, and that was at my father's funeral. My attempt at convincing Bob that I was okay failed, but I did the best that I could under the circumstances. After hanging up the phone, I wept for awhile, shaking and trembling on the edge of the bed. I let my emotions flow unrestrained. Once back to a suitable equilibrium, I put on my pack, glanced at the maid's cache, and pushed north alone.

I returned to the Bridge of the Gods with a dollar in my pocket, thinking that I had to pay a toll to walk across. It turned out that I didn't. (If I'd known that the bill was going to get in my way all day while I tried to retrieve *Databook* pages from my pocket, I would have discarded the money.) After brief introductions and greetings, the woman at the bridge said, "You're the first thru-hiker we've seen this year."

"Could someone else have gone by?"

"No, that's not possible. Unless they passed through very late at night. This bridge has no sidewalk, so that would be dangerous."

The information which she provided me meant that no one had leap-frogged me, so I probably wouldn't be meeting any more thru-hikers. I thanked her, saying my final words in Oregon.

Exhilarated, I walked across the old metal bridge spanning the big river. I stared through the grate beyond my feet at the water directly below. In March I'd climbed the Sydney Harbor Bridge in Australia, so I felt extremely comfortable walking on high bridges. I scanned the water for giant sturgeon, but didn't see any of those prehistoric fish. Whenever I came to a body of water, I looked for fish. My father had taught me this lifelong habit. Fish held many mysteries for me, and I always delighted in spotting them. Sharing a sighting provided even greater joy.

I walked facing bridge traffic, as the woman at the toll-booth had told me to do. The PCT probably hadn't yet been conceived when the bridge had been built. Large trucks drove uncomfortably close to me. I occasionally pumped my fist in the air when no traffic passed by, "Way to go, Ray!" I said out loud. Tears welled up in my eyes. "You can bring it home. Come on, Wall! Be strong!" This type of verbal encouragement always sent goose-bumps up my spine.

My senses felt unusually keen as I crossed the bridge. I could see into the eyes of the drivers whizzing by me. I noticed a variety of smells and sounds which I normally would have missed. Dormant animal instincts seemed to reemerge. I tuned in with my surroundings. Why did I feel more alert here than in the woods? Had I become that much more comfortable in nature?

The bridge spanned a half-mile of the gorgeous river, and I thoroughly enjoyed walking over the water. The sky was perfectly sunny. At only 200 feet above sea-level, the air felt thick. My body put the additional oxygen to use. I carried a heavy load and would be climbing soon to return to the mountains. The anticipation of Mount Rainier and other familiar parts of Washington loomed large. Plus, if all went well, I'd be finished with the trail in less than two weeks.

When I finally reached the boundary of Washington state, my energy left me. That two-states-completed milestone had caused a huge release. My fist-pumping on the bridge had sucked away all my adrenaline. So, by 7:30 am, my tank was empty. Since I hadn't taken a rest-day all summer, *any* disruption to my equilibrium caused a bigger-than-anticipated physical and mental reaction. In this case it meant total energy drainage.

My schedule called for a 36.3-mile day. I'd originally expected this section to be easy, despite its being hilly, hot, and humid. My physical limits had expanded to an entirely new dimension. Somewhere during this last stretch, I'd made a mental transition to thinking that any day's hike of less than 40 miles was easy. This new mindset helped me to surmount greater challenges.

By midday on the 21st I reached Road 2000, at mile 2,170.3. I'd now walked 11.1 miles farther than the length of the Appalachian Trail. Each step was new territory. I approached the ominous-sounding Panther Creek, at mile 2,186.5. The name caught my attention. During this cob-web-covered stretch, I met two women who were headed south. Thanks to them, perhaps I'd lose the cotton-candy look north of here.

The dark-haired woman looked 20. A big Black-Widow-spider tattoo covered her upper arm. She'd rolled up her loose-fitting, T-shirt sleeves, displaying the impressive arachnid. I wondered when and why this young woman had decided to have her arm inked for life. Was it a lost bet? Too much alcohol? Mind-altering drugs? Was she a misanthrope? In my current state of mind, I enjoyed staring at the red-on-black hourglass, so I gave her decision no further thought. The older lady was my age and had graying hair. I could tell that she'd been in the woods awhile, and that the 20-year old had joined her only recently.

The three of us exchanged perceptions of the PCT. Then the older woman blurted out, "I think I know you. I don't mean *know* you know you, but I have seen you before. Did you pass me in Northern California?"

My mind rewound to two weeks earlier, and I, too, recalled our prior meeting. She began our script.

"I was just emerging from my tent, and you said 'hello'."

"And you said, 'Getting an early start'."

"You said, 'Gotta make some miles today'."

"And you said, 'Yeah, the PCT is like that'."

"And you said, 'Good luck'."

We'd duplicated our earlier conversation with a role reversal. It felt fun, and we smiled in front of our audience of one.

I learned that the 40-something woman was section-hiking the PCT over a five-year period, which meant doing 550 miles per year. Her tattooed friend provided company for a short stretch. Having made up a section in northern California that she'd missed last year, she had driven north to Washington and was covering a segment here before returning to Oregon. Our morning meeting in northern California had lasted only two minutes, but somehow she'd remembered me—perhaps because I'd been the first thru-hiker whom she'd seen. This second meeting struck me as remarkable. Without her recollection, I certainly wouldn't have remembered our first meeting. I felt happy that we'd "reunited".

"You've got some miles to make, and we don't want to delay you any longer, so it's goodbye for now."

"See you," I replied, while taking a last glimpse at the spider.

I continued northward alone. Shortly, though, I overtook two male north-bounders. They looked around 20 years old. Their slightly-oily dark hair indicated that they'd been on trail only since Cascade Locks. One fellow planned to hike all of Washington state, whereas his friend intended to hike half of the state, or as far as Snoqualmie Pass, where Superman would meet me. These guys were sitting at a dirt-road crossing when I'd caught them. They'd decided to set up camp on the flat road and appeared to be completely played out. I didn't say anything about their decision to camp on a road. For safety reasons, while alone, I'd never camped on a road, at least not yet.

The two hikers picked my brain about gear, since they couldn't believe how light I was traveling. They complained about their aching feet and sore backs caused by their boots and heavy packs. The guys seemed stunned to hear that I'd walked from Mexico in running-shoes. I talked for half-an-hour without taking off my pack, said goodbye to my new friends, and pushed north again. That evening their campfire would probably be fueled by unnecessary gear.

My recent trail conversations meant that I needed to push the pace to reach Panther Creek before dark. I hiked hard at four-and-a-half miles per hour. Although I was running low on water, I passed up several water-sources in order to save time. I knew that this questionable tactic might impact me later.

The forests in Washington seemed far darker and far more forbidding than those in Oregon. The bigger trees with their giant canopies blocked more light. The forests felt damper. Moss and leafy underbrush thrived. Many spiders extended their webs across the PCT. I noticed that they rebuilt quickly after hikers passed through. Finding campsites late at night in these conditions would be much more challenging than it had been south of here.

I desperately wanted to remain two days ahead of my schedule. While moving at the speed of a slow jogger, I reached Panther Creek at 9:30 pm. The water rustled beneath me. In the pitch darkness my hearing improved. The creek sounded loud. I walked cautiously out onto the wooden bridge which spanned the creek. Panther Creek Campground, where I'd hope to sleep that night, eluded me. I'd passed a couple of hikers off to the side of the trail minutes earlier. Had they been near the campground? I didn't know. Although I felt parched and dehydrated, I decided not to obtain water at the creek because that meant a dark walk on a potentially ankle-breaking trail. Besides, I'd seen many creeklets earlier and guessed that more would flow ahead.

Despite the starry night, the light proved insufficient for hiking, because of the thick canopy. I tripped a number of times. The darkness prevented me from seeing ahead, and I unexpectedly found myself ascending a "Category One" climb of 2,300 feet. I'd hiked 36 miles from Cascade Locks to Panther Creek, and now tacked an uphill battle on to that. That night, though, I'd be more than two days ahead of my schedule. This accomplishment felt significant to me, so I climbed.

My thoughts turned to staying on the invisible PCT and finding a campsite. The trail gained elevation rapidly. I noticed large old-growth trees, bigger than any that I'd seen in a long time. It was a shame to pass through these behemoths in the dark, as they undoubtedly were spectacular. The 150-foot tall giants with 25-foot bellies startled me with their shadowy lunges as I walked by. These monsters created an eerie feeling. Humans, me included, fear dark forests. But I felt blessed and lucky in the presence of these old-timers.

Hiking at night meant walking more slowly and less efficiently. It also meant a higher risk of injury and a lower probability of staying on trail. By 10 pm, despite my dime-sized pupils, I needed to turn on my headlamp. I never liked the lighthouse feeling, but that night I had no choice. My beacon went out into the infinite darkness. The illumination of the Petzl micro changed the environment, and shadows bounced around the majestic forest. My thirst grew as sweat poured off me onto this steep mountain. The slanted land prevented camping. I would need to climb for a long, long time.

The realization hit me that I was now totally dependent on my headlamp bulb not burning out and its batteries not dying. I hadn't practiced replacing a bulb in the dark, nor could I change the batteries in the dark. If either item malfunctioned, I'd be forced to camp exactly where I was. I'd have to get out my sleeping-bag by feel alone, lay it on the steep trail, and lie there until it was light. The PCT becomes an animal Ramblas at night, and lying down on their walkway appealed little. However, the longer that I hiked, the greater the chance of a lamp malfunction. I always delayed turning on my light to conserve the bulb and batteries, and again, I was glad that I'd followed this practice that night.

My thirst overwhelmed me. I hadn't taken a drink for ages. When would I drink? Turn off the thirst switch. Ignore it, I thought. The light rays and the shadows created by my light hypnotized me. Hallucinations painted my brain. I couldn't walk much longer; I couldn't stay vertical much longer. Hiking perpendicularly off to the side of the PCT, in desperation I tried to find any spot that I could call camp. This dangerous maneuver involved climbing over huge blow-downs in the dark.

My neck swirled endlessly to throw light wherever I needed it. The attempt to find a campsite had failed, as had the attempt at not getting dizzy. I returned to the trail with bloody ankles. The slightest brush against the porous bark on the old-growth trees caused my skin to rip. The deep contours provided insects homes, but grated me. Since my head was still spinning, I'd be bumping into a few more little condos before the night was over.

Each uphill step took me farther away from water. So, in addition to having a dry camp that night, I'd be dangerously dehydrated at least until mid-morning. After another Zen-focused hour of hiking, I found a questionable ledge to camp on. I set up the Squall in total darkness, struggling to push in my tent pegs. The stakes barely penetrated the moss on this solid rock ledge, and my shelter balanced precariously.

I went through my bedtime protocol, but skipped brushing my teeth. I'd hiked another 40+-mile day. The good news was that I'd have more free time during the next week, since I wasn't going to advance my schedule past two days. If I stressed myself any further, I'd completely crack both physically and mentally. That night, even in my exhausted state, the hard-rock ledge prevented me from getting more than a few winks.

The next day, after I'd satisfied my enormous thirst at a creeklet, I bumped into a group of day-hikers. Most of them looked to be in their early forties. A more-senior man emerged and approached me. This gray-haired gentleman was holding "class" for a group of teachers. One student looked familiar, but I couldn't place her. We all chatted, and they learned that I was thru-hiking. I told them that I'd come from Cascade Locks a day-and-a-half earlier. Doubt projected silence, and dubious expressions filled faces.

The unwired Oregon town of Cascade Locks lay 60 miles south, mostly downhill. The distance, the climbing, and the heat meant that it was several days away for exceptionally strong backpackers. The familiar-looking woman broke her silence, "He's telling the truth. I saw you cross the bridge on Monday morning." I now remembered seeing her face in one of the SUVs that had driven past me on the Bridge of the Gods. Even though it didn't matter, I felt glad that she'd recognized me and I her. Sometimes our limited perception blocks our understanding and prevents us from seeing the truth.

I learned that the class studied the geology and the history of this unusual area. The instructor seemed knowledgeable. His group went round-robin questioning me. I answered one or two questions apiece— the type of questions that you'd expect from those in mid-life. In fact, now, based on a person's age, sex, and appearance, I could usually guess what questions they would want answered about the PCT. When the questions slowed down, the class wished me well. I said goodbye and pushed north. A mile or so later, I passed a trailside parking lot full of SUVs parked helter-skelter. The group would return to their starting-point soon. I'd be out here for awhile longer yet.

I'd heard many enthusiastic comments about the Goat Rocks Wilderness area. The name alone intrigued. It conjured up images of white Mountain Goats climbing on precipitous cliff-sides. When I entered the Goat Rocks area, the awesome beauty and gorgeous weather astounded me. Whenever I had consulted *Volume II* for Washington, it had indicated that hikers would encounter mist or rain in the area, thus missing out on a spectacular point-of-interest. No rain had fallen on me yet on my trip. The weather thus far had also been phenomenal in Washington.

I'd been prepared to walk with pruned feet and with pruned hands through the entire length of the Evergreen State. Visions of a muddy path, rotting feet, soaked shoes, and moldy gear had been my expectations for Washington. I'd spent years preparing myself for tremendous hardship, so the exhilirating mountain views and crystal-clear skies made this stretch unbelievably satisfying. I surmised that no other hiker would *ever* thru-hike the PCT without rain. The probability of not seeing rain in Oregon and Washington was close to zero. Some people may have thought that I rushed my trip, and, therefore, saw less scenery, but no one else would see as much of Oregon and Washington as I had during that magical summer. I felt blessed and wildly lucky.

I hiked down a steep rocky descent and encountered a hard-breathing white-haired man ascending. With a disgusted look on his face, he said, "Slow down or you'll get a speeding-ticket." Why, I wondered, do people feel it necessary to comment on other people's actions? To him I seemed to be speeding through the most beautiful spot on the planet. To me I flew effortlessly, as happy as I could be. While cutting through the wind on a bike, the faster I ride, the more freedom and excitement I feel. That special feeling was all over me while hiking, and I stored in my library that feeling of being free.

My lungs automatically filled with evergreen-scented oxygen as I glided down the trail. That day was perfect. Beauty herself escorted me through the stunning mountains. I was a ballet-dancer pirouetting along the PCT. During this stage of my Tour, I wore the yellow jersey. My natural movements over the rocky terrain seemed choreographed— all my foot-placements precise. I tripped, but could not trip. My body and my mind synchronized; my existence reached a new plane. Nature and I melded. I became my surroundings and they, me.

"See that pack over there? It's mine," the white-haired man said, pointing three-quarters of a mile away, short-cutting a bend in the trail with his fingers. Having been stirred from my utopia, I looked across the beautiful landscape. "You didn't see a camera, did you?" He'd accidentally left his camera behind. I kept walking, and said only "Enjoy your hike." He trudged uphill in search of his memories, and I floated downhill creating mine.

Ten minutes later I reached his pack, which sat near a 30-foot waterfall. The shower of pristine water fell from almost directly above me. The sunlight brushed icy water into a lovely rainbow. I glanced back at the cameraman, who was now returning. On his huge pack he'd purposely displayed his trail-registration, so that any ranger would see it immediately. After filling a bottle with crystal-clear water, I left a Clif bar on top of the fellow's pack. He wouldn't be arriving here for another 20 minutes or so. I smiled and wondered how he'd react to my unexpected gift. From starvation to giving away food, the PCT was a trail of extremes.

I unwrapped a king-sized MilkyWay and stuffed the entire bar into my mouth, nearly suffocating myself. While moving up steep hills, I wanted to hold only my trekking-poles. I loved to fuel myself while hiking because I could feel the calories rushing into my body. This surge felt euphoric. Insufficient oxygen may have added to my high. Chewing the chocolate and caramel required 10 minutes. I swallowed small pieces of the 500-calorie bar when they were ready. Eating animal-style felt good.

I thoroughly enjoyed the mountains in the Goat Rocks. Many cascading waterfalls dropped refreshing water from the mountains' snowfields. Furry marmots scattered and whistled as if to say "We're having a great time, too." The blue sky, the green fields and trees, the colorful wildflowers, and the whitewater and snowfields blended into a masterpiece that soothed my foot pain. The natural beauty overwhelmed me, and I enjoyed it in total peace.

The beauty of Goat Rocks, especially in these stellar weather conditions, was so dramatic that I had to stop and soak it up. These special moments would never come again. Never again would I be in such a perfect setting. That day was unique, but I didn't regret its passing. I felt blessed to have experienced this setting at all. Every piece fitted together. I sat down and absorbed the situation. A gentle breeze blew on my face. I listened to the absolute silence. My mind settled in a blissful meditative state, my face in a grin.

As incredible as nature was in this awesome scene, I felt a deep longing to be with a loved one. To share this moment with someone whom I loved, and who loved me equally, would have been the ultimate experience. I dreamed of being with that special person: my complement, my lover, my queen. Someone whose name, image, and presence would excite me, increase my heart-rate, yet someone whose kindness, caring, and love would comfort me, decrease my heart-rate, bringing a harmonious equilibrium. Holding her hand, staring into her eyes, kissing her lips . . . .

But I was alone, not with my soulmate. This fact created a painful and deep sadness. My heart ached; a sickness crept over me. Nevertheless, the overpowering beauty of nature made that day one of the most special of my life. Despite my broken heart, somehow I felt content, happy to have approached total bliss. I had discovered heaven on earth, but I did not enter it. I was thankful to add these times to my internal library.

Saturated with reflection, I stood up and resumed hiking. I saw amazing panoramas in all directions. To snap some photos would have been nice, but I could not capture this beauty on film. What made that day spectacular was not just the color scheme, the rugged terrain, and the animals—not just the physical surroundings—but rather the involvement of all my senses. Everything I was and everything I would ever be were there. I saw my life from outside myself.

A picture could never capture my feelings, nor could a print ever bring me back and re-create these feelings. The act of holding a camera in my hand would have caused interference, blocked this nirvana—for I would have needed to decide what pictures to take, look through a viewfinder, and depress a button. Any thoughts or actions, even as simple as these, would have infringed on the purity of the situation. My spiritual existence peaked on that day. I wished with all my heart that all people could experience such a day in their lifetime.

After hiking for awhile in complete tranquillity, I encountered two fathers and their boys. The older men were in their mid-to-late forties, and their sons were in their late teens. The four men formed a strong hiking-team. They'd been off trail enjoying the environment and were returning from their foray. I paused to talk to them, hoping to share this extraordinary day with others. When I stopped to chat with people, I usually took off my pack if I'd be more than a few minutes. This time I didn't unshoulder the G4.

This group knew the PCT here from previous hikes. Anyone who'd ever seen this wilderness would have wanted to return. I told them that this location was the most beautiful spot on the PCT. We all recognized our luck with the stunningly-perfect weather. They had never seen conditions approaching these. We marveled at our extraordinary luck.

One father indicated to me that they hadn't expected to see any thru-hikers so early. They asked me many insightful questions regarding my hike. This team had a good understanding of the trail, and I happily responded to them. They were a pleasure to meet. I thought that one or both of the sons might someday attempt a thru-hike. They seemed inspired by our meeting. Bidding them the best, I left the foursome behind, flying freely up the next climb.

The forests in Washington were chock full of leafy vegetation; they were dense. With the added security of my headlamp, I risked hiking later at night. Combining these two items with the shorter daylight hours made it more difficult to find spots to set up the Squall. This meant that I accepted less-than-desirable campsites, and often slept poorly. Several locations where I had set up the Squall had tested my engineering skills. All locations tested my back.

Elk practically lined the PCT in this region. Since the Elk weren't skittish, I knew that I was in extremely-remote country. Although Elk-hunters had littered the woods in Washington state, none hunted here. Dragging an Elk carcass out to a road from here would have been next to impossible, even with a sled on snow. The Elk knew this fact. Elk and I often startled each other. They plowed through the thick forest, snapping small saplings, and sometimes popped out adjacent to me. We would jump, and they would run. It was a real pleasure to see these animals moving freely in the wild. I estimated that only one-in-a-million people in the world would ever see a wild Elk. This thought seemed unfortunate, and I hoped that my calculations were wrong.

Later that afternoon I encountered a retired man, who was day-hiking. Somehow, we began discussing Panther Creek. I told him that I'd gone through what looked like a beautiful old-growth forest there at night. He confirmed that it was. As an afterthought, he mentioned how polluted the creek was and that it was full of giardia. Since I didn't always treat water at this stage of my trip, I felt glad that I hadn't restocked water there, even though I'd really needed it. A prescence continued to watch over me. One nasty bacteria like Larry Sr. had warned me about, and my dream would have been foiled. I said goodbye to my newest friend and continued north.

Around that time one of my Platypuses sprang a leak. Up until then, each of my Platypuses had worked almost perfectly. The only problem had come earlier when my drinking-tube had become clogged with a rust-colored build-up of mold, particulates, and an assortment of powdered-drink mixes. I'd replaced the putrid drinking-mechanism, when I'd received a plastic tube in the mail. Prior to the much-needed replacement, globs of detritus had calved off, had traveled the gross tube, and had been sucked into my mouth. Unfortunately, I hadn't always been able to spit the gunk out in time. I marveled at the fact that I didn't get violently ill from ingesting such a hideous substance. The taste had been deplorable. No engineer who was brilliant enough to devise an on-trail method for Platypus drinking-tube cleaning has yet been born. The technology would require a scientific breakthrough: a lightweight high-pressure washing-system capable of generating an incomprehensible force.

Although I'd put the leaky Platypus into a plastic bag, I couldn't effectively keep its liquid from escaping onto my pack and the back of my legs. This dripping turned my pack and my legs into fly-paper. The slow leak was more of a minor nuisance than a real drain on my precious fluids. The broken-seamed Platypus constituted one of the few gear failures that I'd experienced on the trip. I never knew what might break next, though, and my biggest concern was a broken pack-strap. That event would have caused a serious problem, since I possessed no means of repairing such a malfunction.

On day 74 of my adventure, on July 24th, I headed toward US Highway 12 near White Pass, at mile 2,298.0. The hiking progressed well, but my emotions ran amok. My timing looked good, and it appeared as though I'd arrive at the Cracker Barrel store at White Pass at around 8 pm. The store lay three-quarters-of-a-mile road-walk from the PCT. I planned to resupply quickly and return to the trail for a few more miles.

Near Tieton Pass, at mile 2,286.5, I descended around a blind corner while belting out a Bruce Springsteen song in a tough New Jersey accent, "Your momma's yapping in the back seat, tell her to push over and move her big feet, or it's the last time that she's gonna be ridin' with me." As I blasted around the bend, I encountered a young couple. They made superhuman efforts to contain their laughter. My embarrassing smile pushed them over their restraint thresholds, and made them burst out laughing.

The wife and husband lived in north-central New Hampshire. Since I had resided in New Hampshire for about 10 years, we shared many similar experiences. I learned that they'd been on the PCT for awhile. They had originally planned to hike all the way to Snoqualmie Pass, but now they intended to stop at White Pass, thereby cutting close to 100 miles from their initial plan. The wife practiced medicine, and the husband served as a high-school guidance-counselor. He and his brother had thru-hiked the AT together.

I immediately took a strong liking to the couple. They seemed genuinely interested in my trip and began asking me a bunch of questions. Several times they generously offered me food, but this time I carried enough with me. Plus I needed to go only another 12 miles before I'd resupply. During the last few miles, I'd been crying a lot. My mental state had plummeted to an all-time low.

My dad and "Killface" my cat, who'd passed away a couple years earlier, filled my thoughts. I felt upset. The New Hampshire section-hikers and I talked philosophy, and, after three hours, during which time I didn't remove my pack or sit down, I pushed on, feeling much better. I thanked them profusely for their support during my rough time. They were kind and understanding. We agreed that I'd visit them in New Hampshire, and I thought how enjoyable that would be. My two most-recent friends kept me going. What would I have done without them?

# 15. Remaining Sane

Having wished my New Hampshire friends good luck and farewell, I pushed on full steam ahead. Three hours had disappeared during our conversation, but those hours were critical in terms of my maintaining my sanity. There was a good chance that I would have curled up into a ball and lain down on the trail had I not met those two. But now I would now have to hike exceptionally hard to make it to the Cracker Barrel store before it closed. Even though the store was located in the middle of nowhere, I hoped that it stayed open until 9 pm. This possibility seemed unlikely, but I hiked hard, putting myself on the rivet for the next few hours.

Highway 12 appeared at 9:15 pm, as I was debouched from the woods onto that asphalt road. Several cars flew past, blinding me with their high beams. Hitch-hiking looked impossible in these dark conditions. I walked uphill seven-tenths of a mile and saw the store. The road-walk had hurt, but not as badly as recent road-walks had done. The Cracker Barrel store had closed hours earlier. This situation was, surprisingly, only a minor disappointment.

On my right a large sign displayed the word "Lodging". The sign encouraged me. I needed to camp near the store that night, since I wanted to resupply there in the morning. The *Databook* hadn't mentioned anything about lodging, so seeing the illuminated sign was completely unexpected. My hunger grew uncontrollably because I'd gone full throttle for three hours. Perhaps I should have accepted food from the New Hampshire couple; I had run out before reaching Highway 12. Across from where I'd seen the lodging sign, loud music emanated from a ski lodge. I instinctively moved toward the music and entered the lodge.

I wandered some vacant hallways. The music lured me upstairs to a dance party. Many athletic boys and girls were dancing to blaring modern music. The kids looked like runners. I entered a small cafeteria area. The establishment had obviously closed for that night, but I went up to a man and asked, "Can I get any food anywhere around here?"

"Are you hiking the trail?"

"Yes; my name's Wall."

"You're early."

"Yeah, I've been hiking pretty hard."

"Alone? When did you start?"

"Yep, I'm solo. Left Campo on May 12th."

"You're *really* moving."

After our brief discussion, I told the cook that I'd pay for any food that he could spare. It turned out that I'd walked in on a cross-country-runners' summer camp. They'd all just finished eating. Fortunately for me, leftovers remained, and the cook liked thru-hikers.

"I could make you a couple burgers. We have cole slaw and angel-hair pasta. You can have soda, too."

"Definitely. That would be great. Thanks."

Within a few minutes, I handed the man a 10-dollar bill for a 5-dollar charge. He had no change, but said that I could return for a paid-in-full breakfast in the morning. The friendly cook handed me a plate with two eye-delighting burgers. I dished up cole slaw and angel-hair pasta, filled a paper soda cup with Coke, and sat down to a replenishing meal.

While I enjoyed my food, I spoke to several of the young runners. The group seemed amazed that I was traversing the United States on foot and doing 40-mile days during this stretch. These serious athletes informed me that they didn't even *run* 40 miles in a week. I reminisced about my high-school cross-country career. Past faces, events, and bus rides made me smile. The lodging sign that I'd seen marked the place where all the kids were staying. They said that I could probably rent a room there. I finished my late dinner, walked to the lodge with three of the coaches, and secured a room.

The unexpected room pleased me. I'd been worried about where to set up the tarptent at this late hour. Once in the fully-equipped room,

I showered, prepared ice-packs for my feet, and readied for bed. I'd learned that the store didn't open until 8 am, so I'd sleep in. Although the lodge housed over 100 teenagers, they'd all gone to bed by 10:30 pm because of the next-day's morning time-trial. I would have enjoyed watching it, but I was entering the final phase of my own epic time-trail. After a bone-chilling, marathon, icing session, I finally turned out my lights at midnight.

In the morning I resupplied at the Cracker Barrel store and made a number of phone calls. I finalized my plans for Snoqualmie Pass. Superman and I would meet there at 5 pm in three days time. He would fly in from Maine. If I could get to Snoqualmie Pass, Superman would bring me home; I felt certain of that fact. After drinking a couple bottles of Gatorade and eating several muffins at the store's counter, I decided not to collect my pre-paid buffet breakfast. I signed the Cracker Barrel register.

7/25/2003 8:15 am

Wall here.

Pushed in last night. Thanks for the talk yesterday. You saved me!

The end is near. I plan to be in Snoqualmie in three days. There I'll meet Superman. He'll bring me home in one week.

Should we be concerned about the number of mosquitoes in Oregon and the number of yellow-jackets in Washington? What about the size of the chipmunks in Washington?

The weather has been perfect, and most days I've been hiking without a shirt.

I love this trail.

Best of luck to all thru-hikers.

My view of glaciated Mount Rainier during the next PCT stretch inspired me. Having lived in Seattle for six years, I'd been to the mountain many times, but never in these extended perfect-weather conditions. I recalled two previous visits to the mountain. The first involved the RAMROD, Ride Around Mount Rainier in One Day, bike-ride. This 156-mile circumnavigation of the mountain is considered one of the five hardest rides in the United States. From my library I viewed myself passing cars at over 50 miles per hour on sinuous descents. I could actually see my wheel, as I did that day years ago, with only one-half of an inch of pavement to its right. I'd leaned over as far to my left as possible, while trying to keep the bike on the road. One-half of an inch farther to the right and I would have crashed into evergreen trees at 50 miles per hour.

The second recollection of Rainier involved a flight over the mountain in a Cessna 170 with two pilot friends of mine. I'd sat behind their tiny cockpit. Sightseeing and enjoying the ice towers on the mountain, marveling at crevasses, and enjoying my good luck, my pilots suddenly became giddy. Shouting, I'd said, "Let's head down!" That day we had flown at 17,000 feet in an unpressurized cabin, and my friends had barely escaped blacking out. Thank God I'd remained clear-headed. The gravity of our earlier situation had become eminently clear, as we'd descended. I never flew with them again.

Despite my yoyo emotions, I left White Pass feeling uplifted. I soon exceeded the 2,300-mile mark, which also boosted my spirits. Days of 37.7, 33.8, and 27.1 miles awaited me on my way to Snoqualmie. Given what I'd already been through, these mileages didn't intimidate me at all. In fact, I looked forward to a day as short as 27 miles. On my very first day on the PCT this summer, I'd hiked over 29 miles. With just three days remaining until my rendezvous with Superman, everything seemed to be going well.

The PCT led me to within 12 miles of Mount Rainier. The 14,410-foot summit appeared to be at arm's length. While hiking near this mountaineer's paradise, I felt more spring in my step. The views of Rainier were the best that I'd ever seen. In my time in Seattle we'd never had a string of perfect-weather days like those that I was enjoying now. I was lucky. As I approached the Chinook Pass vicinity, I hiked strongly.

Near the calm-blue Dewey Lake, at mile 2,324.3, I encountered a couple from the Seattle area along with their Golden Retriever. They'd planned a multi-day backpacking trip like Bruce's group. I learned that they had just reached Dewey Lake, had set up their tent, and had immediately taken it down because of the enormous number of biting insects. They intended to hike back to their car via the PCT and drive home. As far as I was concerned, there were no bugs on the trail in that region, but my perspective had been forever altered by the Sky Lakes Wilderness disaster.

The three of us hiked together to their car, and shared many stories. The husband was a former endurance athlete. He'd competed for the University of Utah's powerful cross-country ski team. Fish's sister-in-law, Laura Wilson Todd, had been the top woman cross-country skier in the United States for a long time, and it turned out that this fellow knew her. We talked about some of Laura's impressive accomplishments. Earlier that summer Rita[1] had run her first half-marathon. She had just moved to Seattle after their recent marriage. Rita owned and operated a cleaning business and was still getting established in the Emerald City.

Rita's husband was in outstanding shape, and he hiked along beside me. Although Rita was fit, she couldn't match our speed, which felt easy to me. I slowed down to wait. If I hadn't been there, she might have walked back alone. Their playful dog liked having us all in a group. He covered at least twice as much ground as we did; he wove in and out, circled, and chased marmots. Their dog brought vivid images of my dogs to mind. I wondered how Julie and Dottie were faring back home. Those old ladies always struggled through Savannah's brutal heat and humidity. I missed my dogs!

Climbing gradually uphill, we reached Highway 410 at Chinook Pass. There I had my picture taken with Rita. The couple generously offered me their remaining water and a number of energy bars. I gratefully accepted. They asked for my email address so that they could send me the picture. I thanked them for their kindness. We said our goodbyes. As I crossed the wood-and-stone pedestrian bridge over Highway 410, I watched them drive toward bug-free civilization. I couldn't help wondering if they'd been arguing before I'd arrived. My presence may have helped to resolve the situation.

I hiked parallel to the mountain highway for awhile. Cold crept into my veins, but at around 7:30 pm, I sat down for dinner anyway. From my sandy ant-laden and narrow dinner perch, Mount Rainier's beauty impressed me. Down across the highway sank a deep valley, where huge fallen trees along the river's edge looked like brown match-sticks. The

---

[1] I don't remember her real name.

enormousness of this view made me feel small. A magnificent sunset was underway. This time of day being my favorite time to hike, I pushed north.

Since I'd been hiking slowly with my latest companions, I wasn't tired. I motored past Sheep Lake and saw a dozen tents there. By that summer's standards the lake seemed grossly congested. I launched myself up a climb of 1,000 feet to reach Sourdough Gap. The words "Chinook", "sheep", and "sourdough" had really stimulated my appetite. Was I just particularly hungry now, despite having eaten recently, or had food items been a part of the PCT's naming-conventions all along? Veggie-Lasagna Crossing, Steak Plate, Burger Flats, Crab-Legs Gap, ... "Snap out of it, Ray!" While munching a Clif bar, I descended 600 feet to meet the Silver Creek Trail 1192, at mile 2,333.0. I felt ready to establish camp.

Usually, at trail intersections, a small flat spot exists with just enough room to position a tent. At this crossing I'd been counting on using such a place. I combed the area, going east and west on the trail perpendicular to the PCT, and north and south on the PCT itself. However, even with my imagination and with my minimal requirements, I couldn't find a viable campsite. The evening scene touched on perfection. I didn't want that day to end, so I kept hiking, enjoying the brisk mountain air and the stunning sunset. Any one of 25 sunsets which I'd seen this summer surpassed all but a few that I'd seen previously. That night's certainly cracked my top five.

While I hiked in search of a camping-place, I questioned my decision to have pushed farther north. Conditions change rapidly in the wilderness, as do moods and energy levels. My lightning-fast ascent of Sourdough Gap had taken something out of me. The PCT followed the side of a heavily-sloped mountain. The air cooled significantly, and I felt cold. I hovered around 6,000 feet. With the breeze, my paucity of body fat, and my minimal clothing, I thought that hypothermia might sneak up on me, but no viable campsites presented themselves.

To my left lay the Crystal Mountain Ski area. Eighteen years earlier my friend Randy "The White Gumby" Day (or "Gumby", for short), a fellow computer-science graduate-student at the University of Washington, had convinced me to race the Crystal Mountain Summit Run. I hadn't been doing much mountain training then, and as I looked over at the steep slopes I remembered how much pain my lower back had been in during that run. The Crystal Mountain Summit Run had taken me up to near 7,000 feet, and that was the highest elevation at which I had run to up until that time. The astounding beauty of that run had started me on a trail-running career that, as of this writing, has now spanned parts of three decades.

Enjoying Crystal Mountain felt special. However, the concerns of freezing and of camping cut my reflective period short. I reached a huge, sweeping, right-hand turn that measured 180°. Rounding the corner I saw a new deep valley and a new grand mountain-range to gaze upon. There simply had to be a flat spot on the land between the turns of this gigantic switchback. I scrambled off trail up a steep 15-foot rise to a 10-foot-wide ridge that separated the two sides of the mountain. After bushwhacking around for awhile, I felt satisfied that I'd found the best possible place to set up my shelter. This aerie would have been a great image to add to Henry Shires's on-line Squall gallery.

From my high point, I gained outstanding views of the surrounding darkening mountains. The stars showed themselves. That night marked another in an unmatched series of cloudless jet-black evenings—a remarkable planetarium show. As on dozens of other perfect nights that summer, I looked out toward infinity and wondered if we were alone. The beauty of the unfathomably distant objects soothed me. I felt comfortable with the unknown; I felt comfortable with what was. At peace, I relaxed for a good night's rest.

The sun and I rose together to a cool morning. Given my delays caused by waiting for the White Pass store to open, my road-walk there, my recent trail conversations, and my hike with the young couple, I'd come up a mile or two short of my schedule's mileage. That day the schedule called for only 33.8 miles, one of my shortest days in ages, so it would be easy to make up a few miles. While my day got underway, the sun drew exquisite shadows on the mountainsides.

The morning's exceptional start led me to think that I might really achieve my goal that summer. When my hike ended, though, I would need to readjust to civilization. I stopped myself from thinking along these lines. Hundreds of miles of rough terrain lay ahead. It would be easy to break an ankle on any of the remaining days of the hike, and I had to make sure that I didn't get injured through carelessness. An

AT-hiker friend of mine broke his ankle in a northbound thru-hike near Maine. His dream had been permanently postponed. I knew that if I didn't break the PCT record that summer, I probably never would. Wild fires burned all over the PCT's three states. I still needed Mother Nature's cooperation.

Pre-occupied with more thoughts than usual, I suddenly heard an alarming noise, thought avalanche, and saw movement 150 feet up to my right. A herd of 11 Elk moved elegantly across the steep slopes above me. I enjoyed the family's passing and kept an eye out for falling rocks. Already on the trip I'd witnessed a number of small rock-falls, including one that was triggered by a particularly fat Marmot. Apparently, he'd escaped uninjured in the mini-avalanche.

I'd seen large Elk herds in Banff National Park in Canada and in Yellowstone National Park, but this sighting felt different. Being alone with the animals made our encounter extra special. There were no tourists to say "Look at how cute the baby is" or "The big one is the mother" or "Where the hell did they sleep last night?" I simply enjoyed the animals, as I pleased. Without having to worry about trying to capture their beauty on film, I observed and reveled in the situation. My internal librarian videotaped everything and stored the reel automatically. I could replay the scene whenever I wanted. This fact let me enjoy the present without fear of losing it to the past.

The gap between Snoqualmie Pass and me decreased significantly over the next several hours. I entered numerous clear-cut areas. These stripped landscapes starkly contrasted with many of the pristine segments along the PCT. A clear-cut unintentionally opened my view, but at what cost? I was surprised to see that many clear-cuts hadn't been replanted. Having lived in Washington state previously, I'd become somewhat jaded to clear-cuts. I recalled shouting "Man did that?", when I'd seen my first clear-cut years ago.

The PCT followed and crossed many logging roads in this region. In the dirt-road labyrinth, navigation without a map would have been impossible. Few trail-signs, if any, existed in the area. The trail was marked only with small rock cairns. When I would emerge at a point where the trail crossed a logging road, I would often need to search extensively before I could continue northward. I stuck to my five-minute rule and fortunately never lost big time in this section.

That day, as on virtually every day that summer, I found myself surrounded by Crater-Lake blue skies. I entered a burned-out forest and encountered thousands of bark-free gray trees with limbs still attached. They stood dead on green hillsides, reaching out to me. Their roots and my feet conversed. I felt their pain. The grass and the undergrowth thrived in the fertile soil. The contrast of the only three colors that I could see—blue, gray, and green—presented another priceless creation. I recorded this spectacular color-combination in my library. Feeling fully in tune with nature, I admired the view but never slowed down.

On the evening of July 26th, I sat a mere 27 miles from Snoqualmie Pass—once again two full days ahead of schedule. I felt a controlled excitement. Many times I'd thought of Superman joining me, and this vision would soon be a reality. He was the only person that I knew who could come in "cold" and hike 260-plus miles in one week. Physically, Superman was indestructible, hence his trail name, and I had no doubt whatsoever that mentally he was up to the demanding trek. I just hoped that his flight had arrived in Seattle on time, and that he had encountered no difficulties in reaching Snoqualmie. Knowing Superman, I felt sure that he'd carried his backpack on board the plane, so I didn't give a second thought to the possibility of lost luggage.

On July 27th I faced my shortest mileage in a long time—27 on the 27th. My feet had actually been recovering in Washington. No longer did I regularly hike 40+ miles a day, and even just three fewer miles made all the difference in the world. As I inched closer to the Snoqualmie Pass area that Sunday, I encountered many day-hikers. To my surprise most of them walked with unleashed dogs. My pet peeve is "He won't bite", since "he" has attacked me in the past. Whenever Dottie and Julie hiked with me, I seemed to be the only person carrying leashes. I liked to let them run freely, but not if they would bother other people.

Three inspirational women in their seventies, who were traveling south on the PCT, struck up a conversation with me. I asked how they were doing. The ladies described their "wonderful" multi-course lunch in great detail while taking turns throwing mouth-watering adjectives at me. I made a feeble *yogi* attempt and asked if they had any dessert left over. Nope. Hiking made them hungry, and they'd consumed everything. Since my increasing appetite needed to be satisfied soon, I wished them well and continued northward.

Four miles south of Snoqualmie Pass, I encountered another group of women in their fifties and sixties. The ladies told me that they were heading to their car. Earlier I'd seen their car parked at a dirt-road crossing. When the women learned that I was thru-hiking, they offered to meet me at Snoqualmie. I agreed and said that I'd probably arrive there before they would. We planned to look for each other. In case I didn't meet them again, I said goodbye.

Snoqualmie Pass held many fond memories for me. I'd been there to ski, bike, climb, hike, and run. When traveling to Eastern Washington from Seattle, I'd usually stopped at the pass for a break. I'd hiked on the PCT south of I-90. My feet landed on familiar ground. Nearby Granite Mountain was my favorite mountain to run up. I'd often gone there with Roach, my little Terrier companion. Thinking of Roach, who'd died 14 years earlier, made me sad. She and I had enjoyed many great adventures. Her trail name was "Roachability Factor". While I reminisced, Snoqualmie Pass came into view.

In bright sunlight I descended across an open ski slope. One woman I encountered there was busy picking blueberries. At the bottom of the slope, I reached a parking lot. I became hyper-alert and on the look-out in case Superman had arrived early to surprise me. If he'd jumped out from behind a tree and scared the wits out of me, I'd never hear the end of it. The bulletin-board at the trailhead didn't contain a message from Superman, so I walked toward the Time Wise Grocery & Deli, where we'd planned to meet. I felt excited.

On the way to "town", I entered an environmental station to ask for directions to the deli. Expanded commercialization in the area had made it hard for me to recognize the place. After providing me with directions to the deli, the rangers bombarded me with questions about the PCT. I thanked them for their help, and said a warm goodbye. They loved their jobs.

When I was no more than 25 feet from the ranger station, a woman came out and said, "Wall, take this candy-bar." I'd rarely turned down food on this trip, and I wasn't turning down this offering, either. However, I wasn't going to backtrack. I said, "Thanks; throw it." She smiled and tossed it. I snagged the flying chocolate-bar; it landed in my stomach seconds later. We both waved.

A few minutes later I stood directly outside of the Time Wise Grocery & Deli. The sun felt hot at the 3,000-foot pass. I'd never been here on a hotter day. Tourists, who were dressed in lightweight summer clothing, milled around. I checked out all of them in my search for Superman. Since I was three hours early, though, I didn't expect to see Superman yet. When had I last seen so many cars and so many people? Was it in San Diego? I couldn't recall. I left the sunlight to purchase snack-food.

When I exited the store, I phoned Superman. He'd arrived in Seattle on schedule. Yippee! At that moment he was standing in line at a Blimpie in North Bend, Washington, roughly an hour from the pass. He would arrive here by 4:30 pm bringing along two large subs for me. Our reunion and upcoming adventure filled us with excitement. I felt that the most difficult phase of my hike was over. My entire summer had been focused on reaching this point on schedule. I breathed a sigh of relief.

My pre-hike plan had been to go into the Seattle area for a break after I reached Snoqualmie—do laundry, take a shower, and drink beer. However, Superman and I faced 260-plus miles in one week. This mileage wasn't bad for me, but seemed brutal for anyone coming from civilization. We had decided that we should return to the trail shortly after he met me. We could hike nine miles that night and get further ahead of schedule; so much for my 27-mile day. Our head start would give us some insurance. Superman was eager to hit the trail, too.

I made a few more phone calls to bring family and friends up-to-date. They encouraged me. In order to relieve my feet, I sat down on the blacktop. From my pavement chair I watched tourists entering and exiting the deli. Everyone seemed to be rushing off somewhere. Now that I'd reached Snoqualmie Pass, I felt relaxed. I drank plenty of fluids and ate salty fatty snack-foods. The final stage of my long-term dream would commence soon.

While anticipating Superman's arrival, I reflected back to the time when Gumby and I had run from Snoqualmie Pass to Stevens Pass in one day. That 75-mile training-run had taken place 17 years earlier. Its route had followed the PCT and had involved nearly 30,000 feet of ascending and descending. I'd found the "run" in my Washington state hiking-book by searching for its most-demanding hike. The book cautioned that this trip required seven days and that a hiker should carry a minimum of eight days worth of food. Our successful run had become a legend in the Department of Computer Science and Engineering at the University of Washington, and our story has been retold there by others countless times. Neither Gumby nor I had repeated the traverse. I looked forward to seeing the terrain which we had been over so many years earlier. Superman and I planned to do this stretch in two days. Even this feat would be exceptionally difficult.

Superman arrived before 5 pm for an emotional reunion. We felt relieved to see each other and exchanged bear hugs. For the moment we focused on gear, resupply, and trail details. I ate my subs, as we repackaged supplies. My leaky Platypus got replaced. This meant no more sticky legs for me that summer. We loaded plenty of Compeed and Advil into our backpacks.

As we were departing, the three ladies who had planned a rendezvous with me at Snoqualmie arrived. They insisted on buying us ice cream. Although I'd just eaten snacks and subs, we didn't turn them down. On the AT Fish had once told me, "Wall, never look a gift beer in the mouth." Since that day, I've been taking candy from strangers. We ate the ice-cream, chatted for awhile, crowded together for a group photo, and waved goodbye to civilization. While catching up on each other's lives, Superman and I flew off into the woods.

Wall at the southern terminus
of the PCT on May 12, 2003.

Wall heading into chaparral near the southern terminus.

Jenny holding a Horned Lizard.

Fish and Wall relaxing at Kennedy Meadows.

A hot Wall with trekking-poles north of Mojave.

Wall at a much-needed water cache in the desert.

A sunburned Wall's lasik surgery;
PCT in the background.

Wall relieving back stress.
Note the PCT marker in the foreground.

Fish and Wall at the PCT
high point, self-portrait.

Fish enjoying perfect weather in the High Sierras.

A tired-of-postholing Fish back
in the water in the Sierras.

Hikers crossing a large snowfield in the Sierras.

A very hungry Wall standing at 12,000 feet at Muir Hut.

Wall crossing a small creek on an easy natural bridge.

Trail angels Karen and Liz at Crater Lake, Oregon.

Generous trail angels buy ice-cream for Superman
and Wall at Snoqualmie Pass, Washington.

Superman in an alpine forest during another glorious day.

Wall standing on a blow-down
in Washington's mountains.

A thin Wall encounters mules on the trail.

Superman ready to hit the trail again after refueling.

Wall with tiny pack approaching a Mountain
Goat in a massive rock-avalanche area north
of Snoqualmie Pass in Washington.

Massive descent, massive ascent in northern Washington.

Smiling Superman and Wall
in Canada on August 3, 2003.

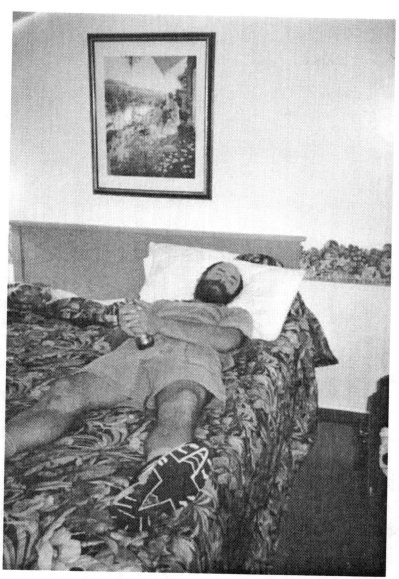

A fading Wall trying to open another beer
on the *very* day that he finished the trail.

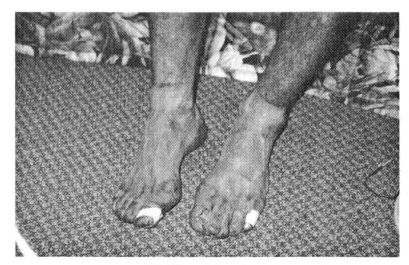

Wall's aching feet.

The incredible cake that we celebrated
with in Sammamish, Washington.

16 Superman Flies in the North Cascades

Only the final leg of my journey remained. On July 27th at 5 pm Superman and I hiked north on the PCT from mile 2,396.3. My birthday present was our reunion. Having Superman accompany me for the duration of the hike meant that my most difficult mental struggles lay behind me. For several weeks I'd been dividing the hike into two parts: the miles until hooking up with Superman, and the last week. I'd completed the first part successfully. If nothing went wrong now, I could finish the PCT—in record time. I worried about the possibility of Superman's getting injured, but he was too strong and too muscular to get hurt. As when Fish had joined me, I felt a strong sense of responsibility for my companion's welfare.

Superman and I had crewed for each other during 100-mile trail runs and had done a number of other sporting events together, including Ironman Triathlons, scuba-diving, and climbing high mountains. We'd been in the Swiss Alps climbing many peaks, including the rock-fall-prone Matterhorn; in Chile climbing Aconcagua; in Russia climbing Elbrus; and in Australia climbing Kosciusko. Superman would push himself to new limits to help me fulfill my long-term dream. Few people understood how much this hike meant to me; he was one of them. Superman's presence and understanding enhanced the trip enormously.

Since we'd just left a road-crossing and a resupply point, we found ourselves climbing. Superman's first steps on the PCT in Washington state were uphill and were a good indication of what lay ahead. We soon passed the 2,400-mile mark—another huge milestone for me. I celebrated with a birthday smile. We traveled light and carried just two-and-a-half days worth of food. In our first six miles we climbed

2,500 feet. Superman breathed hard, but responded well. The mountain views looked spectacular, and the weather felt warm. Having my close friend with me alleviated my foot pain and my mental anguish.

Superman and I exchanged many stories in our early miles, and time passed quickly for us. Superman talked about his family, farm, and company, and I talked about my feet. We reflected on how lucky we'd been in our lives. The two of us felt rewarded by our hard work. We shared a deep love of life and an enormous respect for one another. Our abnormally-high energy-levels allowed us to live our dreams. Our friendship allowed us to dream bigger.

On that night we found a flat grassy area to set up camp. I'd wanted to erect the Squall before dark to assure us a good resting-place. At least for Superman's first evening, I didn't want him sleeping on rocks and on bushes at a 20° tilt. Our campsite marked the best one that I'd found in weeks. We'd stopped early, and I'd enjoyed an easy day—only 36 miles. Combined with his travel to the west coast, Superman had taken full advantage of his time on that day. This man didn't waste many days. The evening provided an outstanding starburst sunset. We fell asleep feeling happy.

My schedule called for days of 39.1, 35.9, 34.6, 35.2, 35.9, 36.6, and 44.8 miles. We'd just hiked nine miles prior to starting into this period. We applied these nine miles to our last day, so we needed to do only 35.8 miles on that final day. I felt good that we'd gotten the jump on my ambitious schedule, since I wasn't sure if we could pull a 45-mile day at the end of this difficult stretch. Superman felt encouraged by our revised plan.

The next day we began early. Superman remained on east-coast time, so he had no problem getting up at first light, at around 5:20 am. He must have been sore from the previous day's climbs, though, but because of his positive outlook and leadership abilities, he said nothing. Our first full day of hiking went great. I described Fish's and my routine to him in terms of having dinner on the trail at 6 pm or so, and then continuing to hike until the day's miles had been completed. He felt comfortable with this plan. We passed through gorgeous mountains and enjoyed phenomenal weather. In one particularly rocky area we circled a mountainside and saw a handful of Mountain Goats. Since I hadn't seen any in the Goat Rocks Wilderness, this sighting felt special.

Seeing certain animals in nature touched me. Moose did, and I now learned that Mountain Goats did, too.

Superman thoughtfully carried a disposable camera. We believed that it had 25 exposures. While maneuvering around, we tried to frame a good shot of the Mountain Goats. These wise-looking animals acted shy, but we did successfully snap pictures of each of us with at least one Mountain Goat. The PCT traversed huge avalanche areas. The Mountain Goats moved with ease on the uneven rocky surfaces, but we twisted and turned our ankles. While whistling their warning calls, Marmots ducked in and out of jagged rock formations. Superman taught himself to imitate their language perfectly. His Marmot conversations made me laugh.

The section between Snoqualmie Pass and Stevens Pass is a popular two-week backpacking trip. We encountered several groups of hikers doing this route. During such meetings, we would share information about trail conditions and our journeys. Although our encounters seemed brief, we felt close to the hikers that we'd talked with. We wished other parties well and vice versa. Everyone we had seen carried at least double the amount of equipment that we did. Our friendly conversations about gear reductions added to our enjoyment.

Because the temperatures in the northern Washington mountains far exceeded those in southern Maine, Superman felt hot. We frequently crossed rivers during that time and obtained as much water as we needed. I hoped that a good water supply would hold out for the remainder of the trek. As my trip drew to a close, I became less concerned about giardia. If I contracted giardia now, the symptoms wouldn't manifest themselves until I'd finished the PCT. For some reason I didn't care what happened to me then. As a result, I no longer treated water from fast-moving streams and creeklets. Superman had lived all over the world, including in many Third World countries, and considered himself to be totally immune to any bacteria, so he nearly always drank the water without treating it. He savored crystal-clear, icy-cold, mountain water. When we added iodine, it just wasn't the same.

Superman and I decided to take a dip in "the chilly tarn", at mile 2,425.6. High, craggy, snowy peaks surrounded the beautiful bowl. We stripped in the hot sun and jumped in naked. Superman said that the ice-cold water felt warmer than what he was used to swimming off the coast of Maine. I smiled. The cold didn't affect him. The water temperature in my outdoor pool in Savannah sometimes reaches 90°F, so this snow-melt tarn felt nippy to me. We savored this swim in case we didn't have time for another dip on this trip.

While I re-bandaged my feet, Superman and I sunned ourselves. After our enjoyable repose, we hiked north, continuing through rugged country. Eventually, we sat down for dinner on the heavily-creosoted Waptus River Bridge, at mile 2,433.4. I had reasoned that fewer bugs flew near the middle of the river. Although the strong-smelling bridge bothered us, I'd guessed right about the bugs, plus we had easy access to drinking-water. Superman ate half the quantity of food that I did. He still had some reserves, but I looked like skin and bones. My schedule had called for us to camp near the Waptus River that night, but we pushed on toward Deep Lake. While accompanied by a friend, I felt comfortable using my headlamp, so we night-hiked more than I had done alone. Having two lights gave us redundancy in case of an emergency.

In the late-evening darkness Superman and I came to a trail junction. Off to our right campers partied around a roaring fire. Much of the woods in the Northwest faced burning restrictions because of extreme dryness. I doubted that their fire was legal. We branched to the left. The pitch blackness prevented us from knowing if this trail was the PCT or a spur. This fact necessitated camping soon. After crossing a large meadow, we arrived at Deep Lake. Relying 100% on the head-lamp lights, we erected the Squall within 10 feet of the lake shore. Amazingly, the bugs barely affected us. I climbed into the Squall first. Superman came in after I'd arranged my gear inside the shelter, since the limited space prevented us from working simultaneously without getting in each other's way.

Superman rose early the next morning and reconnoitered for the PCT. While he was gone, a tame deer meandered into camp. The healthy unconcerned doe sauntered within eight feet of me and didn't blink. I marveled at her beauty. Would she get shot during hunting-season? Enjoy life now, while you can, I thought. Although I've never heard of a deer smiling, she seemed to. This lovely encounter stirred my passions.

Superman was gone a long time. When he finally returned, he indicated that we'd gone past the PCT. Good thing we'd stopped last night when we did. While Superman made final preparations, I hit the trail. I waited for him at the ford of the outlet to Deep Lake. Our shoes got wet on this ford, since the water-level exceeded the height of the stones which someone had placed at two-foot intervals across the creek. The rock bridge allowed us to keep our socks dry, though.

Superman and I hiked hard that day, passing a number of north-bound section-hikers. Our goal was to reach Stevens Pass, at mile 2,471.6, by 6:30 pm, where we'd meet our resupply crew—Laurel, Mac, Lois, and Honey. We flew down a long dusty descent which led to a dirt ski-area parking lot. We arrived at 7 pm. Our crew met us there, as we emerged from the woods. They felt relieved and overjoyed to see us, and we did likewise. We filled them in on the details of the past two days. Our support team carried out folding chairs for us. I felt like a boxer resting in my corner. We'd been beaten up by the PCT, but we would recover before the next round. Our crew made us sand-wiches, filled our water-containers, and gave us to-go bags of grapes and cherries.

In addition to Superman's and my basic needs of food and drink, our crew provided us with much-needed love, encouragement, and good cheer. While they'd been waiting for us to arrive, they'd talked to some other hikers. That conversation had helped them to better understand our needs. They unselfishly gave to us. We felt extremely grateful for their support.

By no means was my thru-hike a done deal—the North Cascades are home to many bears, wildfires burned nearby, we could get injured, and we could get lost. I knew better than most the difficulties that lay ahead. We took several pictures as darkness encroached. Our friend Mac, who was 79 years old at that time and who has had serious back trouble for decades, inspired me greatly when he picked up my fully-loaded pack and put it on my back as we readied for departure. Superman and I said a heartfelt thanks. We crossed Highway 2 at 8 pm in search of the darkening northbound trail.

I felt incredulous that Gumby and I had covered this same terrain from Snoqualmie Pass to Stevens Pass in one day. I have never heard of anyone else doing this stretch in one day, and, reflecting back on that run, our accomplishment was hard to comprehend. On that particular day, I had already biked 30 miles, had swum 2, and had run 5 when the call from Gumby had come that if we were going to do this mega-run, which we'd been talking about, then that night was it. I had agreed.

Gumby and I had driven separately from Seattle to Stevens Pass to drop my old Toyota Corolla there. We had left nothing but a six-pack of cheap beer in its trunk. Then we had driven from Stevens Pass to Snoqualmie Pass, where we had slept for a few hours in the bed of Gumby's truck. We had left early in the morning, carrying almost no gear and almost no food. After an outrageous 40-mile bonk, massive climbs, and deep descents, we had arrived at Stevens Pass to our lone six-pack.

Gumby and I had guzzled the warm beers. We had then driven to Snoqualmie Pass after our 10-minute break. I had headed toward Seattle, falling asleep in rush-hour traffic on I-520, waking up only when the drivers behind me had leaned heavily on their horns. We'd missed the first day of the quarter at the University of Washington, and my illiotibial band had hurt for six months after this epic. Having just hiked over that same terrain, I fully appreciated Gumby's and my earlier effort.

According to the information that Superman and I had received at Stevens Pass, we could expect hot and dry weather for the duration of our hike. My worry about fires had been eliminated when we'd learned that the large blaze burning in northern Washington was a long way east of the PCT. If a section of the trail had been closed due to fire, my dream would have been extinguished. Coping with that disappointment would have been difficult. I had been lucky to reach this point of my hike. Repeating what I'd already accomplished so far that summer within the same time-frame seemed impossible. If the PCT had been closed due to fire danger, my judgment would have been severely tested. Thank goodness that Superman was along to keep me rational.

Superman and I felt bloated after our feast at Stevens Pass. We carried heavy loads in our packs, too. Even though I felt full, I ate my grapes and cherries, spitting the seeds off trail. The dense brush obscured all viable targets, so I had nothing to aim at. Superman decided to save his fruit until the next day. Since the blackberry bushes looked full, we'd figured bears wouldn't bother us over a bag of fruit.

My schedule called for us to hike to Bridge Creek, at mile 2,577.3, in three days with the goal of resupplying at Stehekin River Road, at mile 2,569.3. The revised plan called for a resupply at Rainy Pass's Highway 20, at mile 2,589.1. We hoped to arrive there on August 1st by 9 pm. When we'd left Stevens Pass, the intent was to hike six more miles that night, but we came up short. This fact meant that we needed to cover 115 trail miles in the next three days over unknown and difficult terrain. This distance would test us.

Superman and I hiked in the midst of the warmest and driest summer in over 100 years in the state of Washington. Superman felt affected by the heat, and he drank enormous volumes of water. Each ice-cold stream brought him relief. Superman drank twice the quantity that I drank, and I continued to eat twice the quantity that he ate. Our average hiking speed during this stretch was two-and-a-half miles per hour. So to go 40 miles, assuming no wrong turns, we needed to hike 16 hours. I became concerned that we wouldn't make our resupply rendezvous.

Being on my feet for 16 hours hurt a great deal. My internal switching network functioned well, and it helped me to endure. I wasn't afraid to leave pain switches off this close to the end of the hike. Ignoring my pain was the only way that I could walk 40 miles per day. Adding the time that we spent on bathroom breaks, acquiring water, camp set-up and tear-down, eating, map-consulting, and hiker encounters to the 16 hours that we spent on walking didn't leave a lot of time for sleeping. We made the best of our situation, though.

The night after we'd left Stevens Pass we reached Baekos Creek. We'd descended in the dark to a reasonable campsite near the creek. The steep descent had fatigued us. While I erected the Squall, Superman obtained creek water. We'd passed several pairs of hikers that day. Some of them planned to hike to Manning Park—our final destination. They provided us some security. If we had a total melt-down along the PCT, they'd be coming along behind us. For most of the summer I was too far ahead of those behind me to enjoy such a "safety net".

Superman and I both slept well that night due to our great exhaustion. In the morning we felt thankful for the little bridge spanning the creek. Starting a long day with wet shoes and socks always made for an even longer day. Although we never really talked about it, we knew that for the remainder of the hike we needed to wake up shortly after 5 am. We wouldn't be getting the proper amount of rest until we reached Canada.

The great weather created great views. This combination helped ease our pains. Reaching 5,710-foot Wards Pass, at mile 2,500.6, marked another big milestone for me. Only one more multiple of 100 miles remained. Each time Superman and I saw the majestic Mount Rainier, which I'd gone by ages ago near Chinook Pass, at mile 2,327.5, we'd say in unison "Enjoy it. That's the last view of Rainier." Amazingly, with the tremendous visibility and with the clear skies, we still saw Mount Rainier from near the summit of the 6,500-foot Reds Pass, at mile 2,510.0.

The surroundings made us feel blessed. Mother Nature gave us a show. The massive peaks in Washington popped straight up through the earth's crust and reached skyward, held down only by huge sheets of ice. The extraordinary views of Glacier Peak uplifted us. Superman and I would have loved to have climbed on nearby glaciers, but instead we focused on going north. If our lives permitted, we would come back here.

Early on July 31st, we reached the frigid fast-moving Kennedy Creek. The zero-visibility water was saturated with gray glacial silt. This bridgeless crossing looked treacherous. An avalanche and a flood had wiped out any sign that a bridge had ever stood here. The water-level was far too high to contemplate crossing where the PCT did. Having been through many dangerous fords in the High Sierras, I approached this crossing more lightly than I should have. We planned to hike 40 miles that day, and I didn't want to waste any time reconnoitering the area.

We walked upstream and not too far from the PCT, we encountered a thin log that nearly spanned the creek. This "creek" was, in fact, a raging river. Superman didn't like the looks of the natural bridge, and neither did I. He stepped onto the questionable bridge. It was too thin, too slick, and too unstable. I watched the log vibrate. When Superman attempted to sturdy himself with his trekking-poles, he found the water too deep to reach the bottom. The current flowed too strong, and his poles got swept out horizontally. After a brave attempt, he'd gone forward only seven feet and retreated via unsafe blind backpedaling.

I said that I would make the crossing. On this trip, whenever I'd made such a decision, it was final. I would either make the crossing or fall in trying. Under no circumstances would I retreat. Superman didn't bother trying to reason with me. He knew that doing so would be futile; he understood my mental state and also my new-found abilities. I'd studied the situation, and although it seemed exceptionally dangerous, I felt capable of getting across.

My pack had no waist-belt, so I didn't need to undo any straps. After lengthening my telescoping trekking-poles, I took a good look at Superman. He stared at me. This eye-contact might be our last. If I fell into the boiling glacial water, we didn't know what would happen. The thought of my lungs filling with the ice-cold gray water bothered me. The PCT controlled my destiny, perhaps for the final time.

Gulping several lung-filling breaths of air, I made my way onto the thin blow-down. It immediately rocked. I attempted to find the bottom with my trekking-poles to gain stability, as Superman had done, but even while leaning over as far as possible, my effort made no difference. The water ran too fast and too deep, so prevented me from steadying myself. Glancing down at the ever-changing river to see if I could utilize any rocks, I spotted a few that occasionally broke the surface and poled on them to help me balance.

Looking past the sides of the log in search of pole placements created other problems. First of all it distracted me from my next foot-placement. Secondly, it caused vertigo, since the river raced so quickly. Staring at the silty river produced a sensation that I moved fast, while the water remained stationary. Despite my dizziness, I proceeded. My previous three steps brought me past the point of return. Had I made a big mistake? I dredged up all my courage and my will-power to push out self-doubt.

I stood only one foot above the water's surface. The whitewater splashed onto the narrow log, making my bridge even slicker. The crux of the crossing lay in the next 15 feet. When the final trekking-pole placements disappeared behind me, my chance of losing it increased dramatically. I would go Wallenda-style the remainder of the way. Extreme fatigue overwhelmed me. I felt like I'd been on the log for minutes. Had I? "You need to move, Ray," I said—softly so that my lips wouldn't move and throw me off balance. My legs trembled. I thought that Superman could see them shaking. If he had said anything, I didn't hear it over the roar of the crashing whitewater.

I sucked in another deep breath, being careful not to move my head to either side. As I wobbled forward on the tapering tree, it then occurred to me that I could balance myself better by placing the trekking-poles on the tree itself. The hardened steel tips on my poles had been ground down to stubs hundreds of miles earlier, so I couldn't stick the blunt ends into the wood, but perhaps I could get a slight bite.

While testing out the solution that I'd just thought up, I reached forward with my right hand and placed the trekking-pole on the log just ahead of where I'd step next. This method worked, and I moved forward slowly. When only five feet from the shore, I noticed that the tree had only three more usable feet. My legs and my feet were so battered that I couldn't jump more than two feet. I made one final firm foot-placement and flung myself toward the shore. I landed, painfully, but safely. "Whew!" I exclaimed, exhaling forcefully.

Once on shore, I was able to wipe my brow to prevent any more sweat from entering my eyes. When I turned around, I saw that Superman stood frozen, staring blankly. I couldn't even imagine the thoughts that had gone through his mind during these difficult moments. The whitewater prevented communication. Superman appeared very relieved, but only for a moment. Having witnessed my hairy crossing, there was no way that he would attempt this feat a second time. He bushwhacked upstream, disappearing from my view around a corner. I walked downstream and rejoined the PCT, wondering how long he'd be gone. The crossing had sucked away all my energy. I felt drained. When would the trail get safer? I prayed for that day.

I found a comfortable rock and sat down to stop my trembling legs. From the mesh part of my G4, I pulled out a large bag of as-yet-uncrushed Fritos. While eating handfuls, I occasionally looked upstream for Superman. I wondered how he would make his way back down on the north side of the ford, as a steep cliff fell to the river's edge. Twenty minutes had elapsed, but still no sign. I simply had to wait and to hope for the best. Thoughts of making the dreaded call to his family drowned out everything else.

While I filled my stomach and calmed my nerves, a couple arrived at the south side of the ford. Based on their large packs, I guessed that they were section-hikers. They shouted across to me, and I assumed had asked where I'd crossed. The noisy river and its width prevented me from hearing their voices. I pointed upstream to my narrow-log bridge. They headed off in Superman's direction shaking their heads. As Superman had done, they soon disappeared. Would they find him?

Ten minutes later Superman returned, exhausted. Thank God! He described his harrowing ford, where he'd used a sapling as a vaulter's pole to reach a boulder mid-river. With whitewater gushing all around him, he'd made a five-foot standing jump to safety. He'd walked a long way up river to find his crossing, and it didn't sound as if I could have handled that one. Superman rested for a few moments, his shirt completely drenched in sweat, but we needed to make our daily miles.

Our delay at Kennedy Creek meant hiking another 45 minutes in the dark. At night, even with both of our headlamps on, we could travel at best only two-thirds of our daytime speed. I thought that by now all thru-hikers were at least two weeks behind me and prayed that none of them would find Kennedy Creek at this high a water-level. The crossing would have been dangerous, though, even with just half its present flow.

At Snoqualmie Pass Superman and I had pushed our original re-supply point 20 miles farther north to Rainy Pass from Stehekin River Road. We really needed to hike hard to make this pick-up, and I became concerned that we couldn't. On the other hand, if we successfully made it to Rainy Pass on the evening of August 1st, that meant we would need to hike only 60 miles to complete the PCT and then another seven miles to leave the woods and reach Manning Park. Our penultimate day would be difficult, but our last day would be much shorter than originally planned. Superman and I had no choice but to hike quickly for as long as possible in our efforts to reach Rainy Pass.

The scenery during this stretch impressed us. When the mountains allowed them, the fabulous weather afforded us 100-mile views. We traveled through many passes and past dozens of beautiful lakes. Mica Lake, at mile 2,527.2, housed bluish-green icebergs. A perfectly-shaped evergreen "Christmas tree" floated on one berg. We wondered how the tree had landed on top of the glistening iceberg. The beauty of the lake stirred us. We agreed to return to this picturesque spot at a future time. However, we knew that no circumstances could ever match those of the present. I took another good look, storing the image in my library, and then moved north without stopping.

During this section, Superman and I occasionally applied insect repellent. The mosquitoes weren't horrible, unless you paused. We didn't have time to stop except for bathroom breaks and water refills, so we didn't get bitten too much. I felt thankful that the bugs weren't as bad as those in the Sky Lakes Wilderness. Circumstances could have been much worse. We'd also expected rain every day in Washington. The perfect weather gave us a real boost.

The endless descents trashed our quads in the breath-taking North Cascades. We would reach the top of one pass, see no sign of humankind in any direction, and then plunge for hours, down thousands of feet, to a valley floor. As we descended mountainsides, the forests became denser and the trees larger. Temperatures and humidity soared, as we dropped lower in elevation. Water flowed plentifully in the valleys. Once we'd refilled our water-containers, we always faced huge ascents. We were amazed at how far this National Park sprawled. It stretched in every direction as far as we could see. This remoteness made it exceptionally beautiful, but also scary. If one of us got injured, the other could do little to help. The latter point never became more obvious than when Superman fell.

We'd been walking for many hours, when we arrived at a small creeklet crossing. This one appeared no different from any of the 20 or so that we'd forded recently, except for the fact that someone had placed a debarked log across it. An invisible film of water ran over the stripped log. Superman led the way. When he stepped onto the two-foot-diameter log, his leg shot out from under him. He instantly began falling down the mountainside. Watching from behind, I felt helpless to assist my companion.

Superman apparently had glanced downhill in the fraction of a second that he was permitted. A fallen tree waited to impale him. His body became completely rigid. He hopped once, leaning backward, and miraculously, lay down, thus slipping below the lance. I couldn't comprehend his gymnastic maneuver. Thoughts of what would have happened if he'd been mortally wounded filled my head. Despite being horribly shaken, Superman immediately rejoined the trail. "Great save, Paul!"

In Superman's state-of-shock, he made the same foot-placement that he'd made earlier! This time he slipped and lunged uphill. The danger was far less in that direction, and he recovered quickly. His word-choice expressed utter disgust and anger. Still slightly stunned, he walked directly through the creeklet, soaking his boots. I moved from my three-minute home, following him into the creeklet. My New Balance shoes emerged drenched. I wasn't going to step on the greased log. The PCT could alter our plans in a second.

17 The Home Stretch

To reach Rainy Pass on August 1st by 9 pm, we couldn't be more than 37 miles south of it on July 31st. If we could walk from 6 am until 9 pm at two-and-a-half miles per hour, this plan would give us 15 hours of hiking time for a total of 37.5 miles. Since we'd been starting hiking at 5:30 am, our plan provided a little insurance, too. We achieved our mileage goal on the last day of July, but we had hiked a couple of hours after dark to do it. Also, we had to settle on a less-than-desirable campsite in the black of night.

Superman made an incredible effort to put in the miles that I needed. The mountainous terrain challenged us, as did the hot temperatures. Superman's feet ached, and his body absorbed lots of punishment. He never complained once, but I could tell that he felt exhausted. Superman wanted checkpoints along the trail, so his mind could convince his body that the treadmill would end some day. The knowledge that another mile had been covered comforted him. If we had made a wrong turn, Superman's morale would have suffered a big blow, so I did my best to keep us on track.

We seemed to be in good shape to make our tightly-scheduled rendezvous at Rainy Pass. August 1st, though, was another day when we couldn't swim, wash, or talk much with section-hikers. We focused all of our energy on advancing north. Shortly after crossing Suiattle Pass, at mile 2,550.3, I realized that the gap to the border measured less than 100 miles. This fact meant a lot to me, since I had run over 100 miles in a single day.

With the end in sight, I felt that nothing could stop us now. If I broke an ankle, I'd hike to the border injured. A chill trickled down my spine; my dream would come true! Superman shared my joy. My sustained effort throughout the summer rewarded me with a deep inner satisfaction. Any more thoughts along these lines, though, and I would start crying. Keep hiking. Just keep hiking.

We arrived at Hemlock Camp, at mile 2,557.3, and all appeared well. I scouted the huge campground, but couldn't find the PCT leading through it. After some deliberations we followed a trail leading to our right. We had an uneasy feeling about this trail. If we'd guessed wrong, the answer would be disheartening. The sign that I'd seen marking this trail troubled me. I couldn't help feeling that we were off course. There was little to do, except to keep hiking to see where the trail led.

Superman and I blasted over a number of rolling hills and hiked strongly. The sun shone brightly off to my left. Off to my *left*! S—! Our steps had carried us in the wrong direction. We'd made a wrong turn and had headed south from Hemlock Camp on a trail following the South Fork of Agnes Creek. When we realized my mistake, Superman had looked devastated. I figured that we'd gone at least three-quarters of a mile out of our way. Thank God I'd caught the sun on the wrong side when I did, and that the early- morning hours permitted me to determine our direction. A little farther ahead and the mountains would have blocked the sun. If the time had been closer to noon, we'd have walked south for hours. I felt lucky, but Superman felt depressed.

I decided to hurry back ahead of Superman and scout for the PCT. It was best at this moment to give him a chance to walk alone. While Superman regrouped, I went in search of the PCT. He was probably cursing right and left, following me at a distance. The fast pace that I moved at helped to dissipate my frustrations. My mistake meant hiking another hour that night, and I felt bad about that.

When I arrived back at Hemlock Camp 15 minutes later, I proceeded through the gigantic camp, and sure enough, the PCT continued on the other side. If I'd gone only another 50 feet here 45 minutes earlier, I would have discovered this fact. I sure wished that there'd been a PCT marker in the vicinity. Backtracking to the front of the camp, I sat down and ate a snack, while I waited for Superman. He arrived 10 minutes later, dejected but glad to know that I had re-found the trail. We pushed north, trying to make up time, hoping that no more wrong turns would plague us.

During the next section of the PCT, giant Douglas-firs, huge spruces, and enormous red-cedars greeted us in magical old-growth forests. The Douglas-firs rose straight up at least 150 feet and measured six-to-eight feet in diameter. The spruces topped the biggest that I had ever seen. The red-cedars grew 25-to-35 feet around, and tapered toward the sky, their tips invisible from the forest floor. This stretch contained the most-impressive forests of the entire trip.

The old forests inspired us and lifted our morale. We hiked well through the dark woods, which provided us shelter from the powerful sun. By PCT standards the terrain lay flat and low in elevation, as it reached only 2,500 feet above sea-level. The trees thrived closer to sea-level. If we'd had enough film, I would have suggested a picture here. We had precious few shots left, though. I recorded hundreds of images of trees in my library.

For the remainder of that day Superman worried about our getting lost. If we did get lost, it would be exceptionally hard to make up any time. Our minds couldn't deal with another detour. We pressed toward Canada as hard as we could, and arrived at Rainy Pass a mere half-an-hour behind schedule. Laurel was there alone, in the middle of nowhere, waiting to meet us. Her support meant the world to me. As the temperatures dropped, we crossed a deserted highway and entered a large trailhead parking lot. This damp place marked our last stop. Here at 5,000 feet we would complete our final resupply in total darkness. Realizing that this time was the final time that I'd go through my resupply ritual caused deep reflection and brought emotions to the surface.

Superman and I devoured meat-and-cheese sandwiches, chocolate-chip cookies, potato-chips, and other high-calorie foods. We drank as much Gatorade and Coke as our stomachs could handle. Since we were only two days from finishing, I dumped all unnecessary gear. Although I'd never had any safety net nor redundancy in my gear to this stage, I went even lighter now. The last items to go included my nail-clippers, tooth-brush, and tooth-paste. Superman emptied his pack, too. I even thought of ditching the tarptent, but with two potentially-cold nights of camping and a lame sleeping-bag, I decided to retain the shelter.

Time passed rapidly, and 10 pm arrived too soon. After Superman and I had changed the batteries in our headlamps, we said goodbye to Laurel and returned to the PCT. She had done an amazing job resupplying us and restoring our morale. As we headed uphill with our lights shining, we saw the last of the highway and Rainy Pass. We carried only two days worth of food, so our packs felt light. In the darkness we struggled to Porcupine Creek, at mile 2,590.6, and felt lucky to find a reasonable campsite. We both believed that I would finish the PCT in record time. This anticipation kept us motivated and gave us a great sense of accomplishment. Having Superman to share in the joy made the experience very meaningful.

The next day as we hiked through rugged terrain, I saw a brown-colored bear in the bushes 100 yards off the PCT. He looked at me and bolted. I couldn't tell whether the bear was a Grizzly or a Black Bear. Fortunately, we never got another look at him. Bear-scat littered the trail, and berries appeared plentiful in the woods. In this stretch we often stayed near 5,000 feet. We told ourselves that bears would be lower down, enjoying the berries, which we thought grew better near sea-level. When we passed the 2,600-mile point, I felt a special strength inside me. This mileage barrier would be my last multiple of 100 miles.

On our penultimate day, we'd missed a "pleasant trailside camp-site with water" that we'd been counting on for refilling our bottles. The sunny weather roasted us. Since the Pacific Northwest was experiencing one of the most severe droughts on record, we found several water-sources dry. I hadn't anticipated a lack of water in the North-west. We felt severely dehydrated. Superman's parched lips indicated particularly-bad cotton-mouth.

After finishing the last of my water (his was already long gone), Superman sank to a low point. Being out of a critical resource, cou-pled with the uncertainty of knowing where and when we'd find more, wreaked havoc on our tired minds. Superman's pack seemed to contain only kryptonite. We'd been pushing close to 17-hour days, hiking from 5:30 am until 10:30 pm, and even this man's great stamina approached its absolute limit. Superman's dehydration was extreme.

I needed to do something to obtain more water before Superman fell down. Since it was a Sunday, I hoped to encounter day-hikers. When we were on our last legs, a south-bounder crossed our path. I asked if he could spare any water. The man graciously gave us a full liter. Shortly thereafter, his wife arrived, and she too gave us a liter.

Superman drank most of the water, while I just wet my whistle. We felt thankful. The couple told us of the fires burning to the east, but assured us that the remainder of the PCT to Canada was not ablaze. This news meant that Mother Nature wouldn't stop me.

The two of us hiked north, still dehydrated, but far better off. Before long, we encountered two young women who intended to hike from Snoqualmie Pass to Manning Park. They'd planned a 17-day trip. When they heard that we'd left Snoqualmie only five days earlier, they became interested in our journey. The red-headed Canadian from Vancouver offered me a liter of her water. I accepted and downed the needed fluid within seconds. This prompted her brown-haired American friend to offer Superman a liter. He downed that even more quickly. We repeated the process a second time while we bantered back and forth. After the two section-hikers took a series of photos with us, we thanked them profusely for their kindness, said goodbye, and headed toward Canada.

Superman and I had come nearly 40 miles that day as darkness fell upon us. The elevation measured over 6,000 feet. The cooling temperatures forced us to put on our NorthFace wind-breakers. We wore our headlamps, and I consulted the *Databook* via my spotlight. If we could find Devils Backbone, I could pinpoint our position. Surely a feature with such an intriguing name would be easy to spot. Instead of finding Devils Backbone, we became momentarily lost, perhaps on top of the backbone itself? The starry night appeared beautiful from our vantage-point, but we should have been descending rather than traveling over flat ground, so we couldn't admire the light-show properly. We finally found a series of steep switchbacks and began heading downhill. Superman and I had probably been standing on the backbone.

Concentrating on anything in our state of absolute exhaustion seemed impossible. Superman and I had already been hiking the trail for 17 hours that day. Our minds wandered aimlessly. We couldn't have hiked without the headlamps, but the lighting which they provided was far less than adequate. They opened a fuzzy window of visibility only six feet long and three feet wide. We swiveled our necks in order to see anywhere except directly in front of us. This tedious maneuvering made us even more dizzy. As my fatigue worsened, unpleasant visions of multi-headed Grizzly Bears leaping out of the woods and grabbing us played in my mind. I didn't worry Superman with my delusions.

I'd noted earlier in *Volume II* that just three-quarters of a mile beyond the headwaters of Shaw Creek, at mile 2,629.6, a good campsite existed. Superman thought that he saw the headwaters and, pointing, said, "Over there. You see the lake?"

"That's a rock slide," I said, realizing that the combination of starlight, moonlight, headlamp light, and deep fatigue had fooled Superman's eyes. Or was I wrong?

"No, over there," he insisted, pointing to the exact same spot, which was a rock avalanche leaning at a 45° angle.

"Paul, it's a rock slide. I see it clearly."

Superman and I needed to camp soon. His mind and his body were starting to malfunction, as were mine. A huge debt needed to be paid with rest. We'd pushed ourselves where few dare to go, and our senses failed us. A half-mile later Superman said excitedly, "There! I see the headwaters."

I thought that he pointed to a dead tree which had lost all of its bark. With the moonlight reflecting off of it, the tree appeared to be much larger than it actually was.

"That's a dead tree."

"No, over there!"

"Dead tree."

"Those are the headwaters of Shaw Creek," he insisted again.

"Okay. You're right. That is Shaw Creek," I answered, worried. He's in serious trouble, I thought.

Superman struggled onward with extreme fatigue. I thought that I should hike ahead as quickly as possible and set up camp. However, the idea of us separating in this vast wilderness at night upset me. What if Superman's or my headlamp burned out? What if a Grizzly Bear grabbed one of us? What if one of us fell or became lost? I reasoned that we'd better stay together, until we actually did reach the headwaters of Shaw Creek.

Where the hell is Shaw Creek? I kept wondering. We must have been hiking at only about one-and-a-half miles per hour. Camping on this terrain meant no sleep. Dammit! At this stage we decided that I would walk ahead and set up our camp as soon as feasible. Superman agreed that I should accept the first viable spot. Reluctantly, I moved off and soon couldn't see his headlamp behind me. He coura-geously plodded north, going on sheer will-power. His courage, effort, and stamina moved me deeply. Superman was a wonderful friend and companion. He inspired me.

Hiking alone immediately changed my perspective. My awareness and my fear doubled, as did my concern for Superman. While scanning both sides of the PCT for a feasible site, I maintained a steady pace. No acceptable place presented itself. I really began to worry about Superman. The thought of his headlight burning out haunted me. How long should I wait before I went back for him? I continued ahead. That small trickle we'd seen earlier must have been Shaw Creek. Eventually, I decided to pitch the Squall. I'd come close to a mile and reasoned that I must have missed the campsite mentioned in *Volume II*. In spite of my utmost care, this oversight seemed possible due to the darkness—so much for staying in an established site that night.

The only halfway-feasible place to set up the shelter was a slight widening in the PCT. I'd never yet camped on the PCT itself, nor had I ever planned to do so because of animal traffic. Large mammals, including Grizzlies, Elk, Deer, and Black Bears, prefer to walk on a well-established path rather than through dense forest and undergrowth. The number of animal tracks that I'd seen on the trail over the past two-and-a-half months confirmed this fact. In spite of my worries, I erected the tarptent right on the PCT in pitch blackness. The Squall's large footprint blocked the entire trail. The place that I'd found lay on a 10° slope, so I knew that we'd be sliding into each other all night.

I prayed that Superman would arrive under his own power. It was after 11 pm, and I felt tired. Wherever Superman was, I knew that he was exhausted. I arranged gear inside the shelter and stripped down. It was cold. I crawled into my matted-down bag nearly freezing and begged for Superman's safe arrival. Within 15 minutes, I could see a faint light, or did my eyes play a cruel trick on me? It was Superman! He'd pushed through another set of unknown mental and physical barriers to reach me. His arrival was emotional. We both felt tremendously relieved. I complimented him on his superhuman effort.

Superman had arrived cold and needed to climb into his sleeping-bag right away in order to avoid hypothermia. He placed a trekking-pole on each end of the tarptent to "ward off" bears. The poles would also serve to alert any unsuspecting hikers that people were sleeping in the center of the trail. I knew that no humans would be coming by that night, but I figured that bears might be. We set our alarms for 5:15 am. After popping a few *vitamin A* tablets, I immediately fell into a deep sleep. The next day Superman told me that he'd shivered violently all night. He looked spent.

In the morning it dawned on me that we stood a mere 21 miles from the Canadian border. I felt ecstatic. That day the journey of my lifetime would be successfully completed. I was about to accomplish what I'd set out to do, and, importantly to me, what I'd told people that I would do. Our most major concern, as on nearly every day on the PCT, was not to get lost. I'd started my trip at 7:30 am on May 12th. To finish the trek in less than 83-and-a-half days, we needed to reach the border by 7:30 pm. I'd be over two full days ahead of schedule. Since I rode sky high on emotions, physically, the final 20 miles would feel easy for me.

Superman emerged from the tarptent first. Each morning as we'd moved farther north, he'd spent more and more time bandaging and treating his feet. He'd developed a great appreciation for the amount of foot pain that I suffered as well. For the final time that summer, doing what had become habit, I repacked my gear and moved it outside the Squall. That morning would be the last time that I stuffed the tarptent into its fraying gray stuff-sack. My home for the summer was being put away forever. The Squall had been a reliable and comfortable shelter.

We began hiking before 5:30 am, and within 50 feet, off to the right-hand side, we saw a beautiful camping-spot. It was the one that I'd been seeking the previous night. The groomed site was huge, flat, and even had a bench. I consoled myself by saying that I might have missed it in total darkness, as it was set 45 feet away from the PCT. Without another thought, we pushed north, eagerly anticipating the Canadian border.

The weather remained perfect and the scenery spectacular. This area was Grizzly country, so we paid close attention. If something in the woods moved, we did a double-take. That day we didn't talk much, as we both reflected on the summer, our friendship, and life. Occasionally, I would drift behind Superman. Usually I said, "I'll catch you in a minute; just getting something out of my pack," or "Gotta pee;

be there in a sec." It was obvious to him that I needed a few moments alone. I wept openly, while singing "Bridge Over Troubled Water", "Kathy's Song", "Don't Dream It's Over", "For You", "Annie's Song", and "Slip-Slidin' Away", among others. When I had my emotions under control, I would catch back up to Superman.

Two hikers approached us walking southbound. I had somewhat expected to encounter *flip-floppers* in Washington state, and these two were the first. The Asian man's name was George, and he lived in New York City. I didn't catch his hiking-partner's name. As Superman made for the border, I spoke to the guys briefly. They'd flown from California up to Canada and had left Manning Park the day before with plans to hike south to the point where they'd left the trail. I updated them on what to expect in terms of trail conditions. We spoke of hikers whom we all knew. I wished them good luck, said goodbye, and headed after Superman, who by now had disappeared far up the PCT.

I finally rejoined Superman. That day he was hiking well. The miles ticked off fast. I ran through my favorite trail memories over the summer: having Adrian drop me off at the PCT and take pictures; seeing the beautiful purple flowers in the desert; walking into Idyllwild, meeting Wild Bill, and eating the huge Mexican dinner there; befriending Jenny and singing songs with her; feasting with Fire-Walking Bill and his gang; connecting and hiking with Fish and getting safely through the Sierras; hiking with Freefall, Graham, and Falco; passing through Yosemite, the Ansel Adams Wilderness area, Sequoia National Park, and Kings Canyon; meeting the Millers at Donner Pass; encountering Jill and Stephanie, and eating their crushed Tiger bar; connecting with Shirley at Burney Falls; seeing the towering Mount Shasta; reaching the Oregon boundary; gazing on the beautiful lakes in Oregon; enjoying beautiful sunsets and moonlit nights; hiking with Bruce; talking to Liz and Karen at Crater Lake; resupplying at a vending-machine at Mount Hood; getting to the Washington boundary; seeing Mount Saint Helens, Mount Adams, and Mount Rainier; meeting up with Superman; swimming in the chilly tarn; resupplying in Northern Washington . . . .

"You'd better go ahead on this part," Superman said out-of-the-blue, stepping aside and letting me pass. I thought that maybe he'd seen a Grizzly Bear. Looking up, though, I saw that we stood just 100 feet from the border. His kind and thoughtful gesture brought me to the verge of tears—what a great person and a great friend. I'd cried dozens of times earlier in the trip thinking about that moment.

We reached Monument 78 at 12:30 pm, and embraced each other in a bear hug. Paul understood my feelings.

"Ray, congratulations. You should be very proud."

"Thanks, Paul. Your being here for this week has meant the world to me. I couldn't have done it without you," I replied with a quivering voice.

"Look at the border," he said. We stared at the 20-foot-wide swath of trees that had been cut to distinguish the United States from Canada.

Superman was carrying a disposable camera. One shot remained. He'd saved this final picture so that he could capture my moment of glory at the northern terminus of the PCT. This plan was another in a series of thoughtful gestures that he'd made. I positioned myself near the monument, which looked identical to the one 2,651.5 miles south of here. Superman depressed the button on the camera. To our great surprise, nothing happened.

It turned out that when the camera read '1', there actually weren't any pictures remaining. We were completely out of film. Our disappointment was great. I briefly held out hope that another hiker would come by heading south and would be willing to take our picture. This scenario didn't materialize, though, so there would be no picture of me at the northern terminus. I filed away several images in my library. Later that day we could take a few pictures near the PCT trailhead parking lot.

As I imagined that all thru-hikers did, I climbed up on the end marker and left a pebble on top. A penny filled a crack in the wood atop the monument, and I wondered who'd left it there. We ate and drank, and savored this time. The sun warmed my smiling face. I felt blessed and completely fulfilled.

Part VI

CONCLUSION

The final phase of an epic journey awaited me. I'd faced many difficult moments on the trail. Could I now successfully reintegrate into society? Could I face the next season of my life? Where would life lead me from here?

18. End of an Epic Journey

Superman and I enjoyed our quiet and reflective celebration in solitude at Monument 78 on the United States/Canada border. I'd walked 2,651.5 miles, but we still had another seven miles to hike before reaching a trailhead parking lot. From there we would need to walk another mile to reach Manning Park Lodge. This stretch would be easy walking for both of us—especially for me, though, as an epic journey drew to a close. Superman smelled the barn, too. The first day after Rainy Pass we'd made exceptional progress and would definitely reach Manning Park Lodge long before our originally planned 7:30 pm. We didn't rush things any more, and at one point we sat down to enjoy the day and to eat the remainder of Superman's fatty salty Fritos.

We entered Manning Park Lodge at 3:30 pm, four hours ahead of our revised schedule. This arrival marked only the third or fourth time that I'd been early all summer. I phoned my mother, and let her know that I'd finished the PCT. She was exceptionally happy for me. I felt relieved to deliver this good news to her, and she was moved by what her youngest son had accomplished. Her epic was over, too, as her worries and concerns came to an end. I called Jimbo, who missed my call for only the second time all summer, and left a message for him that I had completed the trail. I'm sure that he felt excited for me and also relieved to hear my voice-mail message. Shortly after he retrieved my message, the hundreds of people who'd been tracking my adventure through the Web also found out that I'd finished, when Jimbo posted the following message:

August 3, 2003 (Day 83.2)

Ray finished! I missed his call, but Ray left a message that he finished today at 12:30 pm! Congratulations, Wall! I'll post more info when I have some.

Superman called his family to let them know that we'd reached Canada safely and that we'd completed this part of our journey. Following the phone calls, we devoured loaded cheeseburgers and drank ice-cold beer at the restaurant across from Manning Park Lodge. This afternoon was a happy and important time. I felt glad to share these life-altering moments with Superman.

Many thoughts weaved their way through my mind during that final day on the PCT. I felt fortunate. I was born to parents, Rox-Ellene and the late Robert, who loved me dearly, educated me, and encouraged me. Most importantly, though, I knew that they'd done their best to raise me. I felt lucky to have them as parents.

My mom's strength carried me through the most difficult times. I could always draw on her mental toughness, strength, and courage. My father possessed a good sense of humor and was resourceful. I was lucky to have Robert, Regina, and Roberta as siblings—all great people whom I deeply respect. I felt lucky to have been born healthy, with a sound mind and body. Genetically, I was never accident-prone nor fragile, and was born with good mechanics. I felt lucky to have such wonderful friends. I was lucky to have dreams.

I thought about my family and their sacrifices during the course of the summer. The limited communication made for a difficult time. Their uncertainty about my safety had been trying. I hold my family in my heart forever, and thank them for the support they gave me, thus helping me to fulfill my life.

I thought back to all of the people whom I'd met along the trail: Joe, the three young guys from New Hampshire, the two elderly ladies near Warner Springs, Wild Bill, the German woman, Jenny, Sharon, Nikki and Dave, Triathlete Dave, Freefall, Graham, Falcor, Liz, Karen, Shirley, Donna, Yogi, Chris, Newsman, Billy Goat, Alistair and Gail, Diesel, Split Pea, Jeff, Strider, Just Mike, Floater, Di, Bergfish, Kit, Northernlights, Tin Cup, Fire-Walking Bill and Gang, Diane, Dan, Stephanie, Jill, Bruce, Pacific Beast, the woman and her friend from

Vancouver, Glory, the southern Washington section-hiker, Fearless, Outward Bound groups, Sightseer, the northern California and Washington section-hikers, Batteries, Happy, Pat, Coach, the Snoqualmie Pass trail-angels, Ryan, the Oregon section-hiker, Just Jane, the group of five from Oregon, Mr. Tea, the newlyweds in Oregon, Masa and Tomo, George, Walt, and many others. Everyone had been kind to me. All these good people had restored my faith in America and in humanity. It felt refreshing to find out firsthand that most people in the United States are good and are willing to help a person in need.

I thought about my body and my mind. As of this writing, I've been running for over 30 years. My health and my well-being were always a priority for me, and the many years of training prevented my body from completely falling apart during this extreme test. My body absorbed a huge amount of stress and responded well. Physically, I became super fit, with only three-to-four percent body fat. My heart-rate had dropped under 40 beats per minute; my blood pressure measured 105–60. My switching network and my library had helped me through the difficult times. My positive thoughts helped me to go beyond usual human endurance limits.

I thought about the incredible inspirational scenery that I'd seen. Through dozens of National Parks, National Forests, and Wilderness areas, the splendors of these 83 days seemed unmatchable. The vastness and remoteness of the western United States inspired me. The contrasts between the flowering desert, the vast snowfields, the volcanic mountains, and the old-growth forests awed me. The crystal-clear nighttime starry skies, the colorful sunsets, and the waning and waxing moons soothed me with their peace and tranquillity. The hundreds of shades of blue waters in the pristine lakes, rivers, and waterfalls stuck with me. I felt humbled by all that I had seen.

I thought about the near-death experiences that I'd been through, including my melt-down in the desert, dangerous snowfield crossings, river fords, Black Bear encounters, Rattlesnake lunges, and Mountain Lion visits. I thought about being completely and utterly lost in an enormous deserted wilderness area. I was lucky to be alive. The fear of death didn't consume me. My will to live and my faith kept me going during my summer's all-out effort, and I felt fortunate that my trip had concluded safely.

I thought about my friends and their amazing sacrifices: Fish-out-of- Water and Superman, two unbelievable athletes, men of unlimited courage, terrific senses of humor, and kings of pain. I love these guys, and what they did for me during the summer of 2003 was extraordinary. Also, there was Jimbo, whose phone support, caring, and willingness to help me in any way possible kept me going. I wouldn't have come close to finishing the trail or breaking the record without his assistance. I love this guy. These three men are incredibly special friends, and sharing this achievement with them meant everything to me. They are my heroes.

This journey helped me to discover myself. When pushed to the breaking- point mentally and physically, I saw my life more clearly. I distilled what was important and meaningful from what was merely required and ordinary. I experienced a series of lifetime lows and a series of lifetime highs. The lows were more than worth enduring for the highs. I would have voluntarily suffered far greater than I did to experience the changes that I underwent and the beauty of that summer. The suffering was an investment in myself and one that I would gladly go through again to reap the benefits. A new inner peace and harmony were born deep inside me.

Throughout the summer months, my fears ebbed and were finally dissolved. Fear of people, fear of snakes, fear of falling, fear of weather, fear of failing, fear of hunger, fear of being alone, fear of the dark, fear of heights, fear of pain, fear of my emotions, fear of bears, fear of the unknown, fear of dying, and the fear of what I would find when I looked more closely at myself all disappeared. The act of overcoming these fears created in me a new-found freedom and an enormously strong will to live and to continue to grow. Fears hold us back, and I knew that I could now go forward to achieve my potential more fully.

To my personal library I added volumes of images of beautiful scenery, recordings of caring people, audio tapes of humorous moments, scenes where I overcame the odds, and a new fresh outlook that allows me to see things more clearly, thereby enhancing my life. I built a repository of these items that will serve me during the remainder of my years—in good times and in bad times. During sad moments or depressing times, I will browse the shelves of this library. I will remember my strength, courage, and will-power from the summer of 2003. I will bring up a happy image or moment; I will endure. In happy moments, I will visit this collection often, and it will always bring a smile to my face and enhance my good feelings. Many of the situations from that summer will be checked out and renewed endlessly. The librarian will say, "But, Mr. Greenlaw, you have checked that out a thousand times before." I'll just grin peacefully with a happy smile as I extend my arm with library-card in hand. Every day of my life, I will select and read my favorites, every single day. This collection was worth developing, and it is worth maintaining. I couldn't have acquired it in any other way.

I have spoken of a presence that followed me and appeared during certain times of my journey. This spirit watched over me and directed me at critical times. Although I don't fully understand this phenomenon, I have learned to be more comfortable with things that I can't comprehend. I have found out where my place is on this tiny earth in the midst of an immense universe. It has been very humbling. I don't need the answers to all questions, nor will I seek them. My life is now less cluttered. I am content with my current level of knowledge and of understanding. I can enjoy what is, rather than speculate about what it all means.

I have opened up more to people and am sharing myself to a greater extent. A number of people have been inspired by my efforts on the PCT, and this fact gives me great joy. To know that I am an inspiration in the lives of others creates a positive feeling inside of me. To hear a young man say, "If Ray Greenlaw could walk over 30 miles a day for an entire summer, then I can run 12 in one day" makes me feel good. To have friends to whose lives I have contributed makes me feel happy. To help others extend their own limits gives me great joy.

I had broken Flyin' Brian's record by over three days. His great achievement had pushed me to higher spiritual, physical, and mental limits. My record might be broken in the near future, or it could last for many years. Mother Nature will be the deciding factor. Variables, including snowfall, fires, flooding, and wildlife, can never be predicted on the PCT. I hope that my record is a source of inspiration, an achievement that people can aim for and surpass, knowing that someone else went before them. I hope that this accomplishment is one that people can use to overcome their own challenges.

Although the late snowfall in the Sierra made breaking the PCT record very difficult, I felt exceptionally fortunate to have hiked in 2003. The bonding friendships that I formed are true treasures in my life. I felt lucky to have enjoyed near perfect weather for my entire trip. I completed the journey without any rain at all. This duration was the longest period in my life that I have gone without rain. It rained the day after I had finished, on the return to Seattle. Not long after I finished the PCT, sections in both Oregon and Washington were closed due to fires, preventing many from the class of 2003 from walking the entire trail. I had been lucky to have hiked the trail pure without missing any sections.

The PCT gave me a new freedom: a freedom to live my life fully. I never have to question myself again about love of life, courage, willpower, or kindness. The qualities that I'd hoped to find were there. I am a person like others—simply finding my way in a complex world. Better understanding my role and enhancing my perspective has given me peace of mind.

My final emotional sign-in at Manning Park Lodge read as follows:

8/3/2003

Wall here.

What began as a dream on May 12th ended on August 3rd. My thru-hike is finished and two days ahead of schedule. :-) It was an epic. I am truly humbled by this experience.

My most sincere thanks and admiration to Peter "Fish-out-of-Water" Solomon (accompanied me 13 days on the trail) and Paul "Superman" Goransson (accompanied me 7 days on the trail). I couldn't have completed this hike without their friendship and support. These guys are world class.

Thanks to James "Jimbo" Wogulis for updating my Web-site during the course of the summer. His support was essential to my success.

I love this trail.

The memories will fade and the muscles will atrophy, but the process and the purity will remain forever.

Thanks to all those who supported me during this hike and to the wonderful trail-angels.

I am going to write a book about this trip, and would like to include interesting stories and anecdotes from other hikers. Please send me an email if you are interested in learning more. Photographs are welcome, too.

Best of luck to all hikers, and thank you for your kindness. You touched my heart. May our paths cross again in the near future.

For You

You made it beautiful.
You made it worthwhile.
You made it fulfilling.
You made it special.
You enhanced my dream.
You are part of me.

I sniffled, returned the register, and began preparations to reintegrate into society. I had finished!

 19. Epilogue

I completed my thru-hike of the Pacific Crest Trail on August 3rd, 2003. The following day, after an American breakfast in Canada, we returned to the United States, arriving in Seattle by early afternoon. As we drove south on I-5, a superhighway which I'd crossed twice while on the PCT, I reflected on life while rain fell around me for the first time all summer. A wonderful, yet sad, feeling swept over me, because that day, for the first time in 83 days, I would not be hiking. Although I'd thoroughly enjoyed my journey, my battered body now needed desperately to rest and to recover.

During my final two weeks on the trail, I had spent time thinking about the transition back into society. This reintegration would be difficult for me, and I would need to exercise patience with myself. My personal traits, which had helped me to succeed on the trail, would also facilitate my readjustment to civilization. I disciplined myself regarding my eating habits by immediately reducing my caloric consumption from 8,000 to 2,000 calories per day. I stopped eating candy, energy bars, sunflower seeds, Fritos, and other types of high-calorie foods that had been staples for me throughout the summer. Since my home diet doesn't include these fatty snack foods, I had little problem avoiding junk food despite the fact that my body still craved calories. Many hikers gain 30 to 40 pounds after completing a thru-hike, and I didn't want this ballooning to happen to me. Combined with other issues, such as losing my daily freedom, missing the beautiful scenery, and returning to work, a significant weight-gain would have brought on deep depression.

Two days after finishing my hike, I drove to a busy Starbucks coffee-house on the outskirts of Seattle to log on and check my email. There I read email for only the third time since departing from Savannah. While I engrossed myself with dated electronic correspondence, the coffee aroma that I smelled and the comfortable chair that I sat in relaxed me. I enjoyed the progressive background music. After replying to the last message in my Inbox and logging off, I headed for the door. Upon exiting the popular Starbucks, I realized that I had no idea what type or color of rental car I'd been driving, nor any idea of where I'd parked the car. Fortunately, I remembered that earlier I'd put a small CVS bag on the back seat of the car.

The huge parking lot, which I now faced, sprawled widely since it accommodated shoppers from a supermarket and two dozen other strip-mall stores, too. Walking around the rows of SUVs and cars in a systematic pattern, I eventually located the back seat containing my car's only identifying feature. (The license-plate number had not been written on the rental-car key chain, where one would have expected it.) The rental-car key fit the door, so I drove away.

This simple search to locate my rental car paled in comparison to the difficult search to locate the PCT in the snowbound Sierras. In my first couple of weeks back from the woods there were many other situations involving trivial details, which pre-hike I had kept track of well, but where lately I had forgotten to make a needed mental note. I recovered from such lapses by using patience and by using persistence. Eventually, I sensitized myself to detail, again. I successfully managed matters other than just the three essentials—food, water, and shelter. This re-adaptation facilitated daily chores.

Post-hike I spoke at length with Fish, Superman, and Jimbo. They supported me and understood what I'd experienced. My close friends knew me and witnessed the changes that I'd undergone. With great feeling I thanked each of them for our wonderful friendship and for their help with my journey. These guys were always there for me. Without their support my transition back into society would have been much harder. Utilizing the help of my support network, I escaped the depression which so often accompanies the letdown that many people feel after they've accomplished a major goal.

My thoughts continued to focus heavily on the PCT because that is what I'd lived and breathed for the past three months. I resumed work just seven days after crossing the Canadian border. Naturally, I wasn't ready to put on a suit and a tie just yet, but I did. My mind and my body took a couple more weeks to acclimate to being cooped up in an office. I missed the beautiful scenery, solitude, hiking, adventure, and freedom. Since colleagues and friends posed many questions concerning my hike, my summer activities remained in the forefront of my mind. As the days passed, I satisfied people's curiosities and then decompressed at my own rate. I entered full swing on my job with the help and support of my highly-capable staff.

Given that I'd eaten more candy during the past three months than over the previous 20 years combined and that I'd brushed and flossed fewer times during the past three months than in any other three-month period which I can remember, one of my first priorities was to get my teeth cleaned. I scheduled the first available appointment at my dentist's office. Kim, my friendly dental hygienist, worked on my teeth much longer than usual, even though she'd cleaned them just three months earlier. In between scrapings and rinsings, I answered her questions about the PCT.

Although Kim worked gently and precisely, my gums hurt considerably more than ever before. Kim indicated that my symptoms were typical of the acidic diet which I'd eaten. I imagined that those of her younger patients who had poor dental habits shared my current issues. This thought gave me a small comfort. My teeth hurt for a few days after the cleaning, but the hyper-sensitivity subsided shortly thereafter. I greatly appreciated having a pain-free and clean mouth.

My aching feet reminded me that they, too, were another important medical priority. As soon as I returned to Savannah, I'd made an appointment with a recommended orthopedist named Dr. Paul Horovitz. When I visited Dr. Horovitz, he couldn't believe how badly traumatized my feet were. We shared a few laughs regarding my hike. He prescribed strong creams for my athlete's foot, and that medication cleared up the tenacious fungus within a few weeks. My custom graphite orthotics, which I'd brought with me to the foot-doctor's office, looked dreadful and lay in tatters. I thought for sure that I would need to purchase expensive new orthotics, but, fortunately, my old ones required only new covers.

Within a week or so of my return to Savannah, word began spreading throughout the hiking community that I had set a new speed-record for hiking the PCT. I don't actually know how this fact first became public knowledge. Glenn van Peski soon posted a note at gvpgear.com that I'd set the new record, as did Henry Shires at www.tarptent.com. Fiddlehead sent his warm congratulations. Shortly thereafter, congratulations began coming in from all over the world via email. Many experienced hikers sent me notes acknowledging how difficult an accomplishment the fastest hike was. I responded to the messages, thanking those who took an interest in my hike. A call from my friend Bob Holtel, who had run the PCT over the course of three summers, was very special.

By mid-August I had started writing this book. For the first week or two of authoring, I felt slow to remember events and to recall details. Because I hadn't taken *any* notes on the trail, I wrote entirely from memory. To my pleasant surprise, the more that I immersed myself in this writing project, the more items that I could recall and the greater my clarity of recollection. Once I focused intensely on this book, the flood-gates opened, and the details of virtually every single summer day became clear. While utilizing my internal library, I relived many of my favorite days and favorite experiences, as I wrote about them.

I mailed a package containing my Leki Super Makalu trekking-poles to a service center. Because the carbide-steel tips had been worn down to stubs, the poles desperately needed refurbishing. Several weeks later when the same package returned containing my "new" walking-sticks, I felt as if two old friends had returned home from the hospital. I'd worn the wrist straps of those poles for almost 850 hours throughout the course of the summer. They'd been part of me. I greatly enjoyed my next hike with the refurbished poles.

I constructed a PCT Web-site and filled the pages with information regarding my journey. Whenever I get the urge, I can now view material on-line from my hike. As friends finished the trail and had their films developed, pictures taken during the course of the summer began trickling in to me. In September and October, I received close to 300 trail pictures from fellow hikers. I installed many of these images in a gallery on my Web-site. Having access to the pictures 24-7 is really great, and through the images and text, others can share in my experience. Whenever I feel a yearning for the PCT (which I often do while traveling), I simply download the photos and text from the Internet and then begin reminiscing. The images sent to me nicely augment my "personal library". Sometimes, I am overcome with emotion when I recall the images and the events from the summer of 2003.

Once I'd returned to Savannah, I resumed weight-lifting and running. I actually ran over 100 miles in one week. This distance was a far cry from my 300-mile weeks on the trail, but 15 miles a day felt big to me while I was working (and writing) full-time. I wanted to race at the Angeles Crest 100 in September 2003 since I was in outstanding aerobic condition. This run would also have given me a chance to revisit a memorable portion of the PCT. My feet told me not to run, though, as they still ached. I felt disappointed about not participating in the Angeles Crest Race, but I let this lost opportunity go. Instead, I entered and ran the Low-Country, Distance-Classic Marathon in October; I felt strong during the Bluffton, South Carolina, race, despite the high heat and the unbearable humidity. A month later I ran strongly at the Atlanta Marathon, too. Twice-daily runs are again my norm. As long as working out is still fun for me and remains an important part of my lifestyle, I plan to continue to race in marathons, ultras, and triathlons.

My trail clothes from Jill and Stephanie arrived, and I sent Jill a "Thank You" letter that included additional postage money for her. I mailed a "Thank You" note to Fire-Walking Bill's gang, too. The Millers mailed me a package containing my ice-axe and a touching card whose outside reads:

> The world is a better place because of those who refuse to believe [that] they can't fly.

Three hand-drawn doves are shown in flight on the front of the card. On the inside the Millers had written "You really raised the bar." Their card meant a great deal to me.

Holding my ice-axe again felt like reuniting with a trusted friend. I phoned the Millers for a long enjoyable conversation. We enjoyed some good laughs.

One day in late September on my voice-mail I discovered and listened to the following message:

> Hi, Ray. It's me! Well, I finished. I'm glad it's over. Yay!

A delightful smile formed on my lips because another friend had fulfilled a life-time dream. While tears ran down my cheeks, I replayed the emotion-filled voice several times. Jenny, one of the first PCT thru-hikers whom I'd met, had achieved her goal. I shared in her happiness and excitement. "Jenny finished," I said out loud. "Yippee!" She's safe, I thought, as I wiped my shirt-sleeve over my eyes. What an amazing woman. (I never did receive a call from Joe.)

Superman had my final pair of shoes which I'd worn on the PCT bronzed and mounted on a beautiful piece of lacquered hardwood. He also had a gold plaque engraved and fastened to the shiny wood. The attractive memento now sits in a prominent place in my office. The plaque on the trophy reads as follows:

Pacific Crest Trail

To Ray Greenlaw, in honor of your epic, record-breaking 83-day, 2,659-mile journey from Mexico-to-Canada in the summer of 2003.
—From your friend and companion
on the final 263 miles,
Paul Goransson

My emotions flowed unchecked while I read this inscription. I am very grateful to Paul for his thoughtful gesture and will treasure his lovely gift forever.

I read several accounts of survival after my trip. In these articles the key personality traits listed for those who do survive disastrous circumstances are (fortunately) all qualities that I possess. Included in the profiles of survivors are the ability to remain calm, to enjoy the journey, to persist always, and to take action. The survival articles read like synopses of parts of my trip. I had experienced tremendous personal growth during my journey from both the distressing moments and from the uplifting ones.

Physically, I mended well. I don't expect any lasting structural damage. My feet have recovered most of their feeling, and all of my soft tissue is fully healed. During my epic out-of-food episodes, I did burn some muscle, including heart muscle. For the moment, though, everything seems to be working well. My heart and my spirit grew many sizes over the course of this adventure.

Once home again, I reunited with the 13-year-old twins Dottie and Julie—my aging German Shepards. I'd thought about Dottie (also known affectionately as Dot, Deezer, and Deezee) and Julie (whose nicknames are Jules, Pep Dog, Pepper, and Pep) every day on the PCT, but I especially missed them whenever I would encounter other friendly dogs on the trail—Bruce's Dalmatian, the famous white-haired dog that had hiked most of the PCT, the Golden Retriever with his own pack, and the dozens of dogs I had met who were accompanied by day-hikers. Dottie and Julie had played such big roles in my life. Together, my pets and I had walked almost three times the length of the PCT as a family. I felt fortunate that "The Poops" had survived the hot Savannah summer and were there to greet me when I returned safely from the PCT. They had waited for me.

The Poops and I spent three more good months together, taking our twice-daily walks, as we'd done almost every day for the past 13 years. Our joint walks were the only significant local walks that I ever took. In early November, rather suddenly, Dottie weakened and died of bone cancer and lung cancer. This happy dog who had taught me how to live also taught me how to die. She never did lose her "famous" appetite, consuming a tasty final meal of three cooked eggs on the day of her death.

Julie could not bear the loss of her soulmate. Julie became utterly distraught and was incapable of eating for six days. I, too, had a broken heart and little appetite. Only two weeks later, Julie was also diagnosed with lung cancer. On our final walk together Julie collapsed underneath the oak tree in my driveway. My two close companions, who had helped me through the past 13 years and the difficult times on the trail, and who had brought so much joy to my life, are now gone. They are together again, after a brief separation. I miss Dottie and Julie terribly.

My PCT trek is a journey of a lifetime, during which I augmented my internal library with many treasures. As time passes since the completion of my 2003 PCT thru-hike, I realize more and more how much of a life-altering event my trip of self-discovery has truly been. I am thankful that I completed the trip successfully, shared the adventure with friends, rediscovered the United States and its people, and returned to nature. Once at a crossroad in my life, I'd lost my path. I have found my path again, and will follow my path, wherever it leads me. If I lose my path again, I am confident that I can find my way now, thanks to the summer which I spent on the Pacific Crest Trail.

 Appendices

Included here are appendices titled:

A. *PCT by Numbers*

B. *Frequently Asked Questions*

C. *Live Web Updates*

D. *Menu del Dia*

E. *Initial Hiking-Schedule*

F. *Preliminary Gear-List*

G. *Backpacking Equipment*

H. *Glossary of Trail Jargon*

A PCT by Numbers

Several of the values reported here are, of course, estimates.

Steps Taken: 6,516,001

Calories Consumed: 500,000

Bears Sighted: 4

Biggest Day: 50+ miles

Biggest Week: 300+ miles

Biggest 25-Day Period: 1,000+ miles

Total Miles Hiked: 2,850

Showers Taken: 6

Total Rainfall: 0 inches

Total Snowfall: 5 inches

Nights in Hotels: 5

Times Did Laundry: 4

Sleeping-Bag Washings: 1, around day 70

Heaviest Pack Weight: 55 pounds

Lightest Pack Weight: 10 pounds

Singings of "Bridge Over Troubled Water": 312,220

Singings of "Slip-Sliding Away": 57

Singings of "Don't Dream It's Over": 341

Beers Consumed: 7

Mail-Drops Used: 3

Mail-Drops Missed: 1

Times Got Lost: 1.38×10^7

Days Cried: 17

Days Laughed: 83

Snake Sightings: 347

Total Hikers Met: 411

Thru-Hikers Met: 89

Times Thought of Quitting: 0

Times Ran Out of Food: 5

Times Ran Out of Water: 4

Injuries: 0

Foot Issues: $> \infty$

Bandaids Applied: 411

Rolls of Adhesive-Tape Applied: 4

Miles Walked in Snow: 250+

Times Ate King Crab: 0

Times Ate Eating King Crab with Butter: 0

Times Thought about Eating King Crab: 100,003

Times Thought about King Crab with Butter: 86,912,221

Average Miles Per Day: Trail: 31.9 (Total: 34.1)

Rest Days: 0

Days Hiked with Fish: 13

Days Hiked with Superman: 7

Trip Cost: $4,500

Mosquito Bites in Oregon: 3,037

Ant Sightings: 12,324,333

Yellow-Jacket Sightings in Washington: 432,112

Times Fire-Walking Bill's Jeans Caught on Fire: 3

B 🥾 Frequently Asked Questions

1. *How long is the Pacific Crest Trail?*

   From the southern terminus at the border town of Campo to the northern terminus at Monument 78, the PCT stretches 2,651.5 miles. From Campo to the border town of Manning Park measures 2,658.7 miles. The length of the trail changes constantly, as sections continually get re-routed.

2. *What was your favorite part of the trail?*

   Many beautiful sections of the trail stand out, and picking just one is virtually impossible. This response depends on the scenery, the weather, your mood, your hiking-companion, food and beverage supplies, and many other factors. Goat Rocks Wilderness (Washington) in perfect weather definitely ranks right up there with any other section of the PCT. I won't ever forget the High Sierras (California) and the North Cascades (Washington).

3. *What did you eat?*

   My diet consisted mainly of junk food. When the trip started, I consumed roughly 5,000 calories per day. This number worked well for 25-mile days. Once I started pushing 40-mile days, this ration rose to 8,000 calories. The ratio of calories to miles scaled amazingly well. I chowed granola bars of every variety, king-sized MilkyWay bars, PopTarts, Hersey chocolate bars, peanut butter, Rice Crispy treats, Spam, sunflower seeds, pumpkin seeds, Clif bars, Luna bars, Tiger bars, Harvest bars, PowerBars, Reese's peanut-butter cups, Skittles, M&Ms, sardines, Wheat Thins, Chicken-in-a-Bisket crackers, Oreos, Slim Jims, cheese, deviled ham, tuna fish, salmon, chicken, Mounds bars, beef jerky, and any powdered drink mixes that I could find, including: Tang, Koolaid, Gatorade, powdered milk, Nestle's Quick, Carnation Instant Breakfast, lemonade, and orange-drink mix.

In the few locations where I feasted at restaurants, I always tried to consume plentiful vegetables and fruits. I savored ice cream in these eating establishments and drank milkshakes, if the cold air didn't nip at me. I often drank classic Coke or root-beer soda in towns, and occasionally quaffed them on the trail itself.

4. *What food(s) did you miss the most?*

   I missed practically all cooked foods, including: shrimp, steak, King Crab legs, chicken, fish, burritos, vegetables, pastas, soups, breads, bagels, pecan and key-lime pies, clam chowder, and pizza.

5. *Were you scared hiking solo?*

   Yes. Many times I shook in my trail-running shoes. The worst three times happened when I traveled alone and became lost in the wilderness. Beating back panic at such times became extremely challenging and took all of my courage. I learned that if I accepted my fate, then I could focus on my survival.

6. *Did you carry a gun?*

   I carried no weapons.

7. *Did you set a new record for the fastest, PCT hike?*

   Yes. My 83.2-day hike sliced three days off Flyin' Brian Robinson's record, and my time has been established as the new record. Several writers have published magazine articles about the record, and a number of prominent Web-sites list the record. My original goal involved hiking the trail in one straight-line shot from south to north in 85 days, so I am very happy.

8. *Would you do it again?*

   Yes. I actually thought of *yoyoing*. I hope to go back on the Pacific Crest Trail and re-hike many of my favorite sections.

9. *Were you lonely?*

Yes. Many times I felt extremely lonely. I'd passed all thru-hikers by Sierra City, at mile 1,191.5, and didn't see any other thru-hikers until the last day of my hike, when I encountered two *flip-floppers*. Over the course of the summer, I talked much more than usual when I would meet day-hikers and others along the trail. Thanks, friends, for listening to me.

10. *How did your body hold up to hiking the PCT?*

During the first week, my legs ached from the ups and downs, my hands and wrists hurt from my trekking-poles, my back and neck suffered from my pack, my feet felt sore from too much walking, and the remainder of my body cried out from sunburn. I told my body to go, and, fortunately, my body became stronger over the course of the trip.

11. *Where do you get your strength from?*

My mother instilled courage, will-power, and determination in me.

12. *Did you carry a GPS unit?*

No. That type of instrument weighed too much for my hike. Tomo and Mr. Tea, a couple of Japanese hikers whom I befriended, carried GPS units, and this technology helped me in the High Sierras for the day that we hiked together.

13. *Did you carry a compass?*

For a short time in the High Sierras, while accompanied by "Fish-out-of-Water", I possessed a compass. I determined my direction from the sun, and the perfect weather allowed me to navigate accurately by this method. Much of my navigation was by dead-reckoning. I strongly recommend that thru-hikers take and use a compass on a PCT thru-hike.

14. *Did you keep a journal?*

No. In order to save weight, I carried no pen, no pencil, and no paper. Being unable to write severely restricted my expressiveness. No communication outlet existed for me, and feelings overwhelmed me occasionally.

15. *Did you carry a camera?*

No. However, many people along the trail offered to take my picture, and my hiking-partners carried cameras. I received many beautiful pictures of my hike. Luckily, I possess a photographic memory, and stored thousands of images in my "library". If I hike the PCT again, I will take a camera.

16. *What inspired you?*

An overwhelming desire burned inside me to hike the PCT. Inspired by the chance to grow, to develop, and to learn about myself, I jumped at this opportunity. My journey induced self-discovery. I also knew that the trip would be beautiful— spiritually, physically, and emotionally. While walking the trail, I encountered many other hikers who were pursuing their dreams; they inspired me. The extraordinary feats of Hermann Buhl, the great Austrian climber, and Walter Bonatti, the great Italian climber, also inspired me.

17. *Did you encounter any animals?*

Yes. I observed many Deer, Elk, Mountain Goats, Marmots, Squirrels, and so on. I also encountered Black Bears in Yosemite, near Seiad Valley in northern California, in the middle of Oregon, and in North Cascades National Park in northern Washington. Several times Black Bears walked north directly ahead of me, and I needed to shoo them off the trail. One young Black Bear almost ran into me in Oregon; we came within 15 feet of each other and stared at one anothers eyes. Luckily, he fled, while I continued north. A couple of Mountain Lions tracked me near Elk Lake Resort in Oregon. That experience bothered me.

18. *Where did you see the biggest trees?*

I marveled at the Redwoods in Central California. Since the trail stays high, you don't really see the true giants from the PCT. Nevertheless, the ancient redwoods touched me spiritually. In northern Washington massive old-growth forests envelop you. Spectacular red-cedars and Douglas-firs raised my eyebrows and raced my heart. These immense and beautiful trees bring true joy to all passersby.

19. *How did the bugs treat you?*

I found essentially no biting bugs south of the Sierras. In the High Sierras in Central California, particularly in the meadows, mosquitoes abound, but nothing extraordinary. Northern California harbored mosquitoes but not bad. In Oregon, particularly in the Sky Lakes Wilderness areas, the bugs ruled the land, the air, and the "sea". Biting flies also chewed me in Oregon. Washington contained mosquitoes and black flies. So, other than in areas in Oregon, where the snow had recently melted or where lakes dotted the landscape, the bugs didn't affect me greatly. Shocking numbers of ants resided in California, and thousands of yellow-jackets flew in Washington. All areas with wildflowers swarmed with bees. Getting stung only three times over the course of the summer, I considered myself lucky.

20. *What is the highest point on the PCT?*

Forester Pass rises to an elevation of 13,180 feet, at mile mark 774.2.

21. *What is the lowest point on the PCT?*

Just north of the Bridge of the Gods on the Oregon/Washington boundary, at mile 2,151.8, the trail dips down to 140 feet above sea-level.

22. *Is there one favorite meal that stands out in your mind?*

Yes. The feed with "Fire-Walking Bill" and the gang just north of Silverwood Lake State Recreation Area, at mile 331.1—the ayce fruit, potato chips, dill pickles, barbecued chicken, smoked salmon, juicy steak, corn-on-the-cob, baked potatoes, and pudding conjure fabulous memories. The ice-cold bottled water, sodas, wine coolers, and Southern Comfort quenched me, too. My dinner at Lake Hughes, at mile 485.2, in the Harley Bar consisting of a large shrimp-cocktail, garden salad with blue-cheese dressing, beer-battered fish and chips, and frosty draft-beer is also forever imprinted in my mind.

23. *How many mail-drops did you send?*

I sent three mail-drops: to Kennedy Meadows at mile 697.0, to Belden Town Resort at mile 1,283.1, and to Elk Lake Resort at mile 1,953.2. I actually missed the mail-drop at Belden, and, because of my fast pace, I needed to forward the package all the way ahead to Seiad Valley, at mile 1,657.0. This miss meant that I wore my haggard shoes and socks for almost an extra 400 miles. Many of my foot problems arose or became worse during that time. At mile 555.1 in Mojave, California, Fish-out-of-Water brought me a package, and I was resupplied on the PCT at mile 2,396.6 at Snoqualmie Pass, mile 2,471.6 at Stevens Pass, and mile 2,589.1 at Rainy Pass.

24. *What would you do differently?*

I would reach the High Sierras after most of the snow had melted, carry *Volume I* and *Volume II* (or their equivalents) for the corresponding sections of trail, take equipment for contingencies, send a few more resupply packages, work out a good communications system, bring pen and paper, carry a camera, and warehouse a surplus of replacement gear ready to ship from home. I would change very little about my experience itself, though. The rewards of the trip felt so great that I actually wanted to turn around, once I'd finished, and walk back to Mexico.

25. *Were you ever worried about super hydration?*

No. I simply drank as much fluid as I could swallow. This system worked well for me. If I worried about every conceivable problem that could have arisen, I wouldn't have enjoyed the trip. I apply this philosophy to my life as well.

26. *What kind of shelter did you use?*

The two-person, 31.2-ounce Squall tarptent designed and manufactured by Henry Shires (www.tarptent.com) became my home. I used one of my hiking-poles to set up the tarptent. This maneuver saved me a few ounces. I carried the tarptent for the entire trip, and while camping in the woods, I slept in this shelter for all but one night.

27. *What kind of pack did you carry?*

I hiked with a custom 25-ounce GVP G4 designed and made by Glen van Peski (www.gvpgear.com). I modified the pack in small ways, such as cutting straps, removing the waist belt, and eliminating unnecessary padding, so the pack dropped a few ounces. The G4 worked best with loads under 30 pounds.

28. *How much did your entire pack weigh?*

Without food or water, the pack weighed anywhere from about 8.5 pounds to 14 pounds. Including large loads of food and drink, the weight rose to as much as 55 pounds. On average, I hauled 25 to 30 pounds.

29. *Did you see any snakes?*

Yes. Many snakes lined the trail, with the highest concentration occurring in the deserts of Southern California. One time an angry rattlesnake actually struck my hiking-pole, and a Mojave Green Rattler once reared up at me. Needless to say, I backed away from this intimidating serpent. I avoided a couple of rattlers in Oregon, but saw none in Washington. One hiker whom I encountered had been bitten on the hand by a rattlesnake. His hand swelled heavily, but I think that he survived the ordeal okay.

30. *Did you see any scorpions?*

No. Nor did I meet any other hikers who'd come across them. I believe that American scorpions live primarily in Arizona and Texas.

31. *What surprised you most about the trail?*

The trail's elevation profile stunned me. Since the route crests the mountains, I knew that it sat pretty high, but I didn't realize that on average I would be up around 6,000 feet and actually spend almost three weeks at or above 10,000 feet. I felt surprised to discover the trail's remoteness, and to discover how poorly marked this national scenic path was.

32. *Did you get a lot of rain?*

Not even a single drop of rain fell on me during the entire summer. This amazing fact blew my mind. On day 66, I encountered a hiker in Oregon, and said, "I can't believe that I haven't received any rainfall in the past 66 days." He told me, "It will be even more surprising if you don't get rain during the remainder of your hike. I can almost believe you didn't get rained on in California." Remarkably, no rain fell in the final 17 days, either. On the drive back to Seattle from Manning Park the day after finishing, the skies opened up, and it poured, as it did for the subsequent days.

33. *Did any snow fall on you?*

Five inches blanketed me on Dick's Pass, where I became pinned down for the night in icy-cold weather. I remember meeting "Pacific Beast" at Echo Lake, and he decided to sit tight rather than push off into the storm. He made the right choice that afternoon.

34. *What was the lowest temperature that you experienced on the PCT?*

The temperature dipped below 20°F a couple of times. The lowest maximum daytime temperature hovered around 70°F, though. On most days the mercury reached 90°F or above. In the sun temperatures soared in all three states.

35. *How hot did the temperatures get out there?*

On most days temperatures exceeded 90°F. In the *shade* in Southern California thermometers must have registered at least 120°F on occasion. I have worked out in saunas before for short periods of time, and a few days the heat approached sauna-level—the type of heat in which your nose burns painfully if you breathe deeply. Temperatures rose to dangerous levels on many occasions.

36. *Did you cross the Mojave Desert in Southern California at night?*

Nearly all hikers I saw wisely dodged the Mojave's deadly heat by sneaking through in the dark. While carrying huge amounts of water, I walked through that unforgiving desert during the day. On my crossing I witnessed many hikers sitting in the minimal shade or in their shelters, trying to keep cool, in the brutal temperatures.

37. *How much did the trip cost?*

I estimate that all my gear cost approximately $1,500, and I should mention that I purchased everything based on quality and on weight. A hiker could spend less and still acquire excellent equipment. I probably spent another $3,000 on food, postage, motels, and miscellaneous items. Since I cashed in frequent-flier miles for both the trip from Savannah to San Diego and the return trip to Savannah from Seattle, I paid nothing for airfare. When I boarded the outbound aircraft with just my backpack and strode to the first-class cabin in my hiking-clothes, the flight attendant asked to see my boarding-card. I didn't take the incident personally.

38. *How much weight did you lose?*

I started the trip at 165 pounds in good shape. My pre-trip training consisted of running 80 to 90 miles per week in Savannah, Georgia. On the trail I shed 10 pounds and plummeted to my lowest weight in many years. During an epic "run-out-of-food episode" on the AT, I'd probably dropped to a similar weight.

39. *Who are "Fish-out-of-Water" and "Superman"?*

"Fish-out-of-Water" is my lifetime friend Peter Solomon. In Pete's college days he was a world-class swimmer. Pete is also known as "King of Pain". He is a highly successful swim coach at Middlebury College in Vermont, having been named Coach of the Year in New England on a number of occasions. "Superman" is my long-time friend and climbing partner Dr. Paul Goransson. I served on Paul's Ph.D. dissertation committee at the University of New Hampshire, where we first met. Paul is an outstanding runner. He founded Meetinghouse Data Communications, a company specializing in security solutions for wireless networks, and works as the President of Meetinghouse. These two guys are amazing friends, people, and athletes. I couldn't have completed my hike without their company. They have added so much to my life and are forever part of me.

40. *Who is "Jimbo"?*

"Jimbo" is my friend of 25 years, Dr. James Wogulis. We roomed together at Pomona College in Southern California. Like Paul and me, Jim received his Ph.D. in computer science. Jimbo works as a software engineer for Borland. Throughout the course of my hike, he maintained my Web-site. Jimbo achieved several notable marks in track-and-field in college, including long-jumping 23' 6", triple-jumping 49' 5", and throwing the javelin 214' 10". Jim's phone- and ground-support proved outstanding, and I depended on him greatly during my hike.

41. *How does the Pacific Crest Trail compare to the Appalachian Trail?*

In 1995 I hiked the AT pure in 97 days total, with six of those being rest-days. On my 2003 PCT hike, I exceeded the entire distance of the 2,159.2-mile-long AT in my first 70 days. I also exceeded the entire distance of the AT in my final 63 days walking from Lake Hughes, at mile 485.2, to Manning Park, at mile 2,658.7. Because I'd aged eight years since my AT hike and pushed myself much harder on the PCT, relatively speaking, for me the AT seemed like a walk to the corner store. The AT is an exceptionally beautiful, steeply graded, and demanding trail, and by no means an easy trail to thru-hike. However, the PCT is more remote, higher, hotter, longer, drier, and generally more dangerous. If the PCT had been snow-free, I might have felt differently. Far fewer hikers take on the challenge of the PCT. In general, the hikers on the PCT possess far more experience than those on the AT, and many of the PCT hikers have already successfully thru-hiked the AT. Both trails hold a special place in my heart and are national treasures.

42. *Did you suffer any injuries?*

I hurt my ankle once while kicking steps in steep hard snow; the ankle throbbed for three weeks. I strained my groin twice as well. My feet experienced serious trauma, but nothing ever broke. My knees felt fine, and the rest of me became stronger.

43. *Do your feet hurt?*

I experienced excruciating foot pain caused in part by deep cracks in the ball of the foot and in the heel. Dozens of cuts criss-crossed my little toes and my big toes. These abrasions resulted in enormous pain in comparison to a blister. In fact, blisters didn't bother me at all, since other far-more-serious issues grabbed my attention. As Fish pointed out, in half-an-hour some other body part will hurt considerably more than whatever is nagging you now. Pain circulates through different channels in the body in an interesting manner. As of this writing, I do still have numbness in my feet, as does Superman. However, a full recovery seems imminent.

44. *Why push yourself to these limits?*

I'll take the[1] fifth on this question.

45. *What's next?*

I hope to hike the Continental Divide Trail and continue with my quest to climb the seven continental summits. As of this writing, I have completed four of the seven summits.

46. *What was your most difficult moment on the trail?*

When I found myself totally lost in the wilderness north of the Sierras, I accepted the thought that I wouldn't ever return home. Having nothing in my possession to write with, I realized that I'd disappear quietly and perhaps never be found. I felt extremely distraught that I couldn't leave a final note.

47. *Any advice for other hikers?*

Follow your dreams, and hike *your* hike.

48. *Do you believe that the first person to reach the border "loses"?*

No. The duration of an event is not what makes it beautiful. The quality of a journey is what matters most; the value of individual experiences and not their quantity is important. I loved my trip, but I felt delighted to reach the border and finish hiking. The experiences from my 83 days on the trail expanded my internal

---

[1] Make it "a".

library greatly. I will continue to seek enriching opportunities each day of my life. Time not spent on the trail is time spent enjoying other aspects of life.

49. *Did you write this book entirely from memory?*

Yes. I took *no* notes while on the trail. While engrossing myself in this project, I felt amazed as the vivid summer details replayed in my mind. Many of my emotions re-surfaced as well, and I periodically became overwhelmed. In writing this book, my PCT memories further crystallized—an occurrence which I am very happy about.

Live Web Updates

This appendix contains the contents of live updates that appeared on the World Wide Web during the summer of 2003. James "Jimbo" Wogulis periodically updated my thru-hike Web-site, and the format here is similar to that which Jimbo employed. Quoted items are either things that I actually said or items extracted directly from someone's notes. Remarks often contain quotes from me, too. The information was transmitted over the phone or via email to Jimbo. Hundreds of people accessed this Web-site over the course of the summer to acquire information about how I was faring. Many Web-surfers said that they couldn't wait for the next installment to appear and that they felt a great sense of drama reading the material in real-time. I have included that content here so that readers can get a sense of how things unfolded "live". Several minor corrections have been incorporated.

May 12, 2003 (Day 1)
Started today, hiked 29 miles.

May 13, 2003 (Day 2)
Reached 62-mile mark.

May 14, 2003 (Day 3)
Reached 87.2-mile mark: dry, sandy wash.

May 15, 2003 (Day 4)

Today Ray reached Warner Springs (110.6 miles) and is 12 miles ahead of schedule. "Feeling very good; the trail is phenomenal. Has seen millions of flowers. It's very hot. Saw 10 snakes. Saw only one person at all through day 4—met 3 young thru-hikers from New Hampshire recently. No physical problems except one blister and one sore hand."

May 17, 2003 (Day 6)

Camped 6th night at Eagle's Nest Perch in strong winds—tent almost blew away but not too cold up there.

May 18, 2003 (Day 7)

Reached Idyllwild at 180.2-mile mark—right on schedule. Hiked 14 miles, hitched into town to resupply, and will hitch back to trail. Reports two close encounters with rattlesnakes. Got shower, groceries, and Mexican food. Hiking well, feeling strong. It's hot and getting hotter now, but saw some snow. Has passed 20 to 25 thru-hikers, and there are 70 to 80 ahead of him. Finding the trail in this part is tricky, and Ray took no map (due to weight), but has lucked out by encountering people with maps at strategic times, and by following footprints and marks in the sand. Has taken a couple of unintended detours, but got back on track fairly quickly.

May 25, 2003 (Day 14)

Reached Cajon Canyon, at mile 344.7. "Ray was in Cajon Canyon Sunday night to resupply. Said he didn't go to Big Bear and was planning to skip some of the towns that were on his schedule if he didn't need supplies. The hike is going well, and he's right on track. It's extremely hot, he said, and he had one very rough day in which he was badly dehydrated. He did finally make it to a river and obtained some water, and is recovered now. He has gotten lost a bit but managed to recover from this, too. He decided to burn off all his excess fat (!) and so went for two days on only 2,000 calories a day (versus the 5,000 or so he's burning). This worked, he says; he's now totally lean."

May 30, 2003 (Day 19)

Ray called me at about 11:30 am from Agua Dulce, at mile 454.4. He is in incredible spirits, injury-free, and as healthy as can be. He is on schedule and anticipates no slowdowns. In a few days he will be joined by hiking-partner "Fish-out-of-Water" in Mojave. Ray figures that he has taken about 20 miles of wrong turns so far, including one that had him hiking through snow up Mt. San Jacinto! It has been extremely hot out there, and he can't wait to get in to the Sierras. His worst day so far was heading to Mission Creek. It was "hotter than hell", and he ran out of water with several hours of hiking left for the day. He was "knocking on heaven's door". Needless to say, there was no time for filtering water, when he finally reached the creek. I think he said that he drank 17 liters of water that day and maybe 18 the next. For the most part Ray has seen very few hikers on the trail. In Agua Dulce "trail angels" Jeff and Donna Saufley are a great help to many. Ray says there are a number of hikers at the Saufleys. We might not get another report from him until he reaches Kennedy Meadows on June 8th.

June 2, 2003 (Day 22)

"He has walked 72 miles in the last 34 hours. Has come through 555 miles of desert intact. It was spectacular but very hot, and he's been carrying 22 lbs of water at a time. The flowers in the desert were "outrageously gorgeous", and there were millions of Joshua-trees. He encountered two Mojave Green Rattlers—one acted very aggressively. He hitched in 12 miles from the trail to Mojave and is staying in a hiker inn awaiting the arrival of Peter Solomon ("Fish-out-of-Water"). Fish is bringing a box of food and supplies, and will accompany Ray for two weeks. They will be in the Sierras for 8 days and will go up to 13,200 feet—will definitely see snow. After the Sierras, Ray will be ahead of most other hikers on the trail.

Ray says he's now "very thin", but his legs are super strong; he has some minor aches and pains, especially in his feet. Ray has encountered numerous trail angels. People have fed him fantastic meals—one included barbecued chicken, salmon, steak, wine coolers, fresh strawberries, and Southern Comfort. At another place, he was fed burritos in exchange for painting part of a picket-fence. There were a number of water-caches in the desert—trail angels keep fresh water just for the hikers coming through—one was an elaborate wine-rack set up with water bottles. Ray's right on schedule, in great spirits, and heartened by the helpful and supportive people that he's encountered."

June 8, 2003 (Day 28)

"Ray and Pete arrived at Kennedy Meadows Sunday morning—a day ahead of schedule. Everything's going great, and they've been doing 27 to 28 miles per day. Pete has held up well in the heat except for one day when he did "hit the wall". Food supplies have been light. Ray reports that seven M&Ms were his breakfast today, and Pete has dropped 10 to 15 pounds in his first five days on the trail. They're leaving Kennedy Meadows with lots of food now and expect to be out seven days. Ray had one narrow miss when a rattler struck his trekking-pole. They encountered a hiker with a hand badly swollen from snakebite. Hikers report having come through the Sierras successfully (snow-level is at perhaps 10,000 feet), so Ray and Pete expect to get through the mountains just fine."

June 3 to June 15, 2003

Click here for Fish-out-of-Water's journal. [Note that the material is still available via the Internet from Ray's Web-site.]

June 23, 2003 (Day 43)

Got a call this afternoon from Ray. He was calling from Echo Lake, at mile 1,089.2 (near Truckee?). He is about a day-and-a-half behind schedule but has been slogging through a *major* amount of snow. Fish-out-of-Water left the hike about 6 days ago, and Ray is going it alone, again. He says he has trekked through about 250 miles of snow out of the last 400 miles. It is quite cold, especially at night, when he wears every stitch of clothing he has, often including his shoes so that they aren't frozen in the morning! He has been sleeping at over 9,000 feet every night for the past two weeks and fording many rivers every day. He wore out a new pair of New Balance shoes in about 6 days! Fortunately, he received another pair at Echo Lake. He is restocking and filling his belly, and will push out of Echo Lake this afternoon. I guess his food was running a bit low as he ate only two Clif Bars in the last 24 hours.

The scenery is incredible, and he saw a bear in Yosemite. On a couple of days he found himself *very* lost but managed to stay level-headed and found his way onward. He now carries the full PCT guide, maps, and a compass. He figures about another week of snow ahead of him and is really looking forward to getting out of it. Fortunately, he hasn't had any bad weather (no storms)—just a lot of cold. There are just three thru-hikers ahead of him at this point. He is in great spirits and still very pumped about the hike. He'll be even happier to get out of the snow.

July 1, 2003 (Day 51)

Ray called around noon today from Hat Creek Resort, at mile 1,373.5. He's doing well; still lots of snow. After leaving Echo Lake, Ray had three days worth of food and was headed into a snowstorm. He got stuck on Dick's Pass and froze his butt off that night. He ended up with four inches of snow on the tent and had to wear every stitch of clothing he had, and still he spent the night shivering. He decided to skip his food resupply at Sierra City and had to stretch three days of food to five. With all the snow covering the trail, Ray found himself *very* lost on several occasions. While his food was running low, he had to push on hard to Belden, doing three 40+-mile days in a row.

At one point he arrived in the Donner Pass parking lot and asked some people if there was anywhere to buy any food, and so they offered him what they had. He was pretty hungry and ate it as fast as they could give it to him. For some reason he decided to give these folks his ice-axe; I suppose he figured that he wasn't going to need it anymore. However, it turned out that shortly thereafter he had to do a huge glissade down about a 60° slope! He ended up losing control and nearly ate it in to some boulders. Fortunately, he was able to stop in time. However, he lost his hiking-poles up the slope and had to hike back up to get them and then slide back down the slope again!

He arrived in Belden, at mile 1,283.1, where he was expecting a package. However, by the time he got to the pickup spot, it was closed! He arranged to have the package shipped ahead to Seiad Valley, at mile 1,657.0. He has been doing a lot of bushwhacking through blown-down trees, some with huge trunks as much as five feet in diameter. His legs are getting pretty cut up from all the scrambling over the trunks. Yesterday he banged out 43 miles. This morning he's done 18 and has another 22 or 23 to go for the day. He figures he's covered about 270 miles in the last week. At Sierra City he passed the last three thru-hikers who were still ahead of him. They had started their hike on April 26th.

July 8, 2003 (Day 58)

Ray called this evening from Seiad Valley, at mile 1,657.0. He got the package that I sent with headlamp, watch, guide-books, and socks, along with another supply package which he had forwarded to himself earlier from Belden. He has been pushing hard to make up some lost time and feels that he can be back on schedule within a few days. He has gone 156 miles in the last three-and-a-half days! His feet are starting to get pretty abused with this kind of mileage and with the very old, dirty, and worn-out socks that he has been hiking in. Good thing he has some new ones now. He figures that he has hiked about 900 miles in those socks! There are still snow-and-ice problems.

When he called today at 6:30 pm, he'd already gone 33.5 miles, and still had to hike up another 4,000 vertical feet once he got off the phone. Ray figures that he consumes about 8,000 calories a day. In a somewhat typical re-supply he might buy 2 entire boxes of Hershey chocolate bars, 10 quarts of powdered milk, 2 jars of peanut butter, sardines, deviled ham, raisins, 10 MilkyWay bars, 10 Clif bars, 20 granola bars, some Tiger bars, Tang, Oreo cookies, Wheat Thins, and Cheezits. This supply would be for about three-and-a-half days.

Prior to reaching Seiad Valley, Ray encountered some very friendly folks one day who were very generous in their offers of food. They may try to hook up with him later on the trail and feed him some more! They emailed me a little bit about their meeting:

> "We met up with him at the Scott Mountain Summit. We were enroute from Foresthill to Shady Cove, Oregon, having stopped in Hayfork to visit Dan's mother. We offered Ray a soda, and started talking to him. After we discovered that he was traveling so far, and trying to keep his pack light, we offered him some cold pizza, soda, dried fruit, water, then gave him some crackers, raisins, and powdered

milk to help tide him over for awhile. He was looking good and enthusiastic. He told us of his mission, and how far the journey has taken him—almost 1,600 miles, according to him. He, so far, has had two bear encounters, and gave away his compass to one of the volunteers setting up for the Western States Trail 100-mile marathon because he didn't feel he needed it any longer, but said he will pick one up near Seattle.

He was heading to Seiad Valley, and told us that he would be coming into Seven Lakes in 10 days or less. Since we will be in Shady Cove, Oregon, for at least 10 days, we gave him our phone number and told him to call us when he crosses Dead Indian Memorial Road on the Pacific Crest Trail—we believe that there is a pay phone about a half-mile from this crossing. We will then bring him supplies (lightweight dry-goods and extra water) to possibly save him having to hitch-hike into town. He didn't want to carry any extra water with him when we saw him—we had offered him a 12-oz jar with water, but he didn't want the weight or the glass in his pack. We will be sure to bring some small plastic bottles of water, and he can decide if he wants to carry some of it or not. He said he has been eating a lot of candy lately to keep him going—10 Hershey bars a day! If he gets ahold of us when he comes near Shady Cove, we will keep you updated."

July 16, 2003 (Day 66)

I got an email today with the following update: "Ray called last night from Elk Lake Resort, at mile 1,953.2 (described by him as in the middle of nowhere). There he picked up two UPS packages with shoes, gear, food, and so on. Ray was *desperate* for *Deet*—he has run out and has been absolutely chewed up by mosquitoes. He badly needs Compeed blister-pads—for his used and abused feet. Ray's now one day ahead of schedule and plans to arrive in Snoqualmie Pass, Washington, at least two days ahead of schedule. He's really looking forward to having Paul Goransson join the hike there. Ray's been putting in 48-mile days and says conditions have been dangerous—he's been tracked by Mountain Lions twice." Fish-out-of-Water sent me some photos from when he had joined Ray. [Note that these are still available from Ray's Web-site.]

July 21, 2003 (Day 71)

I got another email update today with the following information: "Ray called this morning, and he's zooming! Pushed in 43 miles, then 47 miles the last two days to reach Columbia Gorge, at mile 2,150.3, on Sunday night 7/20. He felt overjoyed to see Mount Rainier for the first time yesterday—the huge peak (symbol of Washington state) was welcoming him home to Washington and really made him realize that the end of his long journey is in sight. He will cross into Washington this morning and plans to arrive at Snoqualmie Pass two days ahead of his schedule—this Sunday. There he will pick up Paul Goransson to join him for the last 260-plus miles to Canada. Still plagued by foot problems. He also had a close encounter with a Black Bear. A couple nights ago, he was hiking about 9 pm when a Black Bear charged down the trail directly at him and turned away only about 15 feet in front of him. 'It was a huge adrenalin rush', he said."

July 25, 2003 (Day 75)

Ray called this morning from Naches, Washington. He is currently two days ahead of schedule. Ray spent his first night in a hotel room in a *long* time. He reached Washington state about four days ago. Ray could see Mt. St. Helens and Rainier, and has seen a lot of Elk. It was an emotional high to reach Washington finally. He says the scenery and weather are incredible. It has been about 85 to 90 degrees and not a drop of rain. In fact, he hasn't had any rain the entire trip (he did get some snow in the Sierras, however). He has been hiking mostly without a shirt. Some facts: without food Ray's pack weighs nine pounds. How much did your luggage weigh on your last weekend trip? With food, his pack is about 23 to 24 pounds. He eats about five pounds of food per day. In three more days and about 100 miles he will reach Snoqualmie, where Paul joins him. Paul will hike with Ray for the final week and reach the Canadian border to finish the journey. Ray is very excited about finishing the trip, and is starting to get prepared mentally for this very long journey to come to an end. After nearly three months of very intense hiking, sleeping outside, and eating 8,000 calories a day, he is going to need to shift gears to adjust back to "normal life".

July 27, 2003 (Day 77)

Ray's birthday. For the first time on this entire trip, Ray called when I wasn't home! He left a message saying that he had reached Snoqualmie, at mile 2,396.6, today and was going to meet Paul in about a half-an-hour (5 pm). They were going to try to hike 8 or 9 miles tonight to get a jump-start on their final leg of 260-plus miles that should take seven days. Ray said the last three days were pretty easy (for him!) at about 37 miles per day, which was light enough to help his feet recover a bit. He said that all is well. Ray thought that he would be able to get me another update in a few days. The end is near!

July 28, 2003 (Day 78)

The latest email update: "I saw Ray Sunday at Snoqualmie Pass. He was very happy to see Paul and me. He seems very strong but looks about as haggard as 'The Pianist' after the war. He's pretty thin and quite sunburned. He's very happy to have Paul with him to hike to the end. I'll see them tomorrow at Stevens Pass and will bring a huge picnic dinner as well as an absurd amount of trail food. Ray will at least be well fed from here on out. There's a fire in the vicinity of the North Cascades where he'll be headed next, and I'm in the process of getting information from the Forest Service, but I don't think the trail is closed at this point."

July 30, 2003 (Day 80)

"We met Ray and Paul last night at Stevens Pass and brought them a picnic dinner. They've come 75 miles in the last two days and are holding up pretty well despite the heat. They saw some Mountain Goats and passed numerous alpine lakes that looked very tempting, but they don't have time to stop and swim if they're going to stay on schedule. The next three days are very wild and difficult country, and some of the most scenic, too. They left with as much food as they could carry—Paul is sure that they're carrying too much food, and Ray is concerned that they will run out. Paul clearly has a lot more reserves at this point than Ray has. They left at 8 pm and planned to walk another 6 miles before dark. Five days to go. Ray says he will start being excited about being near the end after they make it through the next 3 days."

Aug 3, 2003 (Day 83.2)
Ray finished! I missed his call today, but Ray left a message that he finished today at 12:30 pm! Congratulations, Wall! I'll post more info when I have some.

 D Menu del Día

This appendix provides a typical daily menu while out on the trail. The operative rule-of-thumb was not to carry any food item unless it provided at least 100 calories per ounce. To obtain adequate energy for hiking *long* days required a strong stomach and extreme flexibility.

ITEM	CALORIES
Beef Jerky	200
Clif Bars	480
Deviled Ham	350
Fritos	700
Gatorade/Koolaid/Tang	1,500
King-Sized MilkyWays	2,700
Mounds Bars	400
Peanut Butter	550
PopTarts	350
Sunflower Seeds	400
Water	0
Wheat Thins	400
Total:	8,030

Initial Hiking-Schedule

A facsimile of my *original* hiking-schedule divided by month follows. This 85.5-day schedule gave me goals to work toward. Only in the beginning, when I kept to the schedule, and at the end, when I advanced two days ahead of the schedule, did I actually camp at the evening locations listed. Most other nights, I slept somewhere in between but usually close to these locations. The plan worked remarkably well, and I finished just over two days ahead of this schedule in 83.2 days.

In the following tables: the "Date" column specifies the day of the month; the "Day" column the number[1] of the days that I'd been on trail; the "Supply" column tells what was available in terms of food and lodging (a 'G' indicates groceries, an 'M' indicates meals, and an 'L' indicates lodging); the "Location in Evening" column shows where I had expected to camp; the "Miles" column specifies the number of miles that I'd planned on hiking that day; the "Avg." column shows the average daily hiking-mileage through this date; and the "Total" column shows the number of miles hiked north of the Mexican border up to this date.

---

[1]This number is *not* the same as the number of 24-hour periods that I'd been on trail.

May

Date	Day	Supply	Location in Evening	Miles	Avg.	Total
12	1		Boulder Oaks Campground	26.1	26.1	26.1
13	2	G	Pioneer Mail Trailhead	26.9	26.5	53.0
14	3		Highway 78	25.1	26.0	78.1
15	4		Barrel Springs	23.8	25.5	101.9
16	5	M	Chihuahua Valley Road	26.4	25.7	128.3
17	6	M	Pines-to-Palms Highway	25.4	25.6	153.7
18	7	G,M,L	Idyllwild	26.5	25.7	180.2
19	8		Falls Creek Road	28.2	26.1	208.4
20	9		Mission Creek	25.9	26.0	234.3
21	10		Arrastre Trail	23.0	25.7	257.3
22	11	G,M,L	Big Bear	19.0	25.1	276.3
23	12		Deep Creek	23.5	25.0	299.8
24	13	G	Silverwood Lake	23.1	24.8	322.9
25	14	G,M,L	Cajon Canyon	21.8	24.6	344.7
26	15		Guffy Campground	22.1	24.5	366.8
27	16		Little Rock Creek	26.6	24.6	393.4
28	17		Big Buck Trail Campground	32.9	25.1	426.3
29	18	G,M	Darling Road	28.6	25.3	454.9
30	19	G,M,L	Lake Hughes	30.3	25.5	485.2
31	20	G	Lancaster	30.8	25.8	516.0

June

Date	Day	Supply	Location in Evening	Miles	Avg.	Total
1	21		Tyler Horse Canyon	23.0	25.7	539.0
2	22	G,M,L	Mojave	16.1	25.2	555.1
3	23		Golden Oaks Spring	24.7	25.2	579.8
4	24		Landers Creek	23.3	25.1	603.1
5	25		Bird Spring Pass	24.1	25.1	627.2
6	26		Trail-Side Campsite	22.7	25.0	649.9
7	27		Canebreak Road	26.2	25.0	676.1
8	28	G	Kennedy Meadows	23.3	25.0	699.4
9	29		Death Canyon	25.6	25.0	725.0
10	30		Guyot Creek	31.0	25.2	756.0
11	31	G,M,L	Independence	28.4	25.3	784.4
12	32		Upper Palisade Lake	29.7	25.4	814.1
13	33		South Fork San Joaquin River	31.0	25.6	845.1
14	34	G,M,L	Vermillion Valley Resort	26.2	25.6	871.3
15	35		Reds Meadows	29.4	25.7	900.7
16	36	G,M,L	Tuolumne Meadows	35.0	26.0	935.7
17	37		Smedberg Lake's outlet	29.4	26.1	965.1
18	38		West Fork West Walker River	33.4	26.3	998.5
19	39		Paradise Valley	32.2	26.4	1,030.7
20	40		The Nipple	34.2	26.6	1,064.9
21	41	G,M,L	Echo Lake	24.5	26.6	1,089.4
22	42		Saddle after Tahoe	32.3	26.7	1,121.7
23	43		Peter Grub Hut	35.6	26.9	1,157.3
24	44	G,M,L	Sierra City	34.2	27.1	1,191.5
25	45		West Branch Nelson Creek	28.7	27.1	1,220.2
26	46		Spring after Bear Creek	33.5	27.3	1,253.7
27	47	G,M,L	Belden Town Resort	29.4	27.3	1,283.1
28	48		Junction to Butt Mountain	36.1	27.5	1,319.2
29	49		Lower Twin Lake	36.5	27.7	1,355.7
30	50	G,M,L	Hat Creek Rim	34.0	27.8	1,389.7

July

Date	Day	Supply	Location in Evening	Miles	Avg.	Total
1	51	G,M	Rock Creek	33.2	27.9	1,422.9
2	52		Deer Creek	38.8	28.1	1,461.7
3	53	G	Castella	38.0	28.3	1,499.7
4	54		Spur Trail to Deadfall Lake	36.7	28.5	1,536.4
5	55		Bloody Run Trail	35.2	28.6	1,571.6
6	56		Babs Fork, Kiddler Creek	36.2	28.7	1,607.8
7	57	G,M	Gridder Creek Footbridge	35.9	28.8	1,643.7
8	58		Lowdens Cabin	33.7	28.9	1,677.4
9	59		Saddle below Ashland Inn	38.7	29.1	1,716.1
10	60	G,M	Junction to Soda Creek	35.8	29.2	1751.9
11	61		Christi's Spring	36.4	29.3	1,788.3
12	62	G,M,L	Crater Lake Lodge	41.5	29.5	1,829.8
13	63		Tipsoo Peak	31.6	29.5	1,861.4
14	64		West Shore of Lake	30.2	29.6	1,891.6
15	65	G	Cluster of Three Ponds	31.2	29.6	1,922.8
16	66	G,M	Elk Lake Resort	30.4	29.6	1,953.2
17	67		Lava Camp Lake	29.9	29.6	1,983.1
18	68		Rockpile Lake	32.4	29.6	2,015.5
19	69	G	Olallie Lake Ranger Station	32.3	29.7	2,047.8
20	70		Crater Creek	36.0	29.8	2,083.8
21	71	G,M	Crest's End	34.4	29.8	2,118.2
22	72	G,M,L	Cascade Locks	32.0	29.9	2,150.2
23	73		Panther Creek	36.3	30.0	2,186.5
24	74		Steamboat Lake Spur Trail	38.8	30.1	2,225.3
25	75		Leave Last Pond	35.1	30.1	2,260.4
26	76	G,M	Naches, Washington	37.6	30.2	2,298.0
27	77		Bullion Basin Trail 1156	37.7	30.3	2,335.7
28	78		Seasonal Creek, Sheets Pass	33.8	30.4	2,369.5
29	79	G,M,L	Snoqualmie Pass	27.1	30.3	2,396.6
30	80		Camp, Waptus River Trail	39.1	30.4	2,435.7
31	81	G	Stevens Pass	35.9	30.5	2,471.6

August

Date	Day	Supply	Location in Evening	Miles	Avg.	Total
1	82		Reflection Pond	34.6	30.6	2,506.2
2	83		Gamma Creek	35.2	30.6	2,541.4
3	84	G	Bridge Creek	35.9	30.7	2,577.3
4	85		Trailside Camp	36.6	30.8	2,613.9
5	86		Manning Park Lodge	44.8	30.9	2,658.7

The *actual* finish date was August 3rd for an 83.2-day total. The final average daily mileage was 31.9.

Preliminary Gear List

This appendix provides my pre-hike gear list that I posted on the World Wide Web prior to commencing my journey. As described in Appendix G, I modified several pieces of gear and from time-to-time deleted or added gear. The sublists given here are sorted in decreasing order of weight. All unlabeled units in this appendix are in ounces (ozs).

Total pack weight (no food and no water): 164.3 ozs =

10 lbs 4.3 ozs

Total weight on person: 71.6 ozs = 4 lbs 7.6 ozs

Key Sleeping-Items and Main Gear: 80.9

▷ 2-person tarptent (Squall) by Henry Shires: 31.2

▷ GVP G4 pack with sleeping-pad plus waist and shoulder pads:

25.0

I plan to dump the waist and the shoulder pads after a week or two.

▷ Mountainsmith Wisp 30°F down, sleeping-bag in stuff-sack: 22.4

▷ nylon rope (50 feet): 2.1
I may cut it to 40 feet once on the trail.

▷ plastic bag to further waterproof sleeping-bag: 0.2

Clothes: 52.3

▷ NorthFace Goretex jacket: 14.5

▷ black, long-sleeve, polypro shirt: 8.5

▷ Thorlo low-cut running-socks, medium weight (3 pairs): 7.2

▷ blue, coolmax T-shirt (short-sleeve): 7.1

▷ nylon-shell pants: 5.8

▷ green shorts: 4.8

▷ Speedo swim-suit: 2.1

▷ balaclava: 1.7

▷ mosquito head-netting: 0.4

▷ plastic clothes-bag: 0.2

Clothes That I Usually Wore: 50.0

▷ New Balance 806 trail-running shoes with custom graphite orthotics: 32.8

▷ brown, long-sleeve, nylon T-shirt: 6.2

▷ black shorts: 4.0

▷ Thorlo medium, low-cut running-socks: 2.4

▷ sombrero: 2.4

▷ Julbo Sherpa sun-glasses: 1.0

▷ bandanna: 0.7

▷ small watch in pocket: 0.5

▷ nothing else on my person: 0.0

Carrying in Hands: 21.6

▷ Leki Super Makalu trekking-poles: 21.6

Miscellaneous: 31.1

▷ Nalgene bottle (1 liter): 3.8
I want a wide-mouth bottle to mix drinks. I want it to be bullet-proof—thus, the heavy Nalgene bottle.

▷ Platypus with drinking-tube (2 liters): 3.7
The tube is a luxury and may have to go.

▷ Polar Pure iodine (empty): 3.2

▷ sunscreen: 3.0

▷ Platypus w/o drinking-tube (4.5 liters): 2.5

▷ floss, tooth-brush, and tooth-paste: 1.7

▷ PCT-related materials (*Databook* cut up): 1.7

▷ Platypus w/o drinking-tube (2 liters): 1.6

▷ bug juice: 1.5

▷ foot-care package: 1.3

▷ GoLite food-bag: 1.2

▷ toilet paper: 1.1

▷ bite-guard: 1.0

▷ nail-clippers: 0.7

▷ Advil: 0.7

▷ GoLite yellow ditty-bag: 0.6

▷ jackknife, one blade and small: 0.5

▷ Lexan spoon (may dump): 0.4

▷ cash (all currency plus two quarters): 0.3

▷ matches: 0.2

▷ lip balm: 0.2

▷ American Express credit-card: 0.1

▷ Mastercard: 0.1

Occasional Gear: 36.5

▷ wind-stopper fleece: 18.0

▷ Raven Pro Black Diamond, titanium 70cm ice-axe: 15.0

▷ Outdoor Research gripper gloves: 3.5

Food and Water

At any given time, I plan to carry a little more food and water than I expect to need. Fully loaded with water, I anticipate carrying about 20 lbs. A maximum food load might approach 25 lbs. I don't ever expect to carry both maximum water and food loads simultaneously.

Backpacking Equipment

Introduction

Closely delving into what I was carrying and why leads to interesting conversations. Learning what I *wasn't* carrying and why leads to even more stimulating conversations. My initial gear list is presented in full detail in Appendix F. I hope that future PCT thru-hikers find that the equipment lists provided here are valuable resources.

I'll break down the gear descriptions into the categories of (1) key sleeping-items and main gear, (2) clothes, (3) clothes that I usually wore, (4) occasional gear, and (5) miscellaneous equipment. When I began selecting gear, I first researched how other hikers had equipped themselves. I searched the Internet for hikers who had actually completed the PCT and then studied their equipment lists. Examining half-a-dozen or so lists and merging all of the items found on any of the lists resulted in a giant number of things. Obviously, I would need to be much more selective. What items were really critical and which weren't? I didn't know; I simply needed to make educated guesses based on my previous long-distance backpacking experience. This meant calling on my AT-thru-hike background.

On my AT thru-hike I'd started later than nearly all other thru-hikers. I passed nearly all of them along the way to Maine. My pace afforded me a great opportunity to meet hikers and discuss, among other things, gear. One couple's thoughts on gear stuck with me. The husband remarked, "At one point we eliminated everything, and then added back whatever we couldn't do without." The wife agreed, "That approach worked and helped reduce our load." I didn't have the luxury of taking this approach since it would be hard to reacquire things that I'd jettisoned, particularly in a timely manner.

Many hikers have a float box that they mail ahead from post office to post office. Using such a method, they can eliminate and then reacquire gear. Since I didn't like going to post offices due to their out-of-the-way locations and limited hours, this system wouldn't work for me. I spent time in my home office, not a good field-testing strategy, thinking carefully about what I needed to bring and what I didn't really need. Everything that I'd planned to take sat in a sizable pile, and gradually I whittled that stack away. I hoped that my selections would work.

As I prepared my gear list electronically, I computer-sorted the gear from heaviest item to lightest item within each category. This obvious step made me realize that I needed to eliminate or reduce the weight of items near the top of each sublist. Removing the elements at the bottom of the list helped, but not much; for example—discarding virtually weightless foam earplugs would save little.

Key Sleeping-Items and Main Gear

At the head of my key sleeping-items and main gear list came the tarptent. I decided to go with this two-person shelter by Henry Shires since I would be joined by a couple of friends along the way. The one-person version tilted the scales only slightly less, and I preferred having the extra room. This choice allowed me to bring all of my equipment, including pack, inside every night. My tarptent, called the Squall, weighed 31.2 ounces. Instead of using the front pole provided by Henry to set up the shelter, I substituted one of my hiking-poles.

The tarptent does have a large footprint and requires quite a bit of room to set up. California, Oregon, and Washington are big states, though, so I worried little about finding sizable campsites. The version of the Squall that I'd custom-ordered came with a sewn-in floor. The lower parts of the sides, the front, and the back were fashioned out of a fine mesh. The accompanying directions indicated that the tarptent could be set up in a mere five minutes. The first time that I set the Squall up I timed myself. I erected the shelter at dusk in my back yard in Savannah, Georgia, in four minutes, including the time spent reading directions. As the trip progressed, I could pitch the Squall in two minutes. Equally important, I could take it down and load its stuff-sack in four minutes. Making and breaking camp took very little time. From my observations I burned far less energy in camp than most hikers do.

For the most part the Squall worked like a charm. In extremely high wind, say over 50 miles per hour, the shelter flapped and rocked. However, as unstable as the Squall was when the wind buffeted it, I suspect that the Squall still performed as well as most other light-weight shelters would have done. The clouds never let loose, so I don't know how the Squall does in wet conditions. My only snow-storm dumped five inches on me, and, although the tarptent sagged under the snow's weight, the shelter held up reasonably well.

Henry had said that in order to avoid excessive condensation the Squall needed to be erected in a breezy place. Most nights I could position the tarptent in a light summer breeze, and little condensation formed. A few times late in the trip when I was unable to follow Henry's guideline, the tarptent would be wet in the morning. Since I never had time to dry the shelter out during the day, I simply erected it at night still wet. Within about five minutes in a comfortable breeze, the tarptent dried. I treated the Squall with great care, except in where I pitched it; luckily, the Squall was never damaged. I bent one tent-peg and ripped the Squall's stuff-sack, but the tarptent itself remained in perfect condition. I wondered how many thru-hikers must have had broken shelters or lost tent-pegs. I felt fortunate with the tarptent.

I used a GVP pack. GVP stands for "Glen van Peski". Glen is an avid hiker and gear innovator. I purchased a custom G4 pack from him. The pack, including sleeping-pad, weighed only 25 ounces. This weight dipped further when I cut some of the straps shorter, eliminated several straps, scrapped a little of the already minimal foam padding, and completely removed the waist belt. The "final" pack tipped the scales at closer to 20 ounces. Several innovative features in this pack are worth discussing.

The pack's shoulder straps and waist belt double as Velcro pockets. By inserting socks or other small items into these pockets, padding can be created out of material which otherwise would merely ride along. The G4 also has a sleeve on each side that holds a standard hydration-system. Velcro holders facilitate positioning a drinking-tube in the proximity of one's mouth. A hiker needs to drink frequently on the often hot and dry PCT, and this system works well.

The pack also contains a large mesh pocket in the back. This feature functions great for storing items that one needs quick access to, for example, candy-bars, sun-glasses, insect repellent, toilet paper, and a water-purification system. The main body of the G4 consists of a simple large compartment. I didn't discover until one-third of the way through the hike that a hidden pocket resides on the inside wall of the pack. This pouch is a good place to stash valuables. The rip-stop nylon from which the pack is made repels water quite well. The lightweight fabric passed the pre-trip "hose test", so I didn't bring a pack cover.

Under heavy food and/or water loads, the pack stressed my back and shoulders, especially after I'd cut off the waist belt. However, loads under 25 pounds didn't cause any stress. The G4 held up remarkably well. The only damage it sustained were two small tears: one caused by my ice-axe, and the other caused when I accidentally walked straight into some sharp rocks. These mishaps both happened before the middle of the trip, and the small pieces of silver duct-tape that I pressed over the slits held for the remainder of the trip. Glen kindly sent me a brand-new pack at the conclusion of my trip. The new pack includes wider shoulder straps, and this improvement was in fact one of the modifications that I would have suggested to Glen. Additionally, the sleeves on the newer version are mesh instead of rip-stop nylon. The mesh saves weight, but may not insulate drinks as well in warm climates. Glen continues to improve the design and to make the pack more usable and even lighter.

I selected a Mountainsmith Wisp 30°F down sleeping-bag. This mummy bag weighed in at a mere 22.4 ounces with its waterproof stuff-sack. Down bags work only if they stay dry and uncompressed. Repeated crunching and repacking causes a bag to lose loft, and thus warmth. I inserted a plastic bag inside the stuff-sack and then put my sleeping-bag inside these two layers. This double protection assured that the bag didn't get wet, at least while it was packed.

Why did I choose a 30°F bag when nights at least as cold as the low 20's seemed imminent? My inner voice told me to use the *same* bag all summer. Since I carried so little padding to sleep on, for cushioning I needed to at least lie down on my sleeping-bag every night.

On real hot nights, a warmer bag would have been uncomfortable. I generally sleep hot, so I opted for a slightly cooler bag than the experts advise. If the mercury plummeted, I planned to wear all my clothes inside the sleeping-bag and seal it up. Mummy bags have a drawstring near the top, so I could completely enclose myself in the bag. Using this technique, almost no body heat escapes. This heat-retention system worked well except for claustrophobia and the fact that breathing became a bit difficult, especially over 10,000 feet in elevation.

In theory a down sleeping-bag can be washed only in a front-loading washing-machine. Since dirt covered my legs by day's end, the inner wall of the sleeping-bag quickly became coated with grime. Nevertheless, I didn't wash my bag until after day 70 on the trail. Cloaked in dirt, my sleeping-bag exceeded its original weight, so I broke the rules and washed the down cocoon in a top-loading machine. Upon retrieving the scrunched bag, I prayed that the dryer would work a miracle. The dryer helped little, and it became rather obvious why you need to use only a front-loading washing-machine. The down feathers had clumped together, and many sections of the bag seemed to have *no* down in them. This compression made for some cold nights in Washington state; the down provided no insulation in its oatmeal condition. Eventually, I restored some loft to the matted down by dedicating five-to-ten minutes each night for "massaging" the bag.

I didn't use the Mountainsmith stuff-sack. Even though their stuff-sack weighed little, I found one slightly larger that weighed even less. This switch meant a tiny weight-savings plus less bag-compression. The more voluminous sack also facilitated repacking the sleeping-bag.

A couple of times my sleeping-bag became damp—for example, when ice on the outside of the bag melted. In these cases I shivered. No single bag met the requirements every night on the trail. Overall, I enjoyed my choice of sleeping-bag. In selecting a bag with the appropriate temperature-rating, one should keep in mind that after a long day of hiking, the tired unreplenished body doesn't heat itself as well as the rested replenished body.

When I began the trip, I brought a 50-foot section of nylon rope that weighed 2.1 ounces. This item was intended to be used for a clothes-line and for hanging food to keep it away from bears. Because I did laundry so infrequently, I never once employed the rope as a clothes-line. Bear concerns forced me to hang my food on four nights around Yosemite. While the idea of hanging food made sense, finding an appropriate branch which would be unreachable by a Black Bear, but which would support my food bag, and which I could lob a rock over was very difficult.

My longer days meant trying to hang food from trees in the dark, and this feat seemed impossible. I glimpsed many ropes and rope fragments stuck in trees where hikers had unsuccessfully attempted to hang or to retrieve their food line. I thought that I would trim the rope to 40 feet to save 0.4 ounces, but I never did. After passing safely through Yosemite, I jettisoned the rope. A few sections of trail have metal bear-proof boxes for hiker use; however, each night when my time to camp arrived, a bear-box *never* sat nearby. Nearly all hikers whom I encountered slept adjacent to their food without incident. I often supported my head and my neck using a food-bag pillow.

The last item under this category was mentioned earlier—the plastic bag to keep my sleeping-bag dry. The kitchen garbage-bag weighed 0.2 ounces. Category 1, key sleeping-items and gear, totaled 80.9 ounces (about five pounds). Once I stopped carrying the nylon rope and modified my G4, my weight in this category fell to 73.8 ounces. Trimming any further weight here would have been difficult. I could have done so by going with a super-lightweight bivvy sack, but it would have been tiny compared with the cavernous tarptent.

Clothes

My NorthFace Goretex jacket outweighed all other items in category 2. This windbreaker differed from a plain shell and actually contained a little insulation. At 14.5 ounces my jacket was grossly heavier than many pure shells, but my jacket was also very durable. An insulated hood and two zippered pockets contributed to the jacket's weight. I felt sentimental about the rainproof coat, having worn it on some big mountain climbs. My favorite clothing article also contained two zippered vents that could be opened to aerate the torso. This design feature helped me to stay a little cooler while hiking uphill in moderate temperatures. The sleeve-openings on the jacket sported Velcro cuffs, so I could tighten them easily for warmth or loosen them for more ventilation. Cold nights forced me to wear the jacket, including the hood, while in my sleeping-bag. I washed the red jacket only once during the summer; prior to that washing it looked black.

Initially I took a black, long-sleeve, polypro shirt that weighed 8.5 ounces. I never actually hiked in this shirt but would often sleep in it. I carried this shirt for about the first half of the trip, dumped it, and then acquired another similar shirt in the middle of Oregon. Prior to adding back the long-sleeve polypro, I carried only a short-sleeve T-shirt and my NorthFace Goretex jacket. If the weather had been bad, I would have suffered without the availability of another dry shirt. I slept in the long-sleeve polypro shirt every night for the second half of Oregon and all of Washington.

I started out with three pairs of medium-weight, low-cut Thorlo running-socks. Some hikers take only two pairs of socks. The Thorlos have padding built-in and are rugged. The socks totaled 7.2 ounces. Occasionally, I carried only one extra pair of socks. One pair of Thorlos always padded the G4 shoulder-straps until the last couple of weeks, when I didn't use any padding. I tried to wash socks each day, but this task was difficult. If my only stream-crossing happened early in the morning and temperatures remained real cold, I didn't want to get my hands cold, so I would delay the washing. The socks housed so much dirt that they often required dozens of scrubbings and wringings before they became moderately clean. Many times I should have sacrificed the hands for the feet; the feet ended up suffering far more than the hands did.

I carried a short-sleeve, REI, coolmax T-shirt when I left Campo. This item weighed 7.1 ounces. At the beginning of the trip, I couldn't really fathom having just one shirt to hike in. However, later in the trek, I happily dumped one of my shirts. I ended up walking the last half of the trail in the well-made REI T-shirt. I would wash this garment in rivers, and it dried very fast. On particularly hot days, I dipped the shirt in ice-cold creeks and then pulled it over the head with a loud "ah". This evaporative-cooling system kept my core body-temperature down on big climbs.

For a short while, I carried a 5.8-ounce pair of nylon-shell pants. I wore these pants only once and wouldn't bring them again. The one time when I needed them, and so naturally didn't have them, occurred when I ran out of insect repellent. The pants would have been a good back-up system for bug protection. They definitely weren't worth their weight, though. In all my years in the mountains, only a couple of times have my legs been cold, and those occasions took place in extreme (−50°F or colder with the wind chill) winter conditions on Mount Washington in New Hampshire.

I brought a pair of green REI shorts that weighed 4.8 ounces. These hiking-shorts had matching pockets and a convenient drawstring around the waist. The pockets held five-to-seven pages of the *Databook* and four-to-six candy-bars. This way I could research the next point of interest while walking and also obtain food without stopping. My shorts would have functioned as gaiters, if the drawstring had broken. As my waistline diminished, the cord gained value. I trimmed the drawstring in conjunction with my disappearing midriff. At the outset of the trip I couldn't really conceive of hiking the trail in just one pair of shorts, but ultimately that happened when I mailed home the green shorts.

I slept in a Speedo racing swimsuit every night. This tiny clothing article helped with hygiene and weighed a mere 2.1 ounces. Before departing on the hike, I'd tried to order a lighter suit over the Internet; the replacement never did arrive. When I thought of jettisoning the Speedo, almost nightly, I always found a reason to retain it. In hindsight, this decision made sense.

I carried a polypro balaclava for about half of the trip. I wore this head cover while hiking on extremely cold mornings but usually for only one or two hours. Once in a while, I wore the balaclava to bed on cold nights. Since we lose so much heat from our heads, the 1.7-ounce balaclava seemed worth retaining at high altitude.

I ended up taking a 0.4-ounce piece of mosquito head-netting. I hate head-netting and never should have brought this material—although after I dumped this protection, of course, times arose when I desperately needed it. Bottom line, I never used the netting and wouldn't take netting on another PCT hike. From time-to-time I would encounter section-hikers who wore netting. They looked like beekeepers, but suffered no facial bites.

Lastly, I carried another 0.2-ounce plastic bag in which I stored my clothes. I threw all my clothes together, dirty and clean. The bag kept the clothes dry.

The total weight for category 2, clothes, tipped the scales at 52.3 ounces. This figure could be reduced further, and as the hike progressed, I eliminated some items. For much of the hike my pack held only 26.4 ounces of clothing. If I wore my NorthFace jacket, my pack contained only one pair of Thorlo socks and my swimsuit. This amounted to just 4.5 ounces of "extra" clothes. In this phase of the hike, I shuddered to think of how cold I might get and worried that I had nothing else to wear. I crossed into hypothermic territory on several occasions. During exceptionally cold times, I thought of Walter Bonatti bivouacking on K2.

Clothes That I Usually Wore

Minimalist hikers frequently boast about how little gear they pack. Their reported weights, though, can be deceiving. For example, some hikers carry a lot of gear in their pockets and don't count these items in their pack weight. Others don't report gear unless they carry it for the whole trip. This section addresses my clothing.

I wore size 11 2E, New Balance 806, trail-running shoes with custom graphite orthotics. These trail-runners weighed 32.8 ounces once I trimmed the shoe laces to the minimum viable length. Since my feet tended to swell over the course of a day and the hike, I took care not to over-trim the laces. For many years I've been a loyal customer of New Balance and typically purchase and wear out seven-to-ten pairs of running-shoes per year. When I was 18 years old, I pulled on a size nine. My running and hiking habits have flattened my feet out two sizes. Prior to the hike, I religiously broke in five pairs of 806's. The first pair of shoes held up great in the desert, and after 700 miles they still looked new. The second pair of shoes didn't appreciate my kicking steps in the snow and ice in the High Sierras, and they rebelled by falling apart in about six days. The toe-box blew open, and the soles shredded. This rapid disintegration of the 806's developed into a serious problem since I couldn't replace them for hundreds of miles.

My custom orthotics started the trip in good shape, but I'd completely trashed them by the end. When I first purchased the orthotics, I remember the doctor telling me to break them in slowly by wearing them a few hours each day, and gradually more and more. Against my better judgment and the foot-doctor's advice, I raced the JFK 50-miler in Maryland the day after I obtained the orthotics. Not surprisingly, intense calf pain plagued me for a few weeks post-race. Immediately after I completed my PCT hike, a podiatrist's technician replaced the covers on the orthotics, and they are still going strong. Since the orthotics cost almost as much as my parents paid for their first house, I delighted in this fact.

I started the PCT wearing a long-sleeve nylon T-shirt called the eco-mesh shirt. Rail Riders, an adventure-racing outfitter, designs and sells these high-tech garments. This light-weight well-vented shirt worked great in the desert. The Velcro pocket located near the chest housed my sun-glasses and candy-bars. Once out of desert conditions about one-fourth of the way through the hike, I ended up discarding the birch-colored garment that I'd grown attached to. Rail Riders calls the eco-mesh shirt one "to-die-for". My large-sized shirt weighed 6.2 ounces, but the Rail Riders catalog lists a weight of 5.0 ounces.

I wore black shorts from REI for most of the trip. They weighed in at a mere 4.0 ounces and dried extremely fast. These shorts featured a drawstring around the waist. Once I lost weight, I trimmed the drawstring a few inches. This shortening probably saved about 0.1 ounces. The shorts contained two pockets that served the same purposes as the pockets in my green shorts. Black didn't show dirt as much as green, and the black shorts elevated when placed on a balance scale with my green shorts. For these two reasons I preferred and kept the durable black REI shorts.

I wore Thorlo medium-weight running-socks which weighed 2.4 ounces. All of my Thorlos possessed a low cut, only to the ankle. These short socks weighed a tad less than your standard above-the-ankle socks.

I always covered my head with a hat. In the desert I began with an Outdoor Research (OR) sombrero for sun protection. This lid weighed 2.4 ounces. Following through on the logic that I was tan enough not to get too sunburned, at Kennedy Meadows, I switched over to a Leadville Trail 100 baseball-cap that weighed 2.3 ounces. This swap saved me 0.1 ounces. My skin cooked a bit in the High Sierras, as the intense sun reflected upward from the snow. I dropped my sombrero into the *hiker-box* at Kennedy Meadows, along with other gear that I'd decided not to continue carrying, including used socks, my first pair of running-shoes, shaving-cream and razor that I'd mailed to Kennedy Meadows, excess food, my loose change, and so on.

For much of the beginning of the hike and for all snow travel, I wore Julbo Sherpa sun-glasses. These glacial glasses provide excellent UV protection and weigh 1.0 ounce. Standard features of the dark shades include eye-cups to reduce glare on the sides of the eyes, plus a strap. After several weeks on the trail, I threw away the strap to save weight. How many fractions of an ounce this maneuver saved, I don't know, since I never weighed the strap separately. Later I also dumped the eye-cups as a weight-saving measure. Lastly, I scrapped the glasses themselves and just squinted. The sun-glasses were critically important for the first half of the trip when the sun beat down intensely. The Julbo's saved my eyes in big snowfields where the possibility of snow blindness loomed large.

I debated back and forth about whether or not to take a bandanna. Up until Donner Pass, I carried yer-old-standard red/black bandanna. Often I would dip the bandanna into a river and then drape the wet cloth around my neck to keep cool. The bandanna doubled as a wash-cloth and towel. Since the bandanna weighed 0.7 ounces, ultimately I tossed it. My shirt functioned as a wash-cloth for the second half of the trip. The coolmax-T dried so fast that this substitution worked well.

My watch holds an interesting story. I usually wear a Timex Iron-man watch, but these timepieces are rather large and bulky. To save weight, I purchased a $4 Casio child's watch. At home I cut off the wrist strap. The modified watch weighed only 0.5 ounces. Apparently, children don't demand alarms or lights, because these features were absent. I carried detailed instructions in order to set the watch. I trimmed the excess paper off these childproof instructions, including the Spanish, French, and other foreign language directions. The watch possessed so few buttons that complex sequences had to be pressed, for example, to set the date. When I needed to hike longer days to keep up with and eventually advance my schedule, I decided to replace the watch with one having five alarms and a light. This way I could get up earlier and tell the time late at night (and hence infer my location on the PCT), while I pressed onward. I ended up giving the Casio child's watch to a thru-hiker named Coach whom I encountered at Seiad Valley. Since his previous watch had died, I am sure that he made good use of the Casio.

The gear for category 3, clothes which I usually wore, totaled 50.0 ounces. With the swapping out and swapping in of the items mentioned previously, the average amount of clothing that I was wearing totaled three pounds. My pockets contained no other gear. Many hikers carry a compass, knife, lighter, GPS, insect repellent, camera, or other small items in their pockets. I carried only *Databook* pages and food in mine. Later in the hike, my pockets also held pages of *Volume I* and *Volume II*.

Occasional Gear

In the High Sierras I carried a Raven Pro Black Diamond titanium ice-axe. This sleek and light-weight tool tipped the scale at a mere 15.0 ounces, including my favorite Grivel hand-strap. I used the 70cm length. The ice-axe provided security on many of the dangerous snow traverses in the High Sierras. In the big mountains of California I also carried wind-stopper fleece (18.0 ounces) and OR gripper gloves (3.5 ounces). These items kept me relatively warm during the high-altitude part of the trip. I probably should have kept the fleece with me longer, but to save weight I unloaded it just north of Donner Pass. I also dumped the gloves around that time. I suffered through many mornings with my hands nearly frozen for the first two hours of the day. Once the sun hit my numb digits, though, they quickly warmed up. If a hiker's hands are the least bit sensitive to cold, warm gloves are a must clothing-item.

Miscellaneous Equipment

If you enter any hiking-gear store, you'll be struck by the number and variety of specialized items, not to mention their prices. Most of these items are unnecessary, although many look cool and have neat color-schemes. Take the carabiner, for example. Approximately 50% of all hikers carry a 6.3-ounce carabiner that does nothing more than attach a 12.2-ounce coffee-mug to their pack. The minimalist hiker needs to be very selective and can not fall into the trap of acquiring sporty or fashionable items. When you are smelly and filthy, you don't look cool regardless of how colorful your pack is. I tried to take only items that I would regularly use.

Initially, I carried a one-liter Nalgene bottle. I wanted a wide-mouth bottle for mixing my classic shake—Nestlé Quick in huge amounts, powdered milk, and Carnation Instant Breakfast. In pouring the powders from a ziplock bag, I needed a big target. To blend these powders together into a 2,000-calorie concoction required vigorous shaking, so I wanted a strong bottle, too. Since I couldn't purchase Nestle Quick or Carnation Instant Breakfast almost anywhere along the trail, though, I dumped the 3.8-ounce Nalgene bottle in favor of a lighter soda bottle.

I carried a two-liter Platypus hydration-system with drinking-tube that weighed 3.7 ounces. Using a restaurant knife, I later cut the drinking-tube in length to save roughly 0.3 ounces.

For water-treatment I used Polar Pure iodine. This product comes in a small brown bottle that contains iodine crystals. After the crystals have been in water for about an hour, the concentrated-iodine mixture can treat up to 5 liters of water. A capful or two of the brown solution added to a liter of water produces drinking-water in 20 minutes. By refilling the bottle of iodine-crystals after each use, the iodine solution is always ready to purify more water. The clever design of the bottle prevents pouring out the crystals themselves. The crystals are sufficient to treat approximately 1,500 liters of water. One bottle lasted me for the entire summer. In theory, I could have treated about 20 liters of water per day using a single bottle of Polar Pure since I spent only 83 days on the trail. I treated far, far less, though, because I often drank water without any purification.

Many long-distance hikers filter their water. Each purification system suffers from some drawbacks. Being mechanical devices, filters can break or malfunction, necessitating that one carry a back-up system. Parts may need to be replaced, and finding them in stores along the PCT can be time-consuming. Filters are heavy. The advantage of a filter is that chemical-free drinking-water can be produced immediately. Iodine does not work against cryptosporidium. Each thru-hiker needs to weigh the trade-offs for the various water-treatment systems before settling on one.

I carried a 3.0-ounce tube of sunscreen at the outset of the trip. When this cream ran out, I didn't replace it. I relied on my clothing and my hat to protect me. My ears and nose did get burned. When a non-hiker encountered another hiker and me one time, I remember his saying, "You people are horribly sunburned." My ears and my nose hurt, so I guess he was right.

I also took a 4.5-liter Platypus which weighed 2.5 ounces without its drinking-tube. When my smaller drinking-vessels became low on fluid, I refilled them from the large one. This system gave me redundancy. If my large Platypus had ruptured, I would have been in serious trouble in the desert. Having my water supply distributed over several containers made me feel more secure.

For dental care I brought container-less floss, a half-length tooth-brush, and a partially-filled, travel-sized tube of tooth-paste. These dental hygiene items lay stashed in a trimmed plastic bag. On trail I couldn't maintain my home brushing-standards. When I returned to Savannah, I immediately went to get my teeth cleaned. The process hurt more than usual.

I included trimmed pages from the *Databook*, starting the trek carrying information on the first 1,400 miles or so. This material weighed 1.7 ounces. When I missed my mail-drop at Belden, I actually hiked by Braille for awhile. That is, I possessed no information about the trail. I eventually acquired the bulky PCT guides: *Volume I* and *Volume II*. While in Central and Northern California, I carried only select pages of *Volume I* if any, but after my Braille experience I carried all of *Volume II* and threw away pages as I went north. I learned that the trail can't be hiked with just the *Databook*.

A third Platypus, another two-liter one (without a drinking-tube) also made it into my pack. This vessel weighed 1.6 ounces. The postal scale, which I weighed gear with, helped me to realize that I really needed only one drinking-tube since even the shortened tube weighed 2.1 ounces or nearly 50% more than the Platypus itself. Sometimes I also carried a quart-sized Gatorade bottle. My maximum capacity for carrying fluid topped out at 11 liters or roughly 22 pounds. Once past Vermillion Valley Resort, at mile 871.3, I rarely hauled more than three liters of liquid. From Vermillion I sent home two Platypuses.

I took a 1.5-ounce bottle of Deet, but never applied insect repellent until I traveled north of Kennedy Meadows. In hindsight, I should have included bug juice in my Kennedy Meadows mail-drop and not carried it unused for 700 miles. When the mosquitoes induced nightmares in Oregon, I armed myself with as many as three containers of Deet. Being unable to consolidate them into a single large container frustrated me. Although I carried an extra ounce or two, it was critical to have plentiful repellent during the worst bug infestations.

My 1.3-ounce foot-care package consisted of unwrapped Band-Aids, adhesive tape without a container or "cardboard center", and un-wrapped Compeed—a thicker and softer Band-Aid-like product that is now sold by Johnson & Johnson. Several times I ran out of Band-Aids and Compeed. Once I actually gave my last Band-Aid to a day-hiker who had developed a pancake-sized blister on the bottom of her foot. She and her friends thanked me profusely, and I felt like a Good Samaritan. Compeed couldn't be acquired on the trail, and I should have carried more of this product at all times. Running out of Compeed definitely ranked as one of my biggest and most painful mistakes.

I used a 1.2-ounce GoLite stuff-sack for my food bag. This green sack contained plenty of room and weighed three to four times less than a typical stuff-sack of comparable size. The sack repelled water, so I didn't need to worry about soggy food.

I usually carried a whopping 1.1 ounces of toilet paper, separately rolled and with no dowel. In this department I thought little about weight-savings. I've heard of some (male) hikers carrying only two squares of TP per day. This extreme seems outrageous. I carried far more than that and never had to resort to leaves. Extra TP was used for cleaning my sun-glasses or for drying a blister before I bandaged it.

For many years I've been grinding my teeth at night. During the trip, I chewed on my custom bite-guard that weighs 1.0 ounces. The bite-guard fit perfectly in my stripped dental-floss container, a con-venience which I discovered only after much pre-trip experimentation. Since the bite-guard cost over $300, I wanted to protect it well. Even-tually, I tossed out the hard-plastic floss container to save weight. I packed the bite-guard with caution. It never broke.

In the past, particularly during 100-mile runs, I have lost many toenails. If a toenail bangs against the front of a shoe millions of times, it will turn black and fall off. Therefore, toenails need to be kept short, so I decided that nail-clippers were required gear. My pair weighed 0.7 ounces. Since I couldn't take nail-clippers on an airplane, I mailed them along with my trekking-poles to San Diego before the hike started.

My "first-aid medicines" consisted of 0.7 ounces of Advil in a plastic baggy. I took almost no Advil until six weeks into the trip. As the summer unfolded, I prescribed Advil for myself both to reduce swelling and to relieve pain. Without popping a few pills before bedtime, sleep would have been just a dream. Since the Advil often wore off after a few hours, I usually set out a few night pills where I could find them in the dark. After I had swallowed them and my pain level subsided again, I'd fall back to sleep.

My 0.6-ounce GoLite ditty-bag held important papers and credit-cards, plus my dental kit, Advil, and nail-clippers. I often thought of throwing away the ditty-bag, but I ended up keeping it. The bag increased my efficiency in locating things, and this factor justified its weight.

I took a small single-bladed jackknife that weighed 0.5 ounces, and used the knife to trim straps and laces, to remove labels from containers, and to cut cheese. Numerous times I thought of unloading the knife, but I carried it for almost the entire trip.

On my AT thru-hike I didn't carry *any* food utensil. In fact, for most of that trip, I possessed nothing relating to food at all except food itself. Similarly, on this hike, I took no stove, no bowl, no cup, and no utensils, save one. On the PCT I carried a 0.4-ounce Lexan spoon. This utensil facilitated eating peanut-butter, melted chocolate, gooey cheese, and items that people gave me. For example, on the way into Vermillion Valley Resort, Freefall cooked noodles for Fish-out-of-Water and me.

The spoon's color was identical to that of my green food-bag. Many times I couldn't locate the spoon inside the bag. I eventually developed a system so that I could find the spoon fast. The "system" involved putting the spoon into a plastic bag with a food item having a con-trasting color—for example, Oreos. Before departing on the hike, my friends from Georgia's Yamacraw Initiative gave me a titanium spork. This spoon/fork combination weighed 0.5 ounces more than my Lexan spoon, so I left the treasured gift at home.

All my cash plus two quarters weighed 0.3 ounces. I later spent the quarters when I realized that I could make phone calls without using change. Regarding currency, I would trade in five ones for a five, two fives for a ten, and so on. If 50 cents or more remained after a purchase, I bought another candy-bar. I always left any spare change in the hiker-boxes.

I carried waterproof matches for part of the trip. The handful I grabbed weighed 0.2 ounces, and I never once used them. When I entered my first wilderness area where extreme fire danger existed, I decided to discard the matches at the next available opportunity. If I became lost in such an area, I wasn't about to light a signal fire that would kill me and hundreds of others in order to "save" me, not to mention that I had no intention of taking any action which could destroy a section of the trail that I came to love. I never possessed any food to cook nor any clothes to dry since it never rained, so lighting a fire for these purposes was not required.

On the PCT lips need protection from sun and dryness. I brought a standard ChapStick lip-balm cylinder which weighed 0.2 ounces. At Kennedy Meadows I removed the label from the cylinder at the suggestion of another hiker. He also suggested getting rid of the cap and winding the balm down farther. I kept the cap to avoid lint lips, but jettisoned the lip balm itself at the Oregon/Washington boundary to save weight.

I possessed an American Express card and a Mastercard which combined weighed 0.2 ounces. Virtually no business establishment along the trail accepted the AMEX card, so I should have destroyed it. I also carried my PCT thru-hiker permit and my driver's license. These two items combined weighed 0.1 ounces. During the last week on the trail, I also brought my entry permit for Canada. I thought about removing the staple attaching the two papers making up the permit but ended up keeping it.

The total weight for category 4, miscellaneous equipment, measured 31.2 ounces at the start. This amount equaled the average weight of miscellaneous gear that I carried throughout the trip. Even though I became more weight-conscientious and removed a few items, the added material from *Volume I* and later *Volume II* balanced my deletions.

Another addition to the miscellaneous gear included a Petzl micro headlight. I included this item at Seiad Valley. For the first 1,657.0 miles, I didn't carry a light. The headlamp allowed me to walk at night and also to read the *Databook, Volume II*, and trail-signs late at night. This illumination critically assisted me when I hiked long days. The Petzl micro weighed 5.1 ounces. (I weighed it after the trip.) I carried two spare AA batteries for awhile. As I approached the end of the hike, I replaced the batteries that I'd been using, even though they weren't dead yet, with new batteries. From that point on, I carried no spares.

In my hands I held Leki Super Makalu trekking-poles that weighed 21.6 ounces. These additional legs helped greatly with balance when fording rivers, when hiking on rough terrain, and when crossing snow-fields. The poles also assisted with uphills, cushioned the downhills, and functioned as tent-support poles.

Notably absent from this list of gear are a compass (which I did carry for a couple of weeks in the High Sierra), camera, journal, pen, flashlight, stove, filter, and GPS unit. Hikers must think carefully about their gear choices and consider equipment as a whole. I don't suggest that anyone travel as light as I did because eliminating some items can compromise safety.

Summary

At the outset of the trip my pack weighed 164.3 ounces or 10 pounds, 4.3 ounces. The clothing that I wore plus my trekking-poles totaled 71.6 ounces or 4 pounds, 7.6 ounces. I always tried to carry as little food and water as possible without compromising my energy or hydration levels. My maximum food load weighed 38 pounds, and my maximum water load weighed 22 pounds. My daily consumption consisted of 5 pounds of food and 20 pounds of water. Typically I walked with 28 pounds on my back. I removed my garbage, no matter how little, whenever I encountered a trash-can. My trash rarely exceeded a pound.

Throughout the trip, I constantly mulled over items to remove. The last items that I considered eliminating were my sleeping-bag and my tarptent. I probably could have dumped one or the other during the last week since I enjoyed perfect weather. However, I felt strong enough toward the end of the trip that I didn't need to worry as much about weight-saving. At the end of the hike, I carried less than nine pounds of gear, and, of course, a few remaining pages of the *Databook* and *Volume II*.

The fact that *I* lost 10 pounds on the hike is worth noting. I accomplished my greatest weight-savings by reducing my body weight rather than via gear selection. On the AT I had lost only five pounds, but there I didn't hike as long days. My usual pack weight on the AT sans food or water measured 20 pounds, or roughly double my PCT-pack weight.

Glossary of Trail Jargon

Appalachian Trail The 2,159.2-mile eastern United States foot-path that passes through 14 states and the Appalachian Mountains from Springer Mountain, Georgia to Mount Katahdin, Maine.

AT Appalachian Trail.

ayce All-you-can-eat.

blow-down A fallen tree, especially one on the trail.

bonk To be completely out of energy.

cache A hidden store of food or water. To hide food or water.

cairn A pile of rocks used to mark a trail.

CDT Continental Divide Trail.

Compeed A thick and soft Band-Aid-like product sold by Johnson & Johnson.

Continental Divide Trail A developing trail that extends 2,700 miles from Mexico to Canada by way of the Rocky Mountains.

Databook The *Pacific Crest Trail Databook* compiled by Benedict "Gentle Ben" Go and published by the Pacific Crest Trail Association.

flip-flop To hike a long-distance trail from one terminus to a point X, be transported to the opposite terminus, and hike back to point X.

ford A bridgeless place where a river requires crossing. The act of walking through a river to cross it.

G4 The fourth in a line of lightweight backpacks manufactured by GVP Gear.

Global Positioning System A location technology that allows for identifying one's position on the surface of the earth.

GPS Global Positioning System.

GVP Glen van Peski, proprietor of GVP Gear.

hiker-box A container located at a resupply point near the trail into which hikers discard items that may be of use to other hikers.

hit the wall A physical breakdown caused by extreme exercise and improper replenishment, and characterized by a total lack of energy, diminishing will-power, and the need to continue to perform vigorous activity.

kickoff The date when the majority of hikers begin their thru-hike; for the PCT this day is usually in the last week of April.

library (internal library) A region of my mind where I stash important life experiences and then "check them out" in times of need. (See page 6 for more details.)

mail-drop A food-and-gear package which a thru-hiker sends for later pickup to a pre-determined spot near the trail.

motor To move ahead rapidly.

pack weight The total weight of the contents of a backpack, including the pack itself.

Pacific Crest Trail The 2,658.7-mile footpath that traverses California, Oregon, and Washington from the Mexican-border town of Campo to Monument 78 near Manning Park, British Columbia.

PCT Pacific Crest Trail.

posthole To fall through snow, especially if it is crusted.

pure hike A thru-hike where no sections of the trail are skipped, where walking is the only means of advancement on the trail, where the hiker carries his/her pack and supplies throughout the entire hike, and where the hike proceeds and finishes in a single direction.

register To write in a trail book for hikers. The actual book itself.

section-hiker A person who walks a segment of a trail.

spur A side trail off a main trail.

Squall The version of the tarptent that I carried.

stealth camp A (temporary) campsite off the trail that is hidden from view.

switch A change of direction or position.

switching network (internal switching network) A grid that I've set up throughout my being that includes "on" and "off" switches relating to pain, senses, and feelings. (See page 6 for more details.)

switchback An abrupt turn (usually close to 180°) in a trail which increases the distance of the path between two points but reduces the intervening grade.

tarptent A combination shelter engineered by Henry Shires that incorporates features of both a tarpaulin and a tent.

thru-hike A walk that covers an entire (mega) trail in a single year.

thru-hiker An individual who walks all of a trail in a one-year period.

trail angel A person who goes out of his/her way to assist hikers.

trail magic Unexpected kindness, usually involving food or drink, that befalls a thru-hiker.

trail name A name bestowed on a thru-hiker that usually points to an interesting trait or experience.

triple crown The AT, CDT, and PCT.

vitamin A Advil, aspirin, or other type of off-the-shelf pain-pill.

Volume I The *Pacific Crest Trail, Volume 1: California* by Schifrin, Schaffer, Winnett, and Jenkins, published by Wilderness Press, 2001.[1] This book has now been split into two volumes: (From the Mexican Border to Yosemite's Tuolumne Meadows) by Jeffrey Schaffer, published by Wilderness Press, 2003; and (From Tuolumne Meadows to the Oregon Border) by Schifrin, Schaffer, Winnett, and Jenkins, published by Wilderness Press, 2003.

Volume II *The Pacific Crest Trail, Volume 2, Oregon & Washington* by Jeffrey Schaffer and Andy Selters, published by Wilderness Press, 2000.

yogi To beg for food subtly.

yoyo To hike a trail from one terminus to the other, and then hike back, all in a single year. (This has never yet been done on the PCT.)

---

[1] This book is the one that I used.

The Fastest Hike:

Quest for the Pacific Crest Trail Record

GLEN "FIDDLEHEAD" FLEAGLE:
"Wall, your book is awesome! I tell you what: it was so good, it makes me want to come out next year and try to break your record!!! It makes me want to do some more extreme adventures. I was totally into it all the way to Canada. What a job you did, not only with the writing, but the hike. How the hell can you remember all of that? I've read a lot of books about hiking, and I know your and my style of hiking doesn't necessarily appeal to many hikers, but it sure does to some, including me. And your style of writing is great. Very professional."

JOHN VELDHUIS:
"I have a new name for you: 'Man of Steel'; you have surpassed the Ironman category."

ROBERT "DR. BOB" ELLINWOOD:
"It's a terrific read! I couldn't put it down. Very intense and powerful. A clear distinction has to be made of a record set through an unsupported hike as opposed to a supported one. I believe no one will ever break your incredible time or effort covering the PCT under your own steam, carrying a pack. Wow. My sincere congratulations. An incredible feat!"

BEN LEAKE:
"Deepest respect to you!"

DAVID "SIGHTSEER" WARREN:
"I am super impressed, and I am even more impressed with the impact that you had on the students of the group that I was with this summer in Washington. I have to tell you too that I experienced a little jaw dropping."

HENRY SHIRES:
"Congratulations on breaking the PCT speed record!"

DAVID "THE RUNNER" HORTON:

"Congrats on your PCT record. If I make it, mine will be the record for an assisted PCT trip. Yours will still be the unassisted record for the PCT. I admire and respect what you did immensely. I can't wait to see some of the places that you talked about in your book."

JAMES "HAN SOLO" BENNETT:

"Congratulations on your 83 days and 5 hours PCT record!"

DAVID MEEHAN:

"Hi Wall, congrats! Man that is awesome. 83 days! We saw your notes that you left along the way—'Hunger Switch Off'. We were thinking about you often."

BOB HOLTEL:

"Congratulations on a job well done!"

RICK AND BARB MILLER:

"You really raised the bar."

A query of "Ray Greenlaw" to any search engine will turn up links leading to Ray's Web-site. From there additional pictures and information can be located.

Ray feeding Red Pandas in Chengdu, China.

Ray "Wall" Greenlaw grew up in East Providence, Rhode Island. At an early age he developed an interest in physical fitness and endurance training. His love for the mountains and outdoors grew during several trips to the White Mountains of New Hampshire. While attending Pomona College near Los Angeles, Ray enjoyed several backpacking trips to Yosemite and the High Sierras. He also took trips into the mountains of Southern California.

Ray moved to Seattle to attend graduate school at the University of Washington. Trips to the mountains became more frequent, and he was able to find peace and solitude on the trails. His first professorship brought him back to New Hampshire. Often, while trail running in New Hampshire and Maine in the late fall, Ray would meet Appalachian Trail thru-hikers coming up from Georgia. They had a certain look in their eyes and conversations with them intrigued Ray.

Ray thru-hiked the Appalachian Trail in 1995. After his thru-hike of the AT, the Pacific Crest Trail was calling to him. This book describes his 2003 thru-hike of the PCT. Ray continues to love the mountains, outdoors, and trails. The Continental Divide Trail is now calling to him . . . .